for the People

What the Constitution Really Says About Your Rights

Akhil Reed Amar and Alan Hirsch

The Free Press
New York London Toronto Sydney Singapore

*f*P

THE FREE PRESS
A Division of Simon & Schuster Inc.
1230 Avenue of the Americas
New York, NY 10020

Designed by Songhee Kim

Manufactured in the United States of America

10 9 8 7 6 5 4 3 2 1

Library of Congress Cataloging-in-Publication Data

Amar, Akhil Reed.
    For the people : what the constitution really says about your
rights / Akhil Reed Amar and Alan Hirsch.
        p.   cm.
    Includes bibliographical references and index.
    ISBN 0-684-82694-1
    1. Constitutional law—United States—Popular works.   2. Civil
rights—United States—Popular works.   I. Hirsch, Alan
II. Title.
KF4550.Z9A43   1998
342.73'085—dc21   97-38241
                                                                    CIP

Contents

Author's Note

THE AMERICAN CONSTITUTION IS one of the most democratic documents in human history. It lays out its bold theme—that all power derives from the people—with force and grace. Yet today, much of the grand democratic design of this great democratic document has faded from view.

In this book, we invite our fellow citizens to join us in considering the Constitution afresh. Our invitation, of course, includes lawyers and judges, but we did not write this book with them first in mind. Too much of what is now said about the Constitution aims only at legal experts, and ignores ordinary citizens. Conversation about a democratic document should itself be democratic—this book is for the People.

Introduction

THE CONSTITUTION GIVES THE PEOPLE of the United States richer rights than have been recognized. The "Conventional Constitution"—the document as understood by the Supreme Court, the legal community, and the general public—protects an assortment of individual rights, many of which apply primarily to persons accused or convicted of crimes. But the "Framers' Constitution"—the document as perceived by those who drafted, ratified, and amended it—includes a grand corpus of democratic rights, rights that have oft been overlooked. This book seeks to illuminate the Framers' Constitution and the rights it protects.

It may seem absurd to speak of a Conventional Constitution reflecting the views of virtually all courts and commentators. Whose Constitution, one might ask: that of conservatives, who protest that liberals invent constitutional rights, or that of liberals, who protest that conservatives ignore constitutional rights? The answer is both. As bizarre as it may seem, partisans on both sides of the current divide in constitutional law share certain basic errors.

First, both sides tend to ignore or undervalue crucial constitutional clauses. These include the Preamble; Article IV, Section 4; Article VII; and the Second, Ninth, Tenth, Thirteenth, Fifteenth, Nineteenth, and Twenty-Sixth Amendments.* While individual scholars may consider one or two of these provisions important, none of these texts has received nearly the attention it deserves.

Second, and closely related, both liberals and conservatives tend to analyze each part of the Constitution in isolation. The resplendent Framers' Constitution comes into view only when we step back and take in the elegant tapestry of the entire document. This entails not only spotting neglected clauses, but also seeing all of the clauses in relationship to one another and to the larger constitutional design.

Third, and deeper still, legal scholars fixate on the so-called "Madisonian dilemma": the tension between majority rule and minority rights. The central issue, in conventional discourse, is the extent to which the Constitution protects the rights of discrete individuals from government encroachment. (The government is equated with the "majority" because elected representatives presumably speak for a majority of their constituents.) To simplify the matter, conservatives like Robert Bork and William Rehnquist believe that, as long as it acts pursuant to powers authorized by the Constitution, the government may generally do as it pleases—the only restraints are a few specific constitutional provisions, which should be interpreted narrowly. Liberals like Ronald Dworkin and William Brennan believe that the protection of rights should be more expansive. For example, liberals see the First Amendment's protection of free speech as encompassing "expression" (such as nude dancing) as well as literal speech. Conservatives scoff. So too, liberals cite the Ninth Amendment ("The enumeration in the Constitution of certain rights shall not be construed to deny or disparage others re-

---

*The reader can look these up in the Constitution reprinted at the end of this book.

tained by the people") as an invitation to judges to identify and protect constitutional rights not spelled out in the document, such as sexual privacy. Again, most conservatives disagree.

To conservatives, the liberal approach does violence to the fundamental principle underlying democracy—majority rule. To liberals, the conservative approach runs roughshod over a basic requirement of a civilized society—a healthy respect for minority rights. Caught up in this debate, the legal community obsesses on questions like abortion. To conservatives, the absence of any mention of abortion in the Constitution means there is no constitutional right to it. To liberals, a right to abortion can be inferred from a more general right to privacy which, though itself unmentioned in the Constitution, derives from the spirit of the document.

The debate over privacy is not unimportant, and neither side's position is frivolous. But focusing constitutional conversation on this question neglects the Constitution's essence. The majority-rule-versus-minority-rights debate ignores a crucial aspect of the challenge faced by the Framers, and their response. To see only the Madisonian dilemma is to miss the Constitution's design.

In our view, both liberals and conservatives are wrong to see almost all constitutional rights as individualistic in nature. We the People can lay claim to a bountiful harvest of constitutional rights, but many of these belong to us less as private individuals entitled to be left alone than as public citizens entitled to act together; such citizens must maintain sovereign ownership of the government and enjoy certain rights that cannot be infringed without damaging the institutions that make our democracy possible. To put the point in more familiar terms, the Constitution's scheme for protecting rights is ultimately more populist than libertarian.

Seeing all this requires careful consideration of the Constitution's tapestry. Today, the Bill of Rights is treated as if it were a jumble of individual clauses protecting particular rights. Thus the First Amendment protects an individual's free speech; the Second Amendment, his or her right to own guns; the Sixth Amendment, the accused's right to a jury trial; and so forth. Such an approach misses the grand design.

The Bill of Rights coheres around a notion of citizenship. This citizenship derives its meaning from membership (actual or potential) in public associations essential to our democracy: the electorate, the militia, the jury. This simple insight casts new light on the specific rights named in the Constitution. The First Amendment is not only about an individual's right to express herself, but even more importantly about the conditions that enable the electorate to make informed choices. The Second Amendment is less about an individual's right to own guns than about the conditions that enable our society to protect and govern itself. The several amendments dealing with the jury, while conferring rights on an accused, more fundamentally establish the conditions that enable We the People to monitor and help administer the criminal justice system and thus keep it from becoming an abusive weapon of the government.

The Framers' vision of citizenship links up with a larger theme. The Constitution's root principle, deeply embedded in its overall structure and in countless clauses, is *popular sovereignty:* rule by the People. This principle and the Constitution's conception of citizenship reinforce one another. Popular sovereignty is an empty phrase unless citizens assume crucial responsibilities, and this they cannot do unless they enjoy a network of rights. And all these rights and responsibilities add up to little if the citizenry does not retain ultimate control of the government.

The last point is key. Today, as noted, most legal scholars assume that the Framers' central task was reconciling the power of majorities with the rights of individuals. (Conservatives and liberals disagree only on the terms of the reconciliation.) In fact, the Framers recognized an issue of even greater importance: how to protect We the People from a self-interested or corrupt *minority government.*

In the current debate, liberals and conservatives alike casually equate Congress and state legislatures with the "majority." Yet America in modern times has combined extremely high reelection rates for incumbents with a pervasive sense that legislators often serve narrow interest groups more than the public interest.[1] As the Framers recognized, the government does not necessarily speak for or on behalf of We the People. The Constitution, in large part, aims to protect the People from a self-dealing government.

In the *Federalist Papers*, James Madison famously declared that it is of "great importance in a republic not only to guard the society against the oppression of its rulers, but to guard one part of the society against the injustice of the other part."[2] For some reason, the legal community focuses almost exclusively on Madison's second issue (protection of minority from majority), while ignoring his first (protection of the people against self-interested government). Yet, the first issue was first in the minds of the Framers.*

The Framers established a representative regime in which the people delegate powers to officials rather than rule directly. This choice stemmed in part from misgivings about direct democracy and in part from recognition that direct democracy is impossible in a sizable country. But the Framers recognized that a representative government poses certain risks. Officials may try to rule in their own self-interest, contrary to the interests and expressed wishes of the people. To minimize such self-dealing, the Framers designed an elaborate edifice. On the most familiar level, they divided the federal government into three branches that would check and balance one another to keep any particular person or institution from assuming tyrannical power. (They further split Congress into two houses, and divided power between competing governments—state and federal.) Equally important, if less recognized, the Framers gave ordinary citizens direct power to restrain all three branches of government. They did so by placing in our hands three primary responsibilities—to vote (in elections), to fight (in militias), and to judge (on juries).

The people at large—as the electorate, in the militia, and on the

---

*To be sure, the need to protect against majority tyranny was the focus of the Reconstruction period, and motivated the Fourteenth Amendment. But the healthy attention to protecting minority rights should in no way obscure Madison's other concern—protection of all the People from a self-dealing government. This concern remains a live issue in America today.

jury—would stand in the way of a self-dealing government. The electorate, of course, could restrain the President and Congress by removing them on Election Day. In addition, the electorate would retain the power to amend the Constitution and thereby wrest from judges or other government officials the final word on virtually any issue. The citizen militias, for their part, were devised as much to guard against a tyrannical federal government as to fend off foreign foes.* And in their service on juries, ordinary citizens would provide a strong check against any government corruption or oppression.

These three institutions were crucial to the Framers. A major complaint with British rule over the colonies was that Americans could not vote for representatives in Parliament. The very first section of the Constitution following the Preamble establishes a representative legislature, and the next section stipulates that one branch of that legislature, the House of Representatives, will be elected by "the people" every two years. If the Framers had stopped there, having written nothing but Sections 1 and 2 of Article I, the Constitution would have gone a good way towards establishing the democracy they sought.

Yet they could not stop there, in part because they had to provide for national security. The militia played the lead role in the Framers' intense deliberations on this subject. Dreading a permanent professional army under federal control, they entrusted the nation's security to citizen soldiers—the militia. They debated issues related to the militia at length, and included three clauses concerning the militia in the original Constitution and yet another in the Bill of Rights.

The jury, too, occupied a prominent place in the Framers' design. The only right secured in all state constitutions penned between 1776 and 1787 was the right of jury trial in criminal cases; and even though the original Constitution omitted a general Bill of Rights, it expressly protected criminal juries. The jury plays a preeminent role in the Bill of

*Lest anyone wonder, today's extremist groups that have appropriated the name "militia" bear little resemblance to the militia of 1787. The Framers' militia consisted of the People at large—*all* voters—whereas today's self-styled and self-selected militias set themselves apart from the general citizenry. See David Williams, "The Militia Movement and Second Amendment Revolution: Conjuring with the People," 81 *Cornell Law Review* 879 (1996).

Rights. Three separate amendments explicitly safeguard juries, and several other amendments and clauses tightly mesh with the jury idea.

The concepts of the electorate, the militia, and the jury, and ideas related to them, weave their way through the Constitution. The ballot (the right to vote in elections, on constitutional amendments, and in the jury room) and the bullet (encompassing a form of military self-government) were both handed to American citizens so they could keep tyranny at bay.

THE VERY FIRST words of the Constitution, "We the People," establish ownership of the government by the populace at large. Much of the rest of the document establishes the means of preserving this ownership. But just what is meant by "We the People"? Who are the People?

The original Constitution uses the term twice. In the Preamble, We the People "ordain and establish this Constitution." Article 1, Section 2, describes the election of members of the House of Representatives "by the People." As these references imply, the notion of the People links up with the concept of citizenship—not in the shallow sense of who is considered a citizen for the purpose of census-taking, but in the deeper sense of who retains ownership over and responsibility for governance. The two references in the original Constitution deal with the electorate, but the Bill of Rights expands the notion of citizenship (and, not coincidentally, makes repeated reference to "the People"). Significantly, the three fundamental constitutional roles of ordinary citizens— to vote, to fight, and to judge—are inherently public, involving citizens in a collective enterprise.

In 1787, each of these central responsibilities was mostly limited to adult white males. All free members of the larger society, including women, enjoyed various civil rights (to enter contracts, hold property, bring lawsuits, and so on) but voting, militia service, and jury duty were tightly clustered *political* rights and responsibilities reserved for full ("first-class") citizens.

History confirms a close link among these three badges of citizenship. For example, the Fourteenth Amendment defined a state's presumptive electorate as all males over twenty-one—almost identical to the definition of the militia. And as blacks, women, and other previously excluded groups won one or two of the three badges of citizenship, the other badges tended to follow. Thus, Abraham Lincoln's initial decision to propose the Thirteenth Amendment outlawing slavery, and the Republican Party's decision to give blacks the vote in the Fifteenth Amendment, were importantly influenced by the fact that black soldiers served the Union during the Civil War. Likewise, Woodrow Wilson and others supported extending the vote to women because of their contribution to the nation's World War I effort. The early women's suffragists also emphasized the close connection between the right to vote and the right to serve on juries. More recently, the Twenty-Sixth Amendment, extending the vote to eighteen-year-olds, grew out of the perceived unfairness of the Vietnam-War gap between the draft age and the voting age.

The three responsibilities of citizenship fit together in another way as well. Apart from their more obvious purposes, both militia service and jury service were expected to educate the citizenry in public affairs and thereby enhance the capacity of the electorate for intelligent self-government. In short, electing representatives at the ballot box, defending America on the battlefield, and administering justice in the courtroom are not simply three discrete activities that happen to be mentioned in the Constitution—they cohere in a vision of citizenship and popular sovereignty.

This vision lays the basis for recognition of a grand corpus of rights enjoyed by We the People. It is often said that rights entail responsibilities. The converse applies with equal force: responsibilities trigger rights. This is partly a matter of fairness to individuals. To take an example alluded to above, if we ask young adults to risk dying for their country, it is unfair to deny them other aspects of citizenship such as the vote—especially since full political participation gives them a say in whether they or anyone else will be asked or told to fight. Equally important, if We the People are to carry out the responsibilities of citizenship, the conditions necessary for effective performance must be assured. Note, for example, that the Second Amendment prefaces the protection of the right to bear arms by declaring a well-regulated militia "necessary to the security of a free State." In other words, the right derives from the need to empower citizens to maintain an effective democratic government.

In sum, the citizenry's responsibilities to participate on the jury, at the polls, and in the military require accompanying rights for two reasons: to ensure that no citizens are second-class citizens and to preserve the vitality of the institutions that safeguard our democracy.

IN THE PAGES that follow, we divide these rights into four "boxes." The first three boxes—the ballot box, the jury box, and the cartridge box—correspond to the three primary responsibilities of citizenship. The ballot box and the jury box are self-explanatory, while the cartridge box refers to citizens' rights and responsibilities with respect to national security.

In Part IV, we consider a very different locus of rights. In America today, the debate over "welfare" concerns money. But the Constitution's primary reference to welfare—the Preamble's declaration that the new government is formed to "promote the general Welfare"—suggests something broader. In Part IV we explore the idea that the Constitution compels the government to provide people the wherewithal to be good citizens. If we expect citizens to care about their responsibilities, we must given them some stake in the country's affairs. This may entail providing citizens with something like "forty acres and a mule"—a democratic grubstake. Similarly, the case can be made that if we expect citizens to serve on juries and vote in elections, we must ensure a reasonable level of education.

The case for such constitutional rights derives from the meaning of citizenship embodied in the clauses concerning the jury, the militia, and the electorate, and receives support from Article IV, Section 4 ("The United States shall guarantee to every State in this Union a Republican Form of Government. . . .") and the Thirteenth Amendment ("Neither slavery nor involuntary servitude . . . shall exist within the United States."). The prevailing view of Article IV, Section 4—that it creates no rights enforceable by courts—is profoundly mistaken. The prevailing view of the Thirteenth Amendment—that it abolished nineteenth-century slavery and then lost most of its significance—is equally erroneous. These great provisions have faded into the background because their broad principles have been ignored.

Thus we offer a fourth box in which rights of the People may reside— what we call the "lunch box." This term has double meaning, and dovetails with the Preamble's broad reference to welfare. "Lunch box" evokes the debate over government's obligation to provide hot lunches for schoolchildren, which in turn implicates the citizen's right to both a degree of material well-being *and* an education.

As should be clear, within each of the four boxes we will make far-reaching claims. There will be much to provoke almost everyone. In suggesting that the Constitution protects many rights that have gone unrecognized, we may unsettle conservatives. They may also dislike some of our specific claims, such as the right of women to serve in military combat. Much of what follows may also disturb liberals. They may resist our reconception of rights away from libertarianism and towards populism. And they, too, may object to some of our specific claims, especially our argument that the Constitution can be amended by a kind of national referendum.

We see this book as an invitation to both liberals and conservatives (and to everyone else) to take seriously the set of issues that we put on the table. Even if some of our specific claims fail to persuade, we think that our general point still holds: The Constitution protects a grand corpus of democratic rights oft overlooked in the current debate.

BEFORE WE ILLUMINATE these rights, we must clarify our approach to constitutional interpretation. We have emphasized that good constitutional interpretation cannot isolate individual clauses. The reader may well wonder why we would bother to make such an obvious claim:

Would anyone deny that a holistic understanding of the Constitution aids interpretation?

The answer, sadly, is that while no one advocates treating individual clauses in isolation, virtually everyone does it. Consider the example of the military draft. In 1918, the Supreme Court upheld the constitutionality of a federal draft in a unanimous opinion[3] that has gone largely unquestioned ever since. Pointing to Article I, Section 8's declaration that Congress may "raise and support Armies," the Court proclaimed it obvious that Congress may conscript. This seems to illustrate the mechanical approach to constitutional interpretation once expressed by the Supreme Court as follows: "Lay the article of the Constitution which is invoked beside the statute which is challenged and decide whether the latter squares with the former."[4]

The problem is that Article I, Section 8, conferring the power to raise armies, is part of a larger document and makes sense only in the context of that document. A mere three clauses after conferring the power to raise armies, the Constitution empowers Congress to "provide for calling forth the Militia to execute the Laws of the Union, suppress Insurrections and repel Invasions." The militia, at the time of the nation's founding, consisted of the general citizenry (that is, adult white males, reflecting the narrow class of full citizens at the time). Thus, the Militia Clause specified three conditions under which the federal government could conscript citizens for military service. If the power to raise armies means Congress can draft citizens for any purpose, the Militia Clause seems pointless: why stipulate that conscription is permitted in situations A, B, and C if it is already permitted from A to Z?

It turns out that, properly interpreted, the Army Clause and the Militia Clause happily coexist. This we explore fully in Chapter 17. For present purposes, we raise the example to convey the futility of treating constitutional clauses in isolation. It won't do simply to say that Congress may "raise armies" and thus must have the power to conscript. To assess the constitutionality of a military draft, one must understand the meaning of "army"—which entails understanding the meaning of its sister term, "militia." This, in turn, means looking to the various clauses in the Constitution that use these terms, and other clauses that interlock with those clauses.

Yet courts and commentators generally eschew this kind of analysis. They do so, in large part, because they lack a theory that makes the Constitution comprehensible as more than a grab bag of clauses. We offer an alternative vision of the Constitution as a rich tapestry weaving together the ideas of citizenship and self-government.[5]

If it is a mistake to interpret individual clauses of the Constitution in isolation, it is an even cruder mistake to interpret all clauses hyperliterally. Consider the Fifth Amendment's prohibition against twice placing a criminal defendant in jeopardy of "life or limb." If we fed the text of the Fifth Amendment into a computer, it would report that double jeopardy is barred only where the potential punishment is death or amputation—but not, say, torture or life imprisonment. Surely the Framers did not intend such a silly result. It makes much more sense to read "life and limb" as a graphic metaphor for all criminal punishment. Similarly, the Sixth Amendment gives the criminal defendant the right to compel "witnesses" in his favor to testify. If we fed this Amendment into the computer, it would tell us that there is no right to subpoena and introduce nontestimonial evidence (such as DNA) that might likewise prove his innocence.

A hyperliteral interpretation of the Constitution would lead to many manifest absurdities: the Vice President would preside at his own impeachment trial (he presides over the Senate and the Senate tries impeachments of government officials); the government could not raise an air force (the Framers, of course, made no mention of one, while expressly providing for "armies" and a "navy"); and Congress could broadly censor television and private letters (which aren't, strictly speaking, "press"). Clearly, a common-sense effort to decipher the meaning of a text, rather than a hyperliteral reading, must guide interpretation. This is especially true when we apply an eighteenth-century document a few centuries later.

A more difficult issue of constitutional interpretation concerns the role of the Framers' intent. Today's legal community seems divided between those who religiously adhere to the Framers' intent and those who pooh-pooh it.[6] As with the debate between conservatives who emphasize majority rule and liberals more concerned about minority rights, our mode of interpretation cuts across this divide. We think the Framers' views are critical. (Indeed, the effort to recover their vision is central to our endeavor.) But these views, while generally the proper starting place for interpretation, are not always the best endpoint. Changed circumstances can render the Framers' outlook on a particular issue anachronistic, and on occasion the text of the Constitution takes on a meaning of its own. Just as a quilter may produce unintended but lovely patterns, so the Constitution's elegant tapestry occasionally displays a pattern that the Framers may not specifically have recognized. In the final analysis, the text, structure, and history of the Constitution all play major roles in sound constitutional interpretation.

Interpretation is not a science; there is no precise blueprint for inquiry that yields a single reliable answer to every constitutional question. But there are better ways and worse ways to approach the Constitution. In our view, the best way—the one that makes the most sense and is most apt to fulfill the Constitution's promise to form a more perfect union for ourselves and posterity—places at center stage the sovereignty of We the People, and the vital rights and responsibilities that follow.

Part One

the Ballot Box

ONE

The People's Right to Amend the Constitution

WE LEARN IN CIVICS CLASS that the principal power of the people in a democracy is at the ballot box. Our "leaders," sometimes called "servants" in recognition of the ultimate sovereignty of the People, must represent us faithfully if they wish to remain in office. Otherwise, we will throw the bums out. In fact, as touched on in our Introduction, the notion that elections assure a responsive government is quaint. Elected officials can (and often do) remain in power despite frustrating the wishes of the people. But even putting aside this large problem, a fundamental obstacle appears to impede fulfillment of the will of the People: the Constitution.

Even when elected representatives eagerly seek to implement the desires of their constituents, they may find their hands tied. Legislation desired by the People may run afoul of the Constitution, in which case legislators, who take an oath to uphold the Constitution, should not pass it. If they do, the President (or governor) can and should veto it. And if both the legislature and the executive move ahead with the legislation, a court can and should strike it down as unconstitutional.

Thus, it may come to pass that the will of the People is frustrated by the Constitution. Ironically, our revered Constitution seems to compromise the basic principle of democracy. Especially since most provisions of the Constitution were written and ratified by persons who died long ago, We the People, far from sovereign rulers of our government, seem slaves to the dead hand of the past. Worse still, the long-deceased Framers were (almost) all white males, many of whom owned slaves. They can hardly be thought of as representative of today's society.

The standard response is that the Framers provided a ready remedy to this apparent problem: the constitutional amendment. As long as the People, at any given time, may amend the Constitution, they retain ultimate authority. But this solution turns out to be itself problematic. Can "the People" really amend the Constitution?

Article V of the Constitution sets forth two procedures for amending the Constitution:

> The Congress, whenever two thirds of both Houses shall deem it necessary, shall propose Amendments to this Constitution, or, on the Application of the Legislatures of two thirds of the several States, shall call a Convention for proposing Amendments which, in either Case, shall be valid to all Intents and Purposes, as Part of the Constitution, when ratified by the Legislatures of three fourths of the several States, or by Conventions in three fourths thereof, as the one or the other Mode of Ratification may be proposed by the Congress.

But Article V fails to preserve the People's authority over the government. First, the Article V procedures do not implement the will and judgment of a simple majority: *two-thirds* of both houses of Congress, or *two-thirds* of the state legislatures, must initiate an amendment, and *three-fourths* of the states must ratify it. Second, the Article V amendment process sits in the hands of government officials, not the People. The *Congress*, on its own or prodded by state legislatures, must act before an amendment even gets off the ground, and may dictate that ratification take place by state legislatures rather than by the People at large.

Since constitutional amendments pursuant to Article V require a supermajority vote of government officials, the amendment process fails to preserve rule by the People. It can be (and has been) the case that a clear majority of the American people wish to amend the Constitution but cannot convince their representatives to initiate or support an amendment.[1] To make matters worse, such resistance is not always principled. To take an obvious example, many representatives oppose an amendment limiting the number of terms a representative may serve; their views are obviously colored by self-interest. Voters may be tempted to dump such representatives at the next election but, of course, the issue of term limits is rarely the only thing separating candidates in a campaign. Moreover, voters in every district have a disincentive to remove their district's incumbent. Given Congress's seniority system, a new representative generally translates into less pork for the district. This raises what economists call a "collective action" problem: Everyone wants to throw the bums out, but most vote to keep *their* bum in.

Where does all of this leave us? If the People are to govern, we cannot be ruled from the grave by those who passed on the Constitution. Self-rule requires that the People be able to amend the Constitution. However, Article V sets forth procedures for amendment that fail to so empower the People.

As it happens, this fundamental problem has a ready solution—one that merely requires a fresh look at the Constitution. A close reading of Article V reveals something interesting: It does not say that the procedures it outlines are the *only* means of amending the Constitution. The best reading of the Constitution, one sensitive to the tapestry of the entire document, yields the conclusion that Article V merely sets forth one mode of amendment—that undertaken by the organs of ordinary government. There also exists a separate means of amending the Constitution: a national referendum (of sorts) by We the People.

This alternate means of amendment does not arise from Article V, which says nothing about amendment by the People directly. Indeed, no clause of the Constitution straightforwardly declares that "We the People may amend the Constitution by majority vote." But the history, text, and structure of the Constitution all support the conclusion that We the People retain the right to do just that.

OUR FOUNDING FATHERS faced a problem similar to that facing We the People today—they were stuck with a document that, at first blush, seemed to defy ready amendment. Many of the thirteen states had written constitutions in place in 1787. These constitutions established demanding rules for amendment—just like our Article V. And, on the surface, various state constitutions were violated when the federal Constitution was adopted and ratified. The Constitution was established in accordance with a process set forth in Article VII (providing for ratification by special conventions of the People), a process that seemingly contravened various state constitutions.

For example, the Massachusetts constitution provided for its own amendment in 1795, if two-thirds of the citizens called for a convention. But when Massachusetts ratified the federal Constitution pursuant to Article VII, thereby dramatically altering the status of its own constitution (which ceased to be the highest law of the state, becoming subservient to the federal Constitution), it did so not in 1795 but in 1788, and not by a two-thirds vote but by a simple majority. Similar provisions in other state constitutions were bypassed when those states ratified the federal Constitution.

Opponents of the new federal Constitution noticed all this. Waving the texts of state constitutions, Anti-Federalists declared that ratification of the federal Constitution under Article VII would be illegal. However, they did not press the point, and for good reason: Federalist supporters of the Constitution had a knockout response. James Madison put it best. At the Constitutional Convention in Philadelphia, a Maryland delegate cited a provision in Maryland's constitution governing its own amendment, and claimed that Maryland was not free to pursue any other mode. Listen carefully to Madison's reply:

> The difficulty in Maryland was no greater than in other States. . . . The people were in fact, the fountain of all power, and by resorting to them, all difficulties were got over. They could alter constitutions as they pleased. . . . [F]irst principles might be resorted to.[2]

What were these "first principles"? Simply that the People are sovereign, and a majority of the people enjoy the inalienable legal right to alter or abolish their form of government whenever they deem fit. This notion may sound radical, but it is quintessentially American. These "first principles" are first indeed—they represent the essence of the American Revolution. In the words of the Declaration of Independence: "We hold these truths to be self-evident. . . . that whenever any Form of Government becomes destructive of these ends, it is the Right of the People to alter or to abolish it, and to institute new Government. . . ." Similar statements dotted the various state constitutions and Bills or Declarations of Rights.

Thus, the ratification of the Constitution was lawful, even in those states that had provisions for amendment of their own constitution that were not followed. Such provisions, read carefully, did not set forth the *only* means of amendment. The adoption of the federal Constitution effectively amended the state constitutions via direct appeal to the People—a method recognized as legitimate, indeed as a "first principle," within all the states.

This account explains something otherwise mysterious: the immediate and widespread acquiescence of opponents of the Constitution once votes were taken in the state conventions. This acquiescence embodied America's animating principle—popular sovereignty. The government belongs to We the People. All exercise of authority must derive from us.

We and only we may change or abolish that government (unless we delegate such authority).

IF THIS IS the case, mustn't we rethink the notion that Article V presents the only means of amending the federal Constitution? Didn't the principle that governed adoption of the Constitution itself—the sovereign right of the People to alter or abolish the government—survive the adoption of the Constitution? Why should Article V block direct amendment by the people any more than analogues to Article V in state constitutions blocked the people from directly amending those documents—by adopting the federal Constitution?

Some may object that this argument renders Article V a nullity. If the Constitution can be amended by the People directly, why did the Framers bother with the elaborate provisions of Article V? The answer is that Article V provides for a mode of amendment that otherwise would have been impossible. Absent explicit authority from We the People, ordinary organs of government (Congress and state legislatures) would not have been presumed competent to amend the document. Without Article V's express delegation of authority from the People, even an "amendment" unanimously adopted by both houses of Congress and every state legislature could not take effect.

But when We the People gave the organs of government the power to amend the Constitution via Article V, we did not deprive ourselves of our independent right to amend the Constitution. Indeed, this right is inalienable—meaning it *cannot* be given up or waived—and was so recognized as a first principle by Jefferson in the Declaration of Independence and by Madison at the Constitutional Convention. The *Federalist Papers,* the Founders' fullest explication of the Constitution's meaning, makes several references to this first principle. For example, in *Federalist* 78, Alexander Hamilton alludes to "that fundamental principle of republican government which admits the right of the people to alter or abolish the established Constitution whenever they find it inconsistent with their happiness."[3]

The idea that constitutional amendments may be undertaken *either* by the government pursuant to Article V, *or* by the People themselves pursuant to the transcendent first principle of popular sovereignty, also draws support from the sharp distinction the Framers drew between government and the People. They understood that government officials were imperfect representatives who might have different interests and judgments from the People they represent. Ultimate control must rest with the People. The inherent tension between government officials and the People also explains why the Framers made Article V so cumbersome. Insofar as a major feature of the Constitution was its restraint of government officials, it would have been self-defeating to permit such officials to easily remove the restraints by amending them away.

The Constitution consists of a set of grants of power by the People to government agents for limited purposes. These agents possess no power outside of such grants. (The Tenth Amendment, discussed in more detail below, made this point explicit.) Article V represents a grant by the people to government officials to amend the Constitution through the procedures set forth therein. It sets forth the mode of amendment *absent participation by the People.* But once again there is no reason to read Article V as binding We the People, who are the masters, not the servants—who are indeed the source of Article V and the entire Constitution.

The Constitution empowers and limits government; it neither empowers nor limits the People. Rather, the Constitution is predicated on the People's preexisting power. As the Declaration of Independence made clear, such power derives from the inalienable right of the People to alter and abolish their government. Even if the People wished to give up this right in 1787, they certainly could not give it up for future generations.

THE ARGUMENT FOR constitutional amendment by the People directly does not rest on history alone. That the Declaration of Independence espoused such a right, that the Framers recognized it, and that such recognition explains the otherwise illegal adoption of the Constitution and the otherwise mysterious acquiescence of its opponents—all this powerfully supports recognition of the sovereign right to amend. But all this, without more, would fail to satisfy those who insist that constitutional meaning trace directly to the text of the document itself. Fortunately, the right of the People to amend the Constitution can indeed be located in the Constitution's text, in the words of and connections among five different clauses: the Preamble, Article VII, and the First, Ninth, and Tenth Amendments.

The Preamble of the Constitution announces that "We the People of the United States . . . do ordain and establish this Constitution." These words say it all. The ringing declaration that We the People create the Constitution embodies the critical principle of popular sovereignty. If We, acting by simple majority in each state, had the authority to ordain and establish the Constitution, how could we lack the authority to alter or abolish that Constitution by the same means?

As the Constitution merged previously separate states into one nation, the relevant majority after its ordainment and establishment became a national majority, not a majority of the people within each state. (An easy modern-day analogy comes from corporate law. Company A and Company B merge, with the approval by lawful majorities of each company's shareholders. After the merger, a majority of the newly-formed company will govern.) But while the Constitution redefined the relevant polity, it did nothing to change the principle of popular sovereignty. To the contrary, the Preamble proudly proclaims popular sovereignty as—literally—the Constitution's first principle.

The Framers recognized a connection between the Preamble and the right of the People to alter or abolish the Constitution. James Wilson, author of the first draft of the Preamble, and one of six men to sign both the Constitution and the Declaration of Independence, argued that the Constitution's "leading principle" is that "the supreme power resides in the people."[4] He saw this principle clearly implied in the Preamble, as his influential remarks at Pennsylvania's ratifying convention make clear:

> This Constitution . . . opens with a solemn and practical recognition of that principle:—"We the *people of the United States, in order to form a more perfect union, establish justice, &c., do* ordain and establish this Constitution for the United States of America." It is announced in *their* name—it receives its political existence from their authority: they ordain and establish. What is the necessary consequence? Those who ordain and establish have the power, if they think proper, to repeal and annul.[5]

Wilson was not alone in connecting the Preamble to the right of the People to amend the Constitution. Similar observations were made by James Iredell (soon to be a United States Supreme Court Justice) at North Carolina's ratifying convention,[6] and Edmund Pendleton (a leading lawyer and the presiding officer) at Virginia's ratifying convention.[7]

Do we need more proof of the link between the Preamble and the People's right to amend the Constitution? If so, we have James Madison himself, hailed as the father of the Constitution. In the First Congress, Madison proposed amending the original Constitution by adding a prefix to the Preamble declaring that "the people have an indubitable, unalienable and indefeasible right to reform or change their Government."[8] The proposal was dropped not because anyone objected to such a right but because it went without saying. For example, one congressman opined that the unamended Preamble amounted to a "practical recognition of the right of the people to ordain and establish Governments."[9] As the Framers recognized, it makes no sense to think of such a right apart from the companion right to *re*ordain and *re*establish the government.

The Preamble, of course, began the Constitution. Article VII ended it. Together, these two provisions are perfect bookends, the Constitution's alpha and omega. While the Preamble announces the People's action in establishing the Constitution, Article VII explains how such action is taken (stipulating the requirement of ratification by conventions of the people). Thus, the Preamble and Article VII, in tandem, declared and effected the right of the People to change their government through direct action.*

If the original Constitution leaves any doubt on this point, the Bill of Rights goes a long way towards removing it. Five separate amendments speak of rights and powers of "the People," and three of them implicitly evoke the right of direct amendment by the People.

The Ninth Amendment announces that the "enumeration in the Constitution of certain rights shall not be construed to deny or disparage others retained by the people" and the Tenth Amendment states that "powers not delegated to the United States by the Constitution, nor prohibited by it to the States, are reserved to the States respectively, or to the people." Both the Ninth and Tenth Amendments have been a source of confusion and controversy. Liberals seize on the Ninth as an invitation to judges to protect individual constitutional rights unnamed in the document, such as sexual privacy. This position infuriates conservatives who, however, offer no serious alternative explanation of the amendment. By contrast, conservatives see the Tenth Amendment as the home of states' rights. This infuriates liberals who, however, offer no serious alternative explanation of the amendment.

Perhaps both liberals and conservatives miss the essence of these amendments. The true meaning of the Ninth and Tenth Amendments emerges when they are seen as intertwined with the Preamble—affirmations that the People retain the right to alter or abolish their government. On a conventional reading, the Ninth Amendment concerns individual rights, the Tenth involves states' rights, and the Preamble offers a bit of prefatory fluff. But look more closely. All three provisions explicitly highlight the role of "the People." If the Ninth Amendment is primarily concerned with individual rights, why does it speak of rights

---

*Just as the Preamble says We the People "establish this Constitution," Article VII explains that ratification by nine states suffices for "establishment of this Constitution." This textual echo reminds us that the adoption of the Constitution involved not just "saying," but "doing"—or, as the name of the document implies, *constituting*. The Constitution is not simply a text, but an embodiment of an action by We the People in the 1780s. The power of the People to amend the Constitution is what gives this original act its ongoing vitality, truly making the Constitution a living document.

of "the people" rather than of "persons"? If the Tenth is exclusively concerned with states' rights, why does it stand back to back with the Ninth and why does it too refer to rights retained by "the people"? And if the Preamble does not affirm and embody popular sovereignty, what in the world does it mean and do?

The history surrounding these provisions, like their language, suggests that the Preamble, the Ninth Amendment, and Tenth Amendment are about much the same thing—popular sovereignty. We have already discussed how the Framers viewed the Preamble. The legislative history of the Ninth and Tenth Amendments confirms their implications for the People's right to abolish or amend the Constitution. Consider this proposed draft that surfaced at Virginia's ratifying convention:

> The powers granted under the Constitution, being derived from the people of the United States, may be resumed by them, whensoever the same shall be perverted to their injury or oppression, and that every power not granted thereby remains with them, and at their will; that, therefore, no right . . . can be canceled, abridged, restrained, or modified by [the federal government] except in those instances in which power is given by the Constitution for those purposes.[10]

Similar language and sentiments, meshing the Preamble with prototypes of the Ninth and Tenth Amendments, and linking the whole package to the right of the People to alter or abolish their government, also appeared in New York's and at other states' ratifying conventions.[11] All of this language, in turn, consciously built on the words of the Declaration of Independence, whose most famous passage affirmed *"the Right of the People* to alter or abolish [Government] and to institute new Government."

Additional evidence linking the Ninth and Tenth Amendments to the Preamble's expression of popular sovereignty emerged during the First Congress's discussion of these amendments. For example, a South Carolina Representative proposed amending an early version of the Tenth

Amendment by adding as a prefix, "all powers being derived from the people," because "he thought this a better place to make this assertion than the introductory clause [the Preamble] of the Constitution."[12]

Eventually, of course, the identical point—that all power is derived from the People—was made by the last three words of the Ninth and Tenth Amendments, which spoke, respectively, of rights retained "by the people" and reserved "to the people." As the South Carolina representative recognized, these clauses echo the Preamble's affirmation that "We the People" have the right to establish (and disestablish) a government.

After ratification of the Bill of Rights, the Ninth and Tenth Amendments formed the Constitution's new omega. The alpha-omega combination of the Preamble and these amendments formed the outer brackets of a Constitution whose inner body consisted of Articles I–VII and the first eight Amendments. By virtue of this structure, the Constitution, read as a whole, did the following:

1. Declared that all power resides in the People (in the Preamble);
2. Delegated many powers to government entities, while also limiting those powers (in Articles I, II, and III);
3. Explained how those entities could amend the Constitution, thereby loosening the restraints (in Article V);
4. Specified additional restrictions on those government entities—rights of the People and of persons that could not be infringed (in Amendments One through Eight); and
5. Clarified that the delegation of power to those entities in no way deprived We the People of our sovereign right to amend or alter the Constitution ourselves (in the Ninth and Tenth Amendments, understood in conjunction with the Preamble and Article VII).

One other piece of this puzzle requires special attention—the First Amendment. It, too, refers to "the people," specifically "the right of the people peaceably to assemble." To assemble where? On the street corner? In our homes? Anywhere? All of the above, no doubt, but there is good reason to believe that the Framers had a specific kind of assembly in mind when they penned the First Amendment.

In revolutionary America, the ideas and words "people," "assemble," and "convention" were invariably found tightly clustered in discussions of popular sovereignty. In 1789, a core meaning of the right of the People to assemble was the right to assemble in convention.* Thus, the First Amendment helps ensure that We the People can exercise our right to alter or abolish the Constitution, by explicitly forbidding the government from abridging our right to assemble at a convention for that purpose.

Finally, one aspect of Article V also lends support to our position. After setting forth the ordinary mode of constitutional amendment, Article V adds a few wrinkles. It declares in effect that the provisions of the Constitution protecting the slave trade cannot be changed until 1808, and that the provision requiring equal representation of states in the United States Senate cannot be amended unless all states agree. On their face, these provisions are difficult to justify—they tie the hands of future generations and thus defeat the first principle of popular sovereignty. However, recognition of amendment outside of Article V solves the problem. The slave trade and equal representation provisions, coming at the end of Article V, are best read as restricting amendments within Article V. Since the People retain the right to amend the Constitution directly, outside of Article V, the provisions entrenching the slave trade and Senate apportionment were not kept off limits to the People.

One key clarification is in order. We have spoken throughout of the right of *the People* to amend the Constitution. But what constitutes the voice of the People? A majority? Two thirds? Unanimous vote only? The Framers recognized the inalienable right of the People to amend our Constitution—but what is the margin necessary to achieve an amendment?

The answer begins with an appeal to logic and common sense: In a

---

*This was not the only meaning, for the text radiates beyond the core, just as the Ninth Amendment's text radiates beyond its core concern about the People's right to amend the Constitution and may encompass additional rights.

regime where all citizens are considered equal, what could reflect the will of the People other than a majority? Simple majority rule has unique mathematical properties; nothing else treats all voters and all preferences equally. Once majority rule is abandoned, there is no logical stopping point anywhere between a 50-percent-plus-one rule and, say, a 99.9 percent rule. And the latter, of course, is surely not rule by the People, since it would treat .2 percent of the people as more powerful than 99.8 percent.*

We need not rest the case only on logic and common sense, however, because there happens to be strong evidence that the Framers accepted, indeed insisted upon, this equation of the People with a majority. For example, the celebrated 1776 Virginia Declaration of Rights—the first Revolution-era Bill of Rights and a model for the rest—declared the "indubitable, unalienable, and indefeasible" right of "a *majority* of the community" to alter or abolish the government. No other state declaration addressed the issue explicitly, and none took issue with Virginia's declaration.

Indeed, in the 1780s, the special status of majority rule was extraordinarily well understood—it literally went without saying in a variety of documents precisely because it was so obvious. While the Declaration of Independence spoke only of "the right of the People to alter or abolish" without specifying that this right must be exercised by a majority, we know that Thomas Jefferson linked popular sovereignty with majority rule. As he wrote James Madison in 1787: "It is my principle that the will of the Majority should always prevail. If they approve the proposed [constitution] I shall concur in it chearfully, in the hopes that they [a majority] will amend it whenever they shall find it work wrong."[13]

This was a recurring theme of Jefferson's. In his first Inaugural Address he described "absolute acquiescence in the decisions of the majority" as "the vital principle of republics," and in another letter

---

*If we think of amendment as a judicial act, we reach the same result. Even judges follow majority rule: On the Supreme Court, five votes beat four. The same principle should apply to America's ultimate Supreme Court—We the People.

declared that majority rule "is the fundamental law of every society of equal rights."[14] Jefferson was not alone. The distinguished judge and scholar Joseph Story, writing about the Declaration of Independence's reference to the right of the People to alter or abolish the government, parenthetically added that the document "plainly intend[ed] the majority of the People" as a proxy for the People.[15] Similarly, Gordon Wood's classic study about America's pre-Constitution confederacy provides instance after instance of contemporaneous references to the right of the majority to alter a governing charter.[16]

Majority rule continued to hold sway throughout the deliberations over the federal Constitution. We find references to it at the Philadelphia Convention of 1787, in the *Federalist Papers* and other writings by both Federalists and Anti-Federalists, and at the state ratifying conventions. James Wilson spoke eloquently of majority rule both at Pennsylvania's ratifying convention and in his 1790 *Lectures on Law*. The Constitution, he noted, belongs to the People, who "have the right to mould, to preserve, to improve, to refine, and to finish it as they please. If so; can it be doubted, that they have the right likewise to change it?"[17] Lest there be any confusion, Wilson added that "A majority of society is sufficient for this purpose."[18]

Even more conclusive than the Framers' words are their deeds. Although Article VII did not specify that majority rule would apply in each state's ratifying convention, this was universally understood. The historical records provide no evidence of a single opponent of the Constitution arguing that a supermajority (say two thirds) should be required for ratification. To the contrary, fervent opponents of the Constitution like Patrick Henry conceded that they must submit to the decision of the convention's majority. In state after state the opponents of ratification acted on this understanding, accepting the legitimacy of an outcome they despised. Indeed, in many states ratification squeaked by: 30–27 in New York, 187–168 in Massachusetts, 57–47 in New Hampshire, 89–79 in Virginia. With so many clever and ardent men opposed to ratification, why did no one point to the absence of a reference to majority rule in Article VII and insist on a supermajority requirement? The answer is clear: majority rule really did go without saying.*

In the final analysis, the history of the Constitution's adoption, and the text and structure of the document itself all point to the same conclusion: The Constitution may be amended by a majority of the People.

IN THE INTRODUCTION, we stated that We the People retain far greater rights than we generally realize. No right is greater, or less recognized, than our right to shape the Constitution. Tremendous power flows from the right to amend our national charter. Could We the People, by majority vote, amend the Constitution so as to establish term limits for members of Congress? Outlaw abortion? Require prayer in schools? Mandate a balanced federal budget? Demand vast redistribution of wealth? Ban discrimination against homosexuals? Set a mandatory retirement age? Expand the President's term to ten years? Set Congress's pay at $25,000?

The answer to all of these questions is yes. Of course, we intentionally selected some examples that will stand conservatives' hair on end, some that will have the same effect on liberals, and some likely to annoy everyone. These provocative examples are designed to spark con-

---

*Because Article VII required ratification by nine of the thirteen states, one might be tempted to see nine/thirteenths, rather than majority rule, as the relevant requirement. That would be a mistake. As Article VII makes clear, any states that did not ratify would not be forced into the Union—the nine/thirteenths requirement had no binding effect on them. The nine states needed for ratification simply represented a term in the new contract, based on what the Framers regarded as necessary for a feasible union. They may have had good reason for choosing the number nine, but it has no significance as a matter of principle—they could just as easily have chosen eight or ten or any other number. The same could not be said for the requirement that ratification in each state required majority approval. As noted, the assumption of a simple majority vote to determine ratification was so universally shared that, even absent its mention in Article VII, no one questioned it. To be sure, the Constitution requires supermajorities for certain actions—ratifications of treaties, convictions of impeachments, overridings of presidential vetoes, and constitutional amendments pursuant to Article V. However, these involve acts by government entities exercising powers delegated to them by the People. As we have said, there is no hint in the Constitution, or elsewhere, that the People delegated away our right to amend the Constitution (which is, in any event, inalienable and thus cannot be delegated away). And that right was understood to reside with a simple majority.

sideration of whether the spacious power of the People to amend the Constitution is a good thing.

Conservatives tend to approve of a wide scope for majority rule, but even they may find themselves nervous about our conclusion in this chapter. It is one thing to give the majority latitude to enact ordinary laws, but to amend the Constitution is something else. Liberals tend to favor expansive rights, but even they may find a popular right to amend too expansive. Is anyone comfortable with a simple majority having the power to enact all the hypothetical amendments listed above?

During the push to enact a constitutional amendment to ban flag-burning, an amendment supported by then-President Bush, one commentator scolded Bush to "keep your hands off Mr. Madison's document."[19] On one level, this was a stunningly inappropriate remark. The Constitution reflects Madison's handiwork, but as Madison well knew, it is not his document: It belongs to the People. Moreover, "Madison's document" was drastically flawed, as blacks and women especially can attest. Had we "kept our hands off it," there would be no Thirteenth Amendment banning slavery, no Fourteenth Amendment requiring states to afford equal protection to all, no Fifteenth Amendment granting black men the right to vote, and no Nineteenth Amendment doing the same for women. One answer to those fearful of constitutional amendments is to point to the inadequacy of the original Constitution, and to the great amendments that remedied many of the original defects.

However, the Thirteenth, Fourteenth, Fifteenth, Nineteenth, and all other amendments to date were passed pursuant to Article V's procedures. They required the action of many government officials, and enjoyed more than mere majority support. Isn't it scary to place our Constitution directly in the hands of a majority of Americans? This important question deserves full and serious consideration—and is the focus of our next chapter.

TWO

Why Amendment by the People Is Not Dangerous

THE AVAILABILITY OF CONSTITUTIONAL AMENDMENT by majority vote should not strike panic in our hearts. As we shall see, there are several reasons to resist the assumption that the citizenry, if made aware of its power to amend, would act rashly, meanly, or foolishly. But even if the American people were as inadequate as some suppose, they would be significantly constrained from wreaking violence on the Constitution and their fellow citizens.

First, not everything in the Constitution is amendable: Since the Constitution recognizes popular sovereignty as an *inalienable* right of the People, then popular sovereignty, and all that it entails, cannot be amended away. We the People can alter our government provided that we do not undermine the very basis of our right—or the right of future generations—to do so. This means, at a minimum, that the People could not amend the Constitution so as to freeze all or part of it. Although the People could pass an amendment repealing Article V (thus retracting our delegation to government entities of the power to amend the Constitution), we could not prohibit future amendments by the People. For that matter, the People cannot pass an amendment forever locking into place some random constitutional provision. Suppose, for example, the People are considering the following proposed amendment: "Christianity is the official religion of America. This provision is not subject to repeal or alteration." This amendment must fail, for it would prevent the People, in the future, from exercising their inalienable right of self-government.

Other amendments, too, would impermissibly impede popular sovereignty. The People cannot abolish elections, or eliminate free speech, or reduce its scope to the point where self-government becomes impossible. (Paradoxically, this part of the First Amendment must be nonamendable in order to preserve the amendability of the rest of the document.) So too, efforts to redefine the polity by stripping the franchise from certain citizens would arguably be beyond the pale.*

Perhaps such limitations on majority amendment will be deemed trivial. The People are less likely to undermine popular sovereignty in

---

*The question arises as to how such restrictions could be enforced. One might think that the Supreme Court would hold improper amendments unconstitutional. However, that approach is unavailing since the People could—legitimately—amend the Supreme Court (or its powers of judicial review) out of existence. The restrictions on the People's right to amend are norms that should guide the amending process and conversation, but that cannot ultimately be externally enforced. This conclusion may seem radical, but is really a matter of logic and common sense. After all, *someone* must be the ultimate interpreter of the Constitution; in a regime where the People are sovereign, that power necessarily falls to them. In the case of ordinary legislation, and even as to amendments passed pursuant to Article V, the People have generally delegated the power of judicial review to the Supreme Court. However, the People cannot irrevocably delegate the power to thwart their own choice to change the government. By analogy, in England certain actions are off limits to Parliament, but Parliament remains the ultimate arbiter. The principle—sovereignty—is the same in America, except that here the People are the sovereign body. The fact that limits on amendments by the People cannot ultimately be externally enforced does not render the limits meaningless. Parliament generally respects limits on its authority; why assume the American people would do otherwise? Direct amendment will occur only if the People recognize their authority. We need to make sure that such recognition is accompanied by recognition of the built-in limits on that authority.

the ways described above than to trample the rights of minorities (electoral minorities as well as racial and other minorities) in various invidious ways. Would not constitutional amendment by majority vote unleash the devastating tyranny of the majority that Madison famously feared? For example, might a nationwide majority deem homosexuality a crime punishable by incarceration? Or resegregate America's schools? Or turn back the clock on the right of women to serve in the military?

This is just the beginning of the potential parade of horribles. Imagine that a group like the erstwhile Moral Majority became a majority in fact as well as name. If the right to amend by majority vote became recognized, wouldn't this group not only overturn *Roe v. Wade*[1] and criminalize abortion, but also reverse *Griswold v. Connecticut*[2] and proscribe birth control? Wouldn't this group be tempted to strip from the Constitution any semblance of a right to privacy?

Under current law, the Constitution's Equal Protection Clause and Due Process Clause prevent these sorts of actions: If Congress or a state passes the kinds of measures described above, the courts will declare them unconstitutional. What happens, though, when a zealous majority realizes that it *can change* the Constitution—not through the cumbersome Article V process, but directly, through a kind of national referendum? What happens if it repeals the Equal Protection Clause and other foundational constitutional protections?

Yes, the parade of horribles is horrible indeed, and the possibility of a tyrannical majority cannot be ruled out. But the above scenarios are quite unlikely. As an empirical matter, many states permit citizens to amend their state constitution through popular vote, and (as we shall see in the next chapter) the overall track record is reassuring. And for good reason. America's unparalleled heterogeneity offers enormous protection. Because each citizen sees herself as in a minority on some issues, each is likely to embrace—consciously or unconsciously—a general idea of minority rights. For example, a conservative Catholic, tempted to constitutionalize his values and ban contraception, will recognize the dangers (and perhaps also the unfairness) of doing so when a very different majority threatens a constitutional amendment that would take away his gun.

Recognizing that their party will not always be in power, most people want limits on governmental authority, out of long-term self-interest if not out of respect for others. Thus strong majorities would generally rally behind some protection of minority or individual rights to property, privacy, free exercise of religion, due process, equal protection, and so on.

Partly for this reason, the American people (unlike certain politicians) generally seem wary about tinkering with the Constitution. Arguably, more danger lies in our collective unwillingness to make needed changes than in our reckless pursuit of change. Many citizens, upon learning of the right to amend the Constitution by majority vote, would recoil from the risk of excessive amendments, and might vote against virtually any amendment, even ones they favor on the merits. Indeed, it appears that in the states permitting constitutional amendment by referendum, the bulk of proposed amendments fail.[3]

Civil libertarians like to point out that polls show most American opposing various provisions in the Bill of Rights.[4] But would we really cast aside these provisions when the awesome moment of truth arrived? It is one thing to register disagreement with a proposition read over the phone by an unknown questioner, and quite another to actually vote to change the venerable Constitution. (Indeed, pollsters rarely tell their subjects that the provision in question is in the Constitution.) Would disagreement with provisions in the Bill of Rights survive a campaign to educate the public about their true effect, and their living history in American constitutional law? For example, would most Americans remain so opposed to the right to a jury trial that we would actually vote to expunge it from the Constitution?

It must be remembered that we are speaking here of a national majority, not simply a statewide one—a majority of the whole, not of a part. As James Madison reminded us, an individual state is far more likely to be dominated by a single tyrannical majority faction than is the nation. The larger polity provides a certain safety in numbers. Indeed, there *are* instances of what might be called tyranny in some states—certainly that's how homosexuals regard laws criminalizing their sexual intimacy—but rarely at the national level.

Where is the national outcry to tyrannize any minority? Those cited by the left and right respectively as dangerous extremists—Pat Robertson's fundamentalist followers, or the American Civil Liberties Union—tend to represent views that are in a distinct minority nationally.

As suggested, the absence of nationwide movements to oppress minorities stems in part from America's heterogeneity. No stable majority emerges across all issues. People know they will sometimes be in a minority, and thus may hedge their bets, exercising restraint when they are in a majority. But something more important may be at work as well: Ordinary American citizens may be more virtuous than they are given credit for.

We say this, of course, not unmindful of the nation's shameful treatment of blacks and other minorities. However, much of the mistreatment has occurred at the local rather than the national level. And, as the Framers hoped, We the People have become more enlightened over time, as the many inclusive constitutional amendments—all of which enjoyed majority support—demonstrate.

Before we assume the worst, we should reflect on the fact that the citizenry's capacity for self-government underlies our nation's experiment with democracy. As James Madison wrote in *Federalist* 55:

> As there is a degree of depravity in mankind which requires a certain degree of circumspection and distrust, so there are other qualities in human nature which justify a certain portion of esteem and confidence. Republican government presupposes the existence of these qualities in a higher degree than any other form.[5]

As Madison went on to say, if people really were devoid of the necessary virtue and sympathy to govern, "nothing less than the chains of despotism can restrain them from destroying and devouring one another."[6]

Looking backward from 1997, we see all the painful exclusions in the founding era (of women, of blacks); but looking backward from 1787, consider the breadth of inclusion. Never before in world history had so many people played so explicit a role in deciding how they and their posterity would be governed: The adoption of the Constitution was, quite simply, the most participatory, majoritarian, and populist event the Earth had ever seen.* Americans did not receive their supreme law from On High, from some Great Man claiming a pipeline to God—Moses, Solon, Lycurgus—or even from some conclave of fifty-five demigods in Philadelphia (who, after all, merely proposed a piece of paper). Nor did our country inherit our supreme law from immemorial custom. Rather, the People ordained and established our Constitution—peacefully, deliberately, inclusively (by the standards of the day) and lawfully—in a way that electrified the world and changed history.

In the ensuing two centuries, the People have remedied many of the defects of the original document, making it far more inclusive. (And while the Thirteenth, Fourteenth, Fifteenth, Nineteenth, Twenty-Fourth and Twenty-Sixth Amendments were passed pursuant to Article V, they enjoyed strong popular support and were driven by ordinary citizens, moral crusaders who took to the streets and the printing presses.) Warts and all, the American experiment with democracy has been a glorious success compared to the experience of most countries.

To a great degree, then, the People have proven themselves worthy of the "esteem and confidence" referred to by Madison in *Federalist* 55. What have we done to deserve distrust? Whenever a David Duke or a Louis Farrakhan receives some enthusiastic support, commentators lament the susceptibility of the American people to demagogues who traffic in scapegoating. But have Duke and Farrakhan won national office? Pat Buchanan's brief success in the 1996 Republican nomination process was the occasion for much handwringing about the gullibility (or worse) of the electorate. But even in his triumphant hour—his victory in the New Hampshire primary—Buchanan failed to win a majority of the votes of his own party. And immediately thereafter, the overwhelming majority of Republican voters repudiated him in state after state. If the American people have a reputation for meanness or foolishness at the ballot box, it is not clear that they deserve it.

*Neither the Declaration of Independence nor the Articles of Confederation had been put to a popular vote, nor had most of the early state constitutions.

Some may argue that, however good or sober the American people may generally be, and however much their sense of fairness or self-interest guards against tyrannical actions, the availability of majority amendment will lead to a certain rashness. Should not something as high-stakes and fundamental as constitutional amendment stem from *deliberation*, not mere nose-counting?

Yes—but there is no reason to assume that majority amendment will eschew the deliberative process. We have, to this point, said nothing about what procedures should be undertaken to implement majority amendment. While that remains largely an administrative matter to be worked out down the road, this much is clear: the majority's right to amend need not entail the right to amend instantaneously or whimsically. In fact, genuine popular sovereignty presupposes a deliberative majority of the collective "People," not a mere nose-counting of discrete individuals. Thus, in the very first sentence of the *Federalist Papers,* Alexander Hamilton reminded the People that they were "called upon to *deliberate* on a new Constitution for the United States."[7] In order to deliberate properly, the People must be exposed to and must engage opposing ideas; a preliminary majority should attempt to reason with and persuade any dissenters, and dissenters in turn should engage the majority in debate. While the judgment of the People must be determined by majority vote, *all* voters are part of the People and thus entitled to be part of the deliberative process.*

Because the requisite deliberations could not occur en masse among all voters in 1787, the Founders had to rely on smaller conventions to speak as and for the People. This prevented extended deliberations and discussions by the polity at large. Today, because of vast improvements in communication and transportation technology—radio, television, ca-

---

*We speak here and elsewhere of the *judgment* as well as the will of the People, to remind readers that amendment is a judical as well as legislative act. The People are not merely the Supreme Legislature; they are also the True Supreme Court and the Ultimate Jury. Just as jurors should not vote to convict a defendant where they believe conviction would be unjust (as we argue in Chapter 10), so too voters should not support any amendment, even one they might otherwise prefer, if they deem the amendment unjust. As with other restrictions on the amending process, this one must be enforced internally rather than externally. (See note on page 21.)

ble, fiber optics, electronic town meetings, etc.—there may be ways to retain the deliberation of the convention while also providing for more direct popular participation akin to referenda. Perhaps citizens could assemble in caucuses in their towns and neighborhoods, and these assemblies could be electronically and interactively linked to focused debate in a central convention assembly. After hearing these debates and having the opportunity to speak up in their local caucus, citizens could vote directly on the proposed amendment, rather than surrendering their proxies to convention members.

In short, there remains considerable room for flexibility in ensuring deliberation. This might include, for example, requiring two separate votes, spaced far enough apart to allow opportunities for true conversation and conversion and to give time for second thoughts to cool fleeting fancy. To acknowledge the majority's right to amend the Constitution does not entail making such amendments easy to get.

Indeed, direct amendment by the People, via majority vote, will not necessarily prove easier than amendment by ordinary government through Article V. We cannot be certain which method will generate more amendments. It may be, for example, that the Eighteenth Amendment (Prohibition) would not have been enacted if the attempt to do so had been made via direct appeal to the people—some evidence suggests that a majority of voters opposed Prohibition at the time of its adoption.[8]

At any rate, our argument in favor of the majority's right to amend does not rest on the notion that the Constitution ought to be easier to amend. Our concern is not how easily amendment should occur but *by whom*—we wish to relocate the final word on the Constitution, taking it out of the hands of government entities and placing it into the hands of the People. (Actually, we wish to spur recognition that it always has resided and must reside with the People.) That can be accomplished without compromising the ideal of deliberation.

It may be feared that, even with extensive deliberation, majority amendments will create instability. The imagined scenario is an endless series of amendments and counteramendments placing constitutional law in constant flux. This, too, is an unjustified fear.

As a practical matter, the states that permit amendments to their constitutions through citizen initiatives and referenda have not experienced wild instability. In California, amendments have passed with some frequency but, for reasons discussed above, it is a mistake to extrapolate from a single state to the nation. California may be particularly unrepresentative. Given its extraordinary growth and rapidly changing demographic structure, it may need frequent amendments to accommodate the changing needs of its people.

Moreover, the People of a state can experiment by amending their constitution precisely because the federal Constitution stands as a secure political safety net—a floor below which the state cannot fall. Under Article VI, Section 2 of the Constitution, the so-called "Supremacy Clause," the federal Constitution is the "supreme law of the land," taking precedence over any state statutes or state constitutional provisions that conflict with it. Thus, for example, if a state amended its constitution to censor certain media, courts would strike down the provision as violative of the First Amendment. For this reason and others, state constitutional amendments lack the self-restraining solemnity of federal constitutional amendments. Even so, we have generally not witnessed a promiscuous approach to constitutional amendments in those states that permit direct amendment by the People.

It may be argued that although voters will show greater prudence and restraint when dealing with the Constitution, the consequences of error are more severe: a constitutional mistake inflicts more damage than a statutory mistake. But of course the majority's right to amend the Constitution does not stop once an amendment is passed; the majority may repeal what it enacts. For reasons stated above, we do not envision a rapid-fire advance and retreat, with amendments quickly and casually passed and then repealed in the same cavalier manner. Still, the opportunity for experimentation followed by observation and, if needed, correction, is not a bad thing.

Indeed, Article V does not necessarily prevent ill-considered constitutional amendments either. The Eighteenth Amendment's constitutionalization of Prohibition poses a sobering example. And while it did not take long for the experiment to be revealed a failure, it took four-teen years for its repeal. If amendments by the People should prove easier to pass (which, as noted, is not a foregone conclusion), the happy corollary is that unwise amendments would be easier to undo. Easy or not, there is little reason to fear that an unwise majority would wreak permanent damage.

Nor does the populace's reaction to calls for constitutional amend-ments in recent years justify concern that amendments by the People would be disastrous. True, the proposed Equal Rights Amendment would likely have passed if the People had recognized their right to amend the Constitution through a kind of national referendum.[9] But while reason-able people may disagree about the merits of the ERA, its prospective passage hardly suggests that the People are wont to shred the Constitu-tion. The fate of the ERA arguably cuts the other way: A majority of Americans, wishing to constitutionalize full equality for women, had their will and judgment thwarted because of the misconception that Arti-cle V monopolizes the constitutional amendment process.

An amendment to mandate a balanced federal budget appears to enjoy popular support,[10] though probably not the necessary enthusiasm to stir the public to initiate, ponder, and pass such an amendment on our own. And if we did? An experiment in mandated fiscal frugality, wise or not, would hardly imperil the nation. Should this assessment prove flawed, the amendment would likely be repealed in short order. Devout supporters of abortion rights might cringe at the thought of *Roe v. Wade*[11] being put to a vote, but in truth they have little to fear—public opinion polls consis-tently show majority public support for the pro-choice position.[12]

In the final analysis, apocalyptic predictions about majority amend-ments do not survive scrutiny. Besides, even if the prospect of direct amendment is a bit scary, so too is amendment via Article V. (For that matter, a system that forbids any amendment would be even scarier, binding Americans in perpetuity to an imperfect document drafted by people long dead.) In our view, an amendment process that puts ulti-mate faith in the People is less scary than one that trusts only self-inter-ested government officials.

Our Founding Fathers recognized that such officials must be restrained by We the People. In terms of military policy, they dreaded a standing army controlled by the federal government; hence their primary reliance on militias, and their insistence that these citizen bodies remain armed. Likewise, in terms of law enforcement, they feared rule by self-interested elites—hence the series of constitutional provisions interposing the jury between the state and persons accused of crimes. So too, in terms of the amendment process, they vested ultimate power in the people, not the government. Whatever concerns the Framers may have had that We the People could run amok did not lead them to question our sovereignty over the Constitution.

BEFORE RESTING OUR case on behalf of the People's sovereign right to amend the Constitution, we wish to clarify one final point, lest our argument be distorted. By arguing that the majority enjoys the right to amend the Constitution, we may seem to come down squarely on the side of conservatives in the modern debate about majority rule versus minority rights. After all, our argument gives the majority even more power than generally demanded by conservatives.

In fact, to place us with conservatives on this issue is to mix apples and oranges—or, more precisely, to mix ordinary laws and the Constitution, and to mix the People and their representatives. Conservative majoritarianism, at least as preached by its foremost proponents such as Robert Bork, maintains that the rights of individuals against majorities (in Congress or, more typically, in state legislatures) should be interpreted narrowly. We don't necessarily agree—and in some cases we strongly disagree. For example, Bork has argued that the First Amendment protects only speech itself, not expression or even symbolic speech such as flag-burning.[13] (At one time he even argued that the First Amendment protects only specifically political speech, though here he has recanted.[14]) We take a more liberal view, believing that a broader interpretation of the First Amendment better nourishes a self-governing citizenry, which popular sovereignty demands. Thus we are more likely than Bork to approve when judges strike down laws as violative of the First Amendment.

Does this contradict our enthusiasm for majority rule, as manifest in our commitment to the majority's power to amend the Constitution? Not at all, because we follow the Framers in sharply distinguishing between government officials and the People. Bork's majoritarianism makes him protective of legislatures (which he, like most legal theorists, casually equates with the majority). Our enthusiasm extends not to rule by the legislature but to rule by the People directly. We are more sanguine than Bork about judges striking down statutes, because we do not necessarily see the legislature as speaking for the People.

Indeed, from this country's earliest days, there have been occasions when the legislature plainly veered from the expectations of the People, and had to be reined in by them. The country's first decade brought one of the most egregious assaults on the Constitution—the infamous 1798 Sedition Act, which made it a crime to criticize the Federalist President or the Federalist Congress. In a remarkable moment in America's rich populist history, the People rebelled, throwing the Federalists out in the landmark election of 1800.

As that episode suggests, the People can speak for themselves. Our brand of majoritarianism demands recognition of their right to do so not only in elections, but also in shaping the Constitution. That is why, for us, majoritarianism and a judiciary that broadly defines and aggressively protects individual rights are not contradictory. Let judges strike down laws as unconstitutional, thereby thwarting the will of the legislature (though not necessarily the People) in service of the Constitution. That's fine, as long as the final word belongs to We the People, who may overturn the judge's decision—or the legislature's—by way of amendment.

As this suggests, the conservatives' brand of majoritarianism extends primarily to statutes, ours to the Constitution. We share with conservatives (and, we hope, with everyone else) an unbending fidelity to the Constitution. But whose Constitution? We respect the Framers, but reject the notion that the People should keep our hands off James Madison's document. The Constitution belongs to We the People, who have the right to change it. This fact should attract liberals and conservatives alike, yet too often it seems lost on both.

IN THIS CHAPTER we have tried to establish that the American people, by virtue of both their good will and their self-interest, will not tyrannize minorities, and that the process of popular amendment can be fashioned in such a way as to ensure deliberation rather than rash action. All that may not suffice to quell fears, because another, deeper concern persists: that the American people are insufficiently educated in public affairs to undertake the awesome task of amending the Constitution. Are the People wise enough to be trusted?

True, polls show that an alarming percentage of Americans cannot identify the Vice President, much less Cabinet Secretaries or Supreme Court Justices. But experience suggests that many of our least educated citizens do not vote and would thus eschew national referenda on the Constitution. In any case, widespread ignorance of public affairs may be misleading. Perhaps the People today are at times irresponsible because they have not been given responsibility and thus have not become trained in the exercise of self-government. The relegation of all constitutional issues to government officials has caused the People's constitutional muscles to atrophy through disuse.

Also, we should be wary of comparing the present to a mythical Golden Age. We tend to think of Americans in 1787 as breathtakingly enlightened, schooled in classical languages and acquainted with political theory. In fact, the Framers were deeply concerned about widespread ignorance, and nervous about whether the people at large could be trusted with self-government. Thomas Jefferson's take on this issue endures as the best response to modern concerns. The remedy for an ignorant citizenry, he insisted, "is not to take [control] from them, but to inform their discretion by education."[15] Jefferson maintained that educating and informing the masses is "the only sure reliance for the preservation of our liberty."

Ironically, widespread ignorance actually counsels in favor of reviving recognition of the majority's power to amend the Constitution. If we take popular sovereignty seriously, we will be forced to educate ourselves and each other. Education will no longer be seen primarily as an issue of individual right but as a requirement of a working democracy, no less vital than speech itself. (This theme is explored in Part IV.) Similarly, when we recognize that popular sovereignty entails deliberations with fellow citizens from all walks of life, we see the need to nurture institutions like the jury and military, vital breeding grounds for public-spirited citizenship. (This theme is explored in Parts II and III.)

THREE

The Right to Make State Law by Plebiscite

IF THE CONSTITUTION BELONGS TO the People, who retain the inalienable right to alter or abolish it, what about the "ordinary" laws that govern the nation and each state? Does not the principle of majority-rule popular sovereignty extend to statutes as well as to the Constitution? We may delegate lawmaking authority to legislatures, but do we not also retain the right to make and change laws ourselves if we so desire?

Americans appear to believe so. Public opinion polls show that most Americans favor the availability of direct lawmaking in states and localities.[1] Many states have in fact established and increasingly use procedures whereby the People at large directly pass laws, rather than relying exclusively on their elected representatives.

While the precise form varies from state to state, "direct democracy" generally involves one of two basic methods. First, if private citizens collect and present a sufficient number of signatures in support of a particular bill, it must be placed on a ballot at a future date. Alternatively, the legislature itself may decide to place a measure on a public ballot. In either case, if a majority of the public votes in favor of the proposal, it becomes law. (The former measure is usually called an "initiative" and the latter a "referendum." We shall use the term "plebiscite" to refer to both.)

On its face, the plebiscite seems to embody democracy in action. Supreme Court Justice Hugo Black cited its emergence as reflecting Americans' "devotion to democracy."[2] But even as this popular method of lawmaking spreads, so too does opposition to it. A chorus of legal scholars assails plebiscites as unwise and even unconstitutional.[3]

The argument rests on an alleged distinction between a republican form of government and a direct democracy. The anti-plebiscite scholars claim that these two forms of government are incompatible and that the Founding Fathers established a republic precisely because they feared direct democracy. They argue that plebiscites contradict the Framers' vision of a representative government. On the federal level, the Constitution clearly sets up a representative democracy as opposed to a direct democracy. It spells out how the people elect legislators who, along with an elected President, make the laws. The Constitution does not specify a system of direct lawmaking by the People. And while the Constitution focuses on the organization of the federal government, it does also address the kind of government permitted within each state. Article IV, Section 4 says the United States "shall guarantee to every State in this Union a Republican Form of Government." Opponents of direct democracy argue that a republican form of government means representative government. Thus, they conclude, plebiscites contradict the Framers' vision and compromise the spirit if not the letter of the Constitution.

In terms of policy, opponents of plebiscites express two principal (and related) concerns: (1) while the legislative process involves genuine deliberation, and concern for the common good, voters in plebiscites act rashly and contemplate only naked self-interest; and (2) plebiscites will produce laws that oppress minorities.

WE BELIEVE THAT careful consideration yields a very different conclusion. While the Constitution does not require them, plebiscites comport with the spirit of the document. And though they do present some risks, plebiscites hold out the prospect of rich rewards. States can and should craft a plebiscitary system that minimizes the risks and maximizes the rewards.

In our Introduction, we noted how James Madison, in *Federalist* 51, cited the two major fears that inspired the new Constitution: a self-dealing government and majority tyranny. The primary value of plebiscites lies in their role in guarding against the former. Citizens have used plebiscites to reform the political processes—through restrictions on lobbying, conflict-of-interest statutes, pay cuts for politicians, and campaign reform. These are measures that politicians usually won't touch, for reasons of crass self-interest. Public participation becomes necessary: Remember term limits. (As noted in Chapter 1, the threat of removing unresponsive representatives will often not suffice. Elections rarely present a simple choice: Each candidate is an intricate combination of positions, record, character, party affiliation, and potential seniority in the legislature.*)

Moreover, concern that plebiscites lack proper deliberation suggests an opportunity as much as a risk. States can (and some do) require mass mailings providing each side's description of the issue and the consequences of its enactment or defeat. This helps ensure that voters possess at least some familiarity with the issue. More significantly, the best model of the plebiscite is not a simple vote in a private booth, but a town meeting or caucus where citizens come together to debate the is-

---

*It is theoretically possible that voters in *every* district prefer the challenger to the incumbent, and would so vote if they knew that voters in other districts would do the same. Instead, fearing that other districts will reelect incumbents, voters may feel compelled to reelect their own incumbent, lest their new representative be low on the seniority totem pole.

sue. This, in turn, contributes to a more deliberative and community-minded citizenry, better able to carry out its various constitutional responsibilities. In other words, we should turn on its head the argument that plebiscites produce laws uninformed by deliberation. Plebiscites should be used to *inspire* deliberation, not only to produce better laws but better citizens.

This vision has been neglected by critics of direct democracy. They have focused instead on the dangers of plebiscites, especially with respect to Madison's other concern: tyranny of the majority. (This is not surprising since, as noted in the Introduction, the legal community generally ignores the Framers' chief challenge—guarding against self-dealing government.) They argue that plebiscites leave minorities—including racial minorities, but also homosexuals, aliens, and other underrepresented groups—at the mercy of majorities. We acknowledge the risk that plebiscite voters will, on occasion, fail to respect the rights of the weak or unpopular. For a variety of reasons, however, we think the fear is exaggerated.

In the previous chapter, we noted that the aura of constitutional lawmaking gives rise to caution. We also argued that the large size and heterogeneous character of America's population militate against a tyrannical majority. Partly for these reasons, we maintained, direct constitutional amendment by the People is not unacceptably dangerous. But these reasons are largely inoperative when it comes to state plebiscites. Most plebiscites involve mere lawmaking (though some states authorize amendment of their constitution via plebiscite), and thus the citizenry's reluctance to tinker with the Constitution is irrelevant. And at the state level the population is smaller and often far less heterogeneous. It might seem to follow that state plebiscites on *non*constitutional issues would be especially likely to oppress minorities. Do not recent plebiscites discriminating against gay men and lesbians illustrate this risk?

Note, however, that legislatures too have oppressed homosexuals. The legislatures of twenty-five states, not the People, have criminalized gay sex. Indeed, as a general proposition, opponents of plebiscites often assume the worst about the People and the best about legislatures. In the states that use plebiscites, majority tyranny has not been the norm.

Only a small percentage of proposed plebiscites have been aimed at re-stricting civil rights, and most of those have been defeated.[4] Many "in-clusive" measures—such as open-housing acts or laws prohibiting gender discrimination—have been passed by plebiscite. In general, cit-izens of the states with plebiscites have shown less eagerness to oppress vulnerable minorities than to reform government processes (such as campaign financing laws), keep their tax burden under control,[5] and protect their environment.

Plebiscites serve no particular ideological agenda—either in theory or in practice. They have been used to enact the death penalty, usually thought of as conservative, and to legalize marijuana, usually thought of as liberal. They have been used to enact antismoking measures and other laws which fall into neither category. Precisely because plebiscites have not produced predictably liberal or conservative re-sults, but have helped keep elected officials from feathering their own nests and corrupting the political process, prominent supporters of plebiscites span the political spectrum—from Ralph Nader on the left to Ross Perot in the center to Jack Kemp on the right. This is as it should be. The case for plebiscites rests not on a particular set of de-sired outcomes but on a principle—the principle that control of govern-ment belongs in the hands of the People.

While plebiscites were neither designed to nor have tended to injure disadvantaged groups, that result undeniably can occur. To take one il-lustration, in a 1992 plebiscite Colorado voters amended the state con-stitution to ban antidiscrimination laws protecting homosexuals. That episode, however, actually illustrates another reason why fear of major-ity tyranny should not induce panic: the measure was held unconstitu-tional by the Colorado Supreme Court and then by the United States Supreme Court.[6] Laws enacted by the People through plebiscites, like laws enacted by state legislatures, are subject to judicial review.*

---

*Some argue that plebiscites should be subject to extra scrutiny by the courts. While we do not embrace this conclusion, a good case can be made that the *nature* of judicial review should differ when a court considers a challenge to a plebiscite. Since legislatures are prone to self-dealing, whereas plebiscites may present an enhanced possibility of majority oppres-sion, the precise focus of a court's inquiry should arguably reflect these respective risks.

Congress offers another potential safeguard. As noted, under Article VI of the Constitution, the laws of the United States take precedence over state laws with which they conflict. For example, were Congress to enact a law banning discrimination on the basis of sexual orientation, the discriminatory practices of many states would be overridden.

Yet another safeguard is the freedom to vote with one's feet. Gay men and lesbians in Colorado, like citizens of every other state, can migrate to a more congenial locale. In this respect, while a tyrannous majority may be more likely to emerge in a single state than nationwide, it is far less dangerous when it does emerge there.*

BEYOND THE SPECIFIC fear of oppression, critics of direct democracy argue that plebiscites yield legislation without reflection, and the triumph of self-interest over the public good. This, too, reflects an unjustified glorification of legislatures and debasement of the public. Legal scholar Lynn Baker (among others) has argued at length that the average plebiscite voter is no less likely than the average legislator to vote in a thoughtful and public-spirited manner.[7] If this conclusion seems fanciful, perhaps it is because we expect too little from the People and too much from legislatures. Legislatures do not always conform to the civics-class model. One California legislator titled his memoirs, *What Makes You Think We Read the Bills?*[8] His book made clear what students of state legislatures already knew—representatives often *don't* read the bills they vote on, nor do they listen to debate. Instead, they respond to their party leaders or to major campaign contributors. Indeed, plebiscites arose out of the Progressive movement around the turn of

---

*We realize that this option is not always practical, and is open to rhetorical exploitation by the enemies of inclusion. (Homosexuals have too often been told, "If you don't like it here, go to San Francisco.") At the same time, the availability of a safe haven for oppressed groups can be a godsend. While it would have been infinitely preferable for blacks to have enjoyed equal rights everywhere, the fact that many southern blacks moved north, where they could vote and enjoy other rights, eased their plight—and helped launch the modern civil rights movement. Our country was founded by people fleeing religious oppression. As long as any forms of oppression exist within our own borders, we should be grateful that we have many mini-polities within those borders, and free movement among them.

this century as a response to the control that party bosses and political machines, themselves tightly enmeshed with corporate interests, had attained over the political process.

We argue not that plebiscites always work better than the ordinary legislative process, nor that states should abandon lawmaking by legislatures in favor of lawmaking by plebiscite. Indirect lawmaking has enormous advantages, especially the benefit of specialization of labor. The legislature can set up committees, gather information, and develop expertise in ways generally not possible for the general public. There is much to be said for a system of government in which a relatively small number of citizens stand in for the polity as a whole in conducting day-to-day affairs.

But we do not confront an either/or proposition. We can benefit from the advantages of a representative system, subject to the availability of plebiscites when citizens find representation lacking. As Woodrow Wilson said, plebiscites are intended "to restore, not destroy, representative government."[9] When elected representatives cannot or will not represent the people, the latter should be permitted to take direct action. Even when they fail to produce laws, plebiscites may serve the salutary purpose of putting issues on the agenda that otherwise suffer neglect from politicians. Lynn Baker has observed that many landmark reforms, eventually enacted by legislation or constitutional amendment, originated as initiatives in the states: women's suffrage, the abolition of poll taxes, and the nation's presidential primary system, among others.[10]

Opponents of plebiscites trot out examples of bills too complicated for voters to understand, or plebiscite campaigns dominated by well-mobilized interest groups. The solution to these problems is not to throw out plebiscites but to fix them. Some commentators actually oppose plebiscites because the poorest, least educated citizens tend not to vote in them. The solution to inadequate democracy cannot be to scale back democracy further. The plebiscite represents an *opportunity* for the disenfranchised, even if they don't always take advantage of it.

Nor, as it is sometimes argued, will the People of a state pass laws promiscuously. Few states average more than a handful of plebiscites per year, and a majority of plebiscites are defeated.[11] The People generally show a reluctance to fool with the status quo, belying the fear that they will haphazardly pass laws that suit their immediate fancy.

Plebiscites (like ordinary legislation) do not always conform to the ideal. But the problems that arise can be corrected, and experimentation in the fifty states will suggest the desirability of certain reforms. For example, some observers protest that bills passed by the legislature have an additional check—a governor's veto—that is absent in the case of plebiscites. But if that is troublesome, we could subject plebiscites to a governor's veto. Or, if in a given state plebiscites become too prolific, the number of signatures necessary to put a measure on a ballot could be raised. If the process seems dominated by financially powerful groups, states could enact certain kinds of campaign reform. Flaws in plebiscites constitute grounds for reform, not abolition. If perfection were required, we should throw out legislatures too.

WHAT ABOUT THE argument that, regardless of its merits, the plebiscite contradicts the spirit and perhaps the letter of the Constitution, particularly Article IV's guarantee of a republican form of government? In fact, since the Constitution rests on a foundation of majority-rule popular sovereignty, it seems implausible that the Framers sought to prohibit or discourage a device that furthers this very principle. The conclusion to the contrary rests on the erroneous idea that they sharply differentiated between a democracy and a republic.

The notion that the Framers regarded a republican form of government as inconsistent with direct democracy derives primarily from a brief passage in James Madison's *Federalist* 10. This passage is a remarkably slender foundation on which to erect an elaborate anti-plebiscite edifice.

The key scrap of language from *Federalist* 10 which allegedly illuminates the meaning of "republican form of government" in the Constitution, is as follows:

A republic, by which I mean a government in which the scheme of representation takes place, opens a different prospect and promises the cure for which we are seeking. Let us examine the points in which it varies from pure democracy. [A] great point[] of difference between a democracy and a republic [is] the delegation of the government, in the latter, to a small number of citizens elected by the rest.[12]

Clearly, in this brief discussion, Madison recognizes advantages of representative democracy over direct democracy, and refers to the former as a republic. But can the passage be read to suggest that the Constitution's guarantee to each state of a republican form of government precludes direct democracy? Here, there are grounds for severe doubt.

Note that in this passage Madison is not discussing the meaning of Article IV's Republican Form of Government Clause. When he and Alexander Hamilton do discuss this clause (in *Federalist* 21 and 43), they make no reference to this scrap of language in *Federalist* 10, nor do they in any way indicate that the clause prohibits direct democracy.[13] Note, too, that Madison seems aware that he is using "republic" in a nonobvious (perhaps idiosyncratic) way: "A republic, by which I mean" as opposed to "A republic, by which is generally meant." By contrast, only three paragraphs earlier, Madison refers unselfconsciously to majority rule as "*the* republican principle."[14] Indeed, the linkage between republicanism and majority rule runs throughout the *Federalist Papers* and the Framers' discourse generally. Opponents of plebiscites can identify no similar pattern linking republicanism with a rejection of direct democracy.

To be sure, Madison refers back to *Federalist* 10 in its sequel, *Federalist* 14, where he repeats his claim that republics, in contrast to democracies, rely on a system of representation.[15] But elsewhere, he pursues a different theme. In *Federalist* 39 and 43, he contrasts republicanism not with democracy but with aristocracy and monarchy.[16] (This was a prominent theme when the Framers discussed Article IV's Republican Form of Government Clause.) Perhaps more to the point, in *Federalist* 39 Madison links republican government with "the capacity of mankind for self-government" where government derives "all its powers" from "the great body of the people."[17] In *Federalist* 55, he reiterates that republican government presupposes "sufficient virtue among men for self-government."[18] Hamilton, for his part, explicitly equated republican government with government "of the people."[19]

Indeed, as we saw in Chapter 1, Hamilton's famous *Federalist* 78 characterized the people's right to change the Constitution as the "fundamental principle of *republican* government." If that isn't clear enough, consider Hamilton's *Federalist* 21, which declares that Article IV's Republican Form of Government Clause *"could be no impediment to reforms of State constitutions by a majority of the people."*[20]

Hamilton was hardly alone in linking republican government to popular sovereignty and majority rule. Samuel Johnson's 1786 dictionary defined "republican" as "placing the government in the people."[21] In a famous Supreme Court opinion in 1793, the great justice James Wilson defined republican government as one in which "the Supreme Power resides in the body of the people."[22] Two years later, Justice James Iredell delivered an opinion noting that in "a Republic" the "sovereignty resides in the great body of the people."[23] As noted in Chapter 1, Thomas Jefferson described majority rule as "the vital principle of republics." Similarly, Caleb Strong, a former delegate at the Constitutional Convention, noted that "in republicks, the opinion of the majority must prevail."[24]

Of course, it is conceivable that some of these references to self-government entailed nothing more than citizens casting ballots to elect representatives. But the scraps in *Federalist* 10 and 14 at most establish that Madison had misgivings about direct democracy. They do not prove that these misgivings were shared by other Framers, or that they were reflected in the Republican Form of Government Clause.

The available evidence suggests neither. In the South Carolina ratifying convention, Charles Pinckney, who had been a delegate to the federal convention, described a republican government as one where "the people at large, *either collectively or* by representation,"[25] form the legislature. At Pennsylvania's ratifying convention, James Wilson pointedly equated a "republic" with a "democracy" (contrasting both to a monarchy or aristocracy). In both, "the people at large retain the supreme power, and act *either collectively or* by representation."[26] Later in the convention Wilson referred to representation itself as the "*democratic* principle."[27]

In the many debates over the Constitution, republican government was regularly distinguished from monarchy and aristocracy, rarely from democracy. Madison himself, who in *Federalist* 10 offers a "*republican* remedy for the diseases most incident to *republican* government,"[28] at the Philadelphia Convention described this very same scheme as a defense against "the inconveniences of *democracy* consistent with the *democratic* form of Govt."[29] Note too, that in the 1790s various political groups sprang up, some labeling themselves "Republican Societies," some "Democratic Societies" and some "Democratic-Republican Societies." The political party Madison cofounded in that decade began as the Republican Party but later became known as the Democratic Party.

The etymology of these two words supports their similarity. "Republican" derives from the Latin *res* (thing) *publica* (public). This idea of the "public's thing" expresses a rough Latin equivalent of the Greek "demoskratia"—rule *(kratos)* by the people *(demos)*. Founding Father Roger Sherman nicely captured this etymological truth in a 1789 letter to John Adams, noting that "what especially denominates [a government] a republic is its dependence on the *public* or *people* at large."[30] Like the Constitution's explicit reference to "the People" in the Preamble and the First, Ninth, and Tenth Amendments, Article IV's guarantee of re*public*an government consciously taps into the principle of popular sovereignty. And plebiscites, properly administered, do not violate this principle; they implement it.*

PUTTING ASIDE ARTICLE IV, what about the more general claim that the Framers regarded elected officials as adequate to represent the People? It should go without saying that elected officials are not even close

---

*Even if "republican form of government" does indeed refer to a representative democracy, the availability of plebiscites would not necessarily compromise such a scheme. All states do have representative governments, most of which are structured similarly to the federal government. Plebiscites supplement this scheme of representation rather than replacing it.

to perfectly representative of their constituents. Consider, first, the federal government. In the United States House of Representatives, the more accountable of the two branches of Congress (since its members face election every two years), each member has close to a half million constituents. This fact alone renders it impossible that a "representative" will wholly represent the average voter. Worse, still, this representative spends most of his time in a one-industry town of lawyers and power brokers—a lifestyle hardly representative of the average citizen's.

Frequent elections do require that congressmen pay some attention to what their constituents think. However, elections also require lots of money, and the constant pressure to keep wealthy donors happy further loosens the bond between representative and ordinary citizen. (From the standpoint of representativeness, the situation in the Senate is even worse: the ratio of constituent to Senator is higher, the average term of office longer, the cost of campaigns more astronomical.)

The Framers were acutely aware of the differences between the most popular branch of government and the People themselves. In *Federalist* 71, Alexander Hamilton noted disapprovingly that representatives "seem sometimes to fancy that they are the people themselves."[31] Precisely for that reason, Madison argued that "the people ought to indulge all their jealousy and exhaust all their precautions" to restrain "the enterprising ambition" of our representatives.[32]

Though the Framers knew well that representative democracy does not permit anything resembling perfect representation, they also knew that the country was too large for direct democracy.[33] As for the states, apart from requiring them to have a republican government (which, as noted, meant a government where power resided with the people, as opposed to a monarchy or aristocracy), the Framers left them free to devise their own precise form of government.

If the Framers, then, are to be brought into the debate on plebiscites, we must look to the principles they espoused. Such an inquiry does not yield the conclusion that they would have frowned upon plebiscites. To the contrary, as noted above, plebiscites generally comport with the idea of popular sovereignty so central to the Framers' vision.

Plebiscites give the People greater control over their government, greater ability to keep their representatives honest and responsive, and an enhanced capacity for civic responsibility. Rather than cave in to fears about the worst of our fellow citizens, we should appeal to the best in them. Let us argue, in state after state, for better, fairer laws. Let us enhance plebiscites by making them more interactive and deliberative. Let us not resort to tying the hands of the People. Above all, let us not do so by making the false argument that the Constitution distances the citizens of each state from their own laws.

WE MUST REITERATE that we take seriously the concern that plebiscites may be (mis)used to punish the weakest or least popular members of a community. However, this concern rests on the vision of an ignorant and atomized citizenry voting its fears, prejudices, and unenlightened self-interest. To the extent that this phenomenon exists (rendering the safeguards discussed above indispensable), we should not regard it as unalterable. If the citizenry lacks civic virtue, that may be because we citizens have been alienated from our civic duties. Involving people in the process of making laws is a step in the direction of fostering public-spiritedness.[34] By contrast, allowing people to vote only for representatives, who often duck hard choices and fail to represent their constituents faithfully, is a prescription for a selfish, uninformed, and apathetic citizenry. To the extent that a plebiscite system can bring citizens together to debate issues of concern to the community and to participate in collective self-government, it should prove a partial corrective. (Again, our preferred mode of plebiscite would make greater use of caucuses, town meetings, and other forms of collective deliberation than is currently the norm.)

Plebiscites are certainly no panacea, but they must not be viewed in isolation. Indeed, if we are to reap the full rewards of plebiscites, while minimizing the risk that they will be used to persecute minorities, we must strengthen the other institutions—the jury, the military, the schools—that the Framers saw as sustaining communities, educating people in public affairs, and inculcating a public-spiritedness that would produce superior citizens.

The remainder of this book explores how these institutions fit within the mosaic of popular sovereignty.

Part Two

the Jury Box

FOUR

The Jury: What's the Big Idea?

IN THE JURY BOX, as at the ballot box, the People can lay claim to more constitutional rights than have been recognized. Mainstream discourse tends to see constitutional rights as belonging solely to discrete individuals. Nowhere is this tendency more pronounced than in debate over the jury. We tend to think of the jury in terms of its service to the parties in a case, overlooking its much larger function as a space for popular sovereignty.

The right to a jury finds expression in three amendments in the Bill of Rights. The Fifth Amendment safeguards criminal grand juries, the Sixth protects criminal trial juries, and the Seventh preserves civil juries. In recent times, these amendments, especially the Sixth and Seventh, have become controversial. Some commentators argue that today's complex civil litigation involves issues beyond the ken of ordinary citizens.[1] Others maintain that jurors are governed more by sympathy for injured parties than by a rational assessment of the facts.[2] Likewise, the criminal defendant's right to a jury trial has come under fire. Acquittals or hung juries in high-profile cases invariably produce talk of jury incompetence. The chief complaint is that juries allow guilty defendants to walk.[3]

In many quarters the jury system receives a vigorous defense. Social scientists argue that jurors can indeed process complex material and do base their decisions on facts rather than emotions;[4] and civil libertarians believe that a criminal defendant's rights are paramount, and thus juries should err in that direction.[5]

Both sides in this debate tend to oversimplify the issue, envisioning the Constitution primarily in libertarian terms and neglecting its crucial populist and republican underpinnings. The value of the jury transcends its ability to reach a correct verdict in particular cases. The "big idea" behind the jury is not so much protecting discrete individuals (though that is certainly important) as preserving a democratic culture.

The jury is a *public* institution, an engine of self-government. While the Framers regarded the jury as a reliable body for meting out individual justice, even in this regard their emphasis differed from that of the jury's defenders today. Supporters of the jury today sing paeans to jurors' common sense, or the fact-finding superiority of a body of twelve to a judge of one.[6] To the Framers, the value of the jury derived more profoundly from another consideration: the role of ordinary citizens in thwarting various forms of government oppression, corruption, and self-dealing.[7]

In this connection, there exists an elegant symmetry between the legislature and the judiciary. One branch of our two-part Congress, the Senate, is somewhat removed from the People, by virtue of infrequent elections. However, the legislature as a whole remains sufficiently close to the People by virtue of the other part, the House of Representatives, whose members are subject to frequent elections. Likewise, the courts have two parts—judges and juries—with the latter far closer to the People. In the judiciary, as in the legislature, the more representative body checks and balances the less representative and helps preserve the People's sovereignty over their government.

Because judges are in some respects the most insulated government officials (federal judges face no elections, and virtually all judges are lawyers, members of a professional cadre with similar backgrounds), they must be checked and balanced by the most representative participants in government: jurors, ordinary citizens who perform their service and return to the community. Judges, like all public officials, might be led astray by bribery or political affiliation. As Thomas Jefferson explained, "It is left therefore to the juries, if they think the permanent judges are under any bias whatever in any cause," to ensure that justice is done.[8]

Federal judges are sometimes well positioned to safeguard our rights, since life tenure insulates the judiciary from political pressure. But life tenure is no cure-all. Federal judges, appointed by the President (and subject to promotion) and paid by Congress (and eligible for salary increases), may well wish to remain in the good graces of one or the other branch. Juries are beholden to no one, and thus in a unique position to ensure that justice is not defeated by a self-dealing government.

The Framers also recognized a second component of the jury's "checking" role, one even more important than ensuring fairness in each case. The jury helps prevent the formation of an ongoing tyranny in which the political branches, counting on the cooperation of judges, oppress certain groups or stifle dissent (by punishing opposition press or speech, for example).[9]

This leads to another aspect of the jury that tends to be overlooked today—verdicts in individual cases sometimes have far-reaching implications for larger political issues. As Tocqueville observed:

> To regard the jury simply as a judicial institution would be taking a very narrow view of the matter, for great though its influence on the outcome of lawsuits is, its influence on the fate of society is much greater still. The jury is therefore above all a political institution.[10]

So too the grand jury. Founding Father James Wilson emphasized the grand jury's capacity to "suggest publick improvements, and the modes of removing publick inconveniences: they may expose to publick inspection or to publick punishment, publick bad men, and publick bad measures."[11] Wilson's repeated use of the word "publick" was no accident: "All the operations of government," he observed, "are within the compass of [the grand jury's] view and research."[12] This sense of the jury's public function dovetails with the structure of the Constitution. The Sixth Amendment calls for not only jury trial but also *public* trial. And the role of ordinary citizens in the criminal-justice system exemplifies self-government, thus evoking Article IV, Section 4's guarantee to each state of a re*public*an form of government.

Finally, and perhaps most importantly, the Framers saw the jury box as a breeding ground for good citizenship, providing a valuable education in civic affairs and preparing citizens to play their other public roles. Tocqueville characterized the jury as a "free school which is always open and in which each juror learns his rights"[13] and added that "I do not know whether a jury is useful to the litigants, but I am sure it is very good for [the jurors] . . . [It is] one of the most effective means of popular education at society's disposal."[14]

The jury box provides a unique forum for interaction among citizens who might otherwise never engage each other, people who live in different neighborhoods, attend different schools, worship in different congregations. Today, people tend to confront one another in hierarchical or impersonal arrangements such as employer/employee, seller/buyer, drivers at an intersection, or spectators at a ballgame. In the jury box, we meet citizen to citizen, face to face, not just to exchange greetings or currency, but to listen to, learn from, and work with one another in the solemn task of self-government. Nowhere else, not even in the voting booth, must Americans come together in person to deliberate collectively about fundamental matters in our shared public life. Democracy is well served by the dialogue that takes place in the jury room.

A number of commentators have deplored Americans' increasing iso-

lation from one another.[15] They have lamented the decline of various institutions that traditionally brought people together, such as religious
congregations, trade unions, and schools. Yet they overlook one of the
most important public spaces, one which brings together a cross-section
of the community not for social or personal reasons, not to strengthen a
group or advance an agenda, but to perform our constitutional duties as
citizens and represent the People at large.[16] We are losing the sense of
the jury box as a vital public space—and thus losing touch with our
Constitution.

It is almost impossible to exaggerate the jury's importance in the constitutional design. No idea was more central to the Bill of Rights—indeed, to America's distinctive regime of government of the people, by
the people, and for the people. As noted in the Introduction, the right to
a jury in a criminal case was the only right secured in all state constitutions written between 1776 and 1787. This right was one of only a few
explicitly protected by the original Constitution, and the Constitutional
Convention's only discussion of whether to add a more elaborate Bill of
Rights took place in response to concerns about protecting civil juries.[17]
When the Constitution neglected such a provision, Anti-Federalists
pounced on the omission. As a result, jury-protection clauses topped
the wish lists at the state ratifying conventions. Of the six such conventions that floated ideas for amending the Constitution, five put forth two
or more explicit jury proposals.[18]

At first blush, all of this attention, and the fact that the eventual Bill
of Rights devoted three specific amendments to the jury, might suggest
a disproportionate concern with a single institution. After all, the Bill of
Rights names only a handful of rights. It offers no explicit protection of
the right to travel, the right to privacy, or even the right to equal treatment by the government, to name just a few items one might consider
essential. Is it odd, then, that the Framers included three amendments
dealing with the right to a jury?

No, not when we keep in mind that the jury is less about the rights of
individual litigants than about the right of the People to control their
government. Indeed, the jury not only appears in the Fifth, Sixth, and

Seventh Amendments, but also tightly meshes with several other provisions in the Bill of Rights.

Start with the First Amendment's ringing defense of a free press. This right includes the doctrine of "no prior restraint": Whatever punishment one may face for saying or publishing certain material, the government may virtually never censor speech in advance.[19] A prior restraint ("You may not publish X") could issue from a judge via an injunction, and be enforced through contempt proceedings that excluded a jury. By contrast, postpublication punishment, such as a libel judgment, takes effect only if a jury can be persuaded to rule against the publisher. Thus, the prohibition against prior restraints ensures that major restrictions on the press cannot occur without the imprimatur of ordinary citizens. And as the eighteenth-century trial of John Peter Zenger famously showed, a jury may well side with the press.

Next, consider the Second Amendment, which provided a right to bear arms for the explicit purpose of ensuring a well-regulated militia. Like the jury idea, the Second Amendment empowers the People to participate in a public institution. The militia and the jury were close cousins, local bodies composed of ordinary citizens carrying out collective governmental responsibilities. They represented twin duties of citizenship and, roughly speaking, those eligible to serve on one (adult white males) were eligible to serve on the other. Both the militia and the jury reflected suspicion of paid, professional officials: a standing army on the one hand, and judges, prosecutors, and bureaucrats on the other. And both the militia and the jury were valued as forums for educating the citizenry in the skills and knowledge necessary for self-government more broadly. (The constitutional vision underlying the militia is spelled out in detail in Part III.)

Likewise, the Fourth Amendment's protection against police searches (stating that search warrants require a determination of probable cause and must set forth with specificity the place to be searched and the things to be seized) links up with the jury idea. Search warrants were disfavored[20] precisely because they issued from paid government bureaucrats and cut the jury out of the loop—just like a prior restraint.* And should government officials conduct an unreasonable search without a warrant, the citizen-target could bring a lawsuit against the official. The Seventh Amendment would then come into play, assuring the plaintiff a jury trial. In such a trial, the key issue would invariably be whether the government's search or seizure was "reasonable"—a standard jury question requiring the judgment of ordinary citizens.[21]

The jury concept hooks up with various other provisions in the Bill of Rights as well. The Fifth Amendment's protection against double jeopardy immunizes a criminal jury's acquittal from reversal by a court of appeals. (In a similar vein, the Seventh Amendment's specification that "no fact tried by a jury shall be otherwise re-examined in any Court" makes it difficult for appellate judges to overturn a civil jury's verdict.) Next consider the majestic Fifth Amendment phrase, "due process of law." This grand phrase traces back to common law scholar Lord Coke, who defined it, in words well known to eighteenth-century lawyers, as "indictment or presentment of good and lawful men"[22]—that is, a grand jury. Likewise, the Eighth Amendment's prohibitions of unreasonable bail and cruel and unusual punishments are inextricably linked to the jury idea. Of course, bail hearings and sentencing hearings are often held by judges sitting alone, without juries—but this only proves our point. Precisely because judges acting without juries were suspect, the Bill of Rights had to put special limits on them—just as the Bill of Rights provides special protection against prior restraints and search warrants, since these too could issue from judges and other officials acting without juries.

---

*The connection between the First and Fourth Amendments runs deep. The Fourth Amendment requires that warrants specify the places and things to be searched. The Framers' aversion to general warrants stemmed, in part, from the fact that the British had used them to restrict free speech. Indeed, the famous 1763 English case of *Wilkes v. Wood*, 19 *Howell's State Trials* 1153 (C.P. 1763), 98 Eng. Rep. 489, well known to the Framers, was just such a case. John Wilkes, a flamboyant member of Parliament, published an anonymous pamphlet attacking the majesty and ministry of King George III. The ministry responded by issuing a general search and arrest warrant against the pamphlet's publishers and printers. No names were listed in the warrant; it essentially authorized henchmen to round up the usual suspects.

What about the Ninth and Tenth Amendments? Both amendments speak of rights and powers of the "People," echoing the Preamble's triumphant declaration of the right of "We the People" to self-government. Indeed, no phrase appears in more of the first ten amendments than "the people." The core idea conjured up by this phrase is popular sovereignty—the People's control over their government. In large measure, this very idea underlies the jury trial. As Thomas Jefferson exuberantly put the point in 1789, the jury represents trial "by the people themselves."[23]

In all the above-mentioned ways—preventing tyranny, playing a role in the formation of public policy, bringing citizens together in a vital public forum to exercise and improve their capacity for self-government—the jury serves an inherently populist and republican function far transcending the role of meting out justice to the parties in a case.

If we shift our focus on the jury away from the litigants and towards society at large and the jurors and potential jurors themselves—citizens with the right and the responsibility to participate in public affairs—we enormously expand our field of constitutional vision. This perspective enables a number of important conclusions to emerge, which we consider in the ensuing chapters. Before doing so, however, we note here three basic analogies that will frame our analysis: (1) the bicameral analogy, suggesting similarities between the judge/jury two-part judiciary and the Senate/House two-part legislature; (2) the legislative analogy, noting the role jurors play in representing the People;[24] and (3) the voting analogy, which emphasizes the similar function and activity of jurors in the jury box and voters at the ballot box.

These analogies have gone largely unnoticed. To the legal community, the "judiciary" means judges, "representatives" imply legislators, and "voting" refers to election of candidates. When we see jurors as members of the judiciary, who represent the People and cast ballots, new insights into the jury emerge. The next chapter provides an illustration. Drawing heavily on the analogy between jurors and voters, we argue for a heretofore unrecognized constitutional right to jury service.

FIVE

The Constitutional Right to Serve on Juries

WE HAVE SEEN THAT THE jury idea links up with various aspects of the Constitution. One link warrants independent consideration, because it both helps clarify the essence of jury service and suggests recognition of a constitutional right that has somehow gone unrecognized—the right to serve on a jury.

The clearest analogy to the citizens' role in the jury box is their role at the ballot box. The juror ultimately undertakes the same activity as the voter—she votes. And the vote in the jury box, as at the ballot box, represents self-government in its most pristine form.[1] Tocqueville called the jury system and the election system equally "direct and extreme" consequences of the "sovereignty of the people."[2] He thus regarded it as "essential that the jury lists should expand or shrink with the lists of voters"[3] and noted that historically this did in fact happen—with few exceptions, "in America all citizens who are electors have the right to be jurors."[4]

Women's suffragists, among others, understood that these two rights are tightly linked. As legal historian Barbara Babcock observes, "From the beginning, their struggle was also about the right to serve on juries. The two causes were the twin indicia of full citizenship both in the minds of women suffragists and in the attitudes of American society."[5]

Yet, under current doctrine, two major distinctions separate voting from jury service. First, several amendments to the Constitution—the Fifteenth, Nineteenth, Twenty-Fourth, and Twenty-Sixth—prohibit denying the vote to certain groups. The Fifteenth protects the right to vote of blacks; the Nineteenth, women; the Twenty-Fourth, poor people; and the Twenty-Sixth, young adults. However, courts and commentators have construed these amendments to apply only to the ballot box, not to the jury box. We disagree, for several reasons.

As a matter of plain meaning, these amendments protect the right to "vote," which is exactly what jurors (after deliberation) do. As a matter of legislative history, the Framers of these amendments did not focus narrowly on the right to pull the lever in an election. Rather, they tended to see the right to vote as part of a cluster of political rights that included jury service. Moreover, the voting-rights amendments interact with many state law provisions that explicitly link voting and jury service. And, as a matter of logic, it makes no sense to treat these rights differently. Why would we regard anyone as qualified to vote but not to serve on a jury, or vice versa? (These points are developed in detail in Chapter 8, dealing with the right of young adults to serve (and vote) on a jury.)*

Completely apart from the amendments specifically protecting the

---

*To be sure, the Supreme Court has not been oblivious to the relationship between voting in elections and jury service. In a few recent opinions, the Court has analogized these two activities. See *Edmonson v. Leesville Concrete Co.*, 500 U.S. 614, 625–26 (1991); *Powers v. Ohio*, 499 U.S. 406–08 (1991). It is also noteworthy that, with the exception of young adults, the groups protected by the voting rights amendments (blacks, women, the poor) have been protected from jury discrimination by the Supreme Court—albeit by resort to constitutional clauses that are less germane. See Vikram Amar, "Jury Service as Political Participation Akin to Voting," 80 *Cornell Law Review* 203, 247–51 (1995).

rights of certain groups to vote, the Supreme Court has on several occasions declared a general constitutional right to vote.[6] Commentators casually declare the existence of such a right as if the point were too obvious to require elaboration.[7] Yet, inexplicably, there is no clearly recognized federal constitutional right to serve on juries. (A number of state constitutions do explicitly recognize such a right.)

In the aftermath of the passage of the Nineteenth Amendment, this distinction was crucial. Citing their newly-won right to vote, women challenged their exclusion from jury service. Some states denied their claim on the ground that voting is a right of citizenship while jury service is merely a privilege or duty.[8] While the Supreme Court eventually required equal treatment of women with respect to jury service, it did so without reliance on a constitutional right to jury service. The Court has not made clear whether such a right exists. For example, in a case striking down race-based exclusions of potential jurors, the Court equivocated: "[W]hether jury service be deemed a right, a privilege, or a duty, the State may [not] extend it to some of its citizens and deny it to others on racial grounds."[9] Some lower courts and legal scholars have been less equivocal, explicitly *denying* that there is a right to jury service.[10]

We certainly do not quibble with the Court's recognition of a general right to vote. Such a right follows directly from the very premise of a democratic government, especially one explicitly established by "We the People" and guaranteeing each state a *republican* form of government. But such structural considerations apply with equal force to the jury, which, like the electorate, embodies the People and the public. So why the distinction between voting and jury service?

The Supreme Court has suggested that the right to vote is implied by Article I, Section 2's provision that "The House of Representatives shall be composed of Members chosen every second Year by the People of the several States."[11] On this reasoning, in mandating elections the Framers implicitly established a right to vote. After all, how can there be elections without an electorate? And how can we assure an electorate without guaranteeing a right to vote? But this inference is no stronger than the inference of a right to jury service from the fact that the Constitution mandates trial by jury. You can't have a jury without jurors any more than you can have an electorate without voters.

It may seem that acknowledgment of a general right to vote in elections, but not a parallel right to jury service, is a trivial matter of semantics. For with respect to both voting and jury service two rules govern actual practice. First, any putative right is not absolute; notwithstanding a recognized right to vote, restrictions are permitted. For example, most states forbid voting by convicts and children. As the Supreme Court has observed, the right to vote applies to "qualified citizens" only.[12] Second, some bases for exclusion are impermissible; notwithstanding its lack of recognition of a general right to serve on juries, the Supreme Court has forbade the denial of jury service on the basis of race and gender.[13] Why, then, should we be concerned about this gap—the recognition of a general right to vote but the denial of a general right to jury service? The difference appears inconsequential.

In fact, the distinction between the two rights matters in several respects. First, under current doctrine, there *are* people whose right to vote in elections is protected but who are denied the right to serve (and vote) on juries—young adults, for example. Second, the formal recognition of a right shifts the presumption governing actions that might restrict it. That is, if a constitutional right to jury service is recognized, we will be slower to make or tolerate exceptions: The governmental interest behind any exclusion would have to be especially strong. For this reason, recognizing a constitutional right to jury service could have immediate practical consequences for jury selection. (These are explored in the next several chapters.) Last, but not least, recognizing a constitutional right to serve on a jury would signal the need to rethink our attitudes about jury service. It has come to be regarded as a burden, something to escape if at all possible. People receiving a summons to jury duty often react with dismay rather than pride. This is cause for alarm, and not just because it leaves us with juries that underrepresent whatever segments in our society are more apt to evade service. The very notion of self-government becomes imperiled when the People regard their participation as a nuisance rather than a proud responsibility.

Rights entail responsibilities. Just as the right to amend the Constitution entails the responsibility of deliberation and respect for others in the amendment process, the right to vote in elections and shape the lives of fellow citizens triggers duties toward those fellow citizens, including the duty, when called, to deliberate with them. In Chapter 3, we suggested that those who wish to vote in plebiscites should deliberate in convention or caucus. Similarly, those who avail themselves of the right to vote in elections should not shirk the responsibility to serve on juries.

The Supreme Court has said that "with the exception of voting, for most citizens the honor and privilege of jury duty is their most significant opportunity to participate in the democratic process."[14] Today, too few citizens regard jury service as such an opportunity, much less an honor and a privilege. Recognizing that citizens have the constitutional right to serve on a jury would be a step towards recapturing the vision suggested by the Court and at the heart of American self-government.

Once again, this does not mean that everyone must be permitted to serve on a jury. Just as reasonable restrictions may be placed on the right to vote (and most other rights), so may they be placed on jury service. The state may deny jury service to those who abuse their citizenship (by committing crimes) or don't take it seriously (and fail to register to vote). Indeed, in rare cases, even some voters should not be eligible for jury service. For example, Americans who do not speak English but follow current events by reading foreign language newspapers would make good voters but poor jurors in trials and deliberations conducted in English. We claim only a *presumptive* right to jury service. The citizen in good standing, who reveals no infirmity to serve on a jury, cannot legitimately be denied such service. Just as the Supreme Court recognizes a right for "qualified citizens" to vote, we should extend the same recognition to jury service. We now turn to some important ramifications of all this.

SIX

The Unconstitutionality of Peremptory Challenges

THE PEREMPTORY CHALLENGE ENABLES THE attorneys in a case to dismiss a certain number of jurors for no articulated reason. If our analysis in the previous chapters is sound, this practice is problematic in two respects. First, the peremptory challenge undercuts the "big idea" behind the jury discussed in Chapter 4. By enabling attorneys and parties to determine the composition of the jury, it gives the search for adversarial advantage precedence over the values of public education and participation. If the jury is a vital public space in which citizens learn from one another and carry out self-government, and a political institution that represents the People, we should be extremely reluctant to permit the litigants to exclude certain people and perspectives from the process.

Second, once we recognize a right to serve on a jury, we must be suspicious of a practice whereby prospective jurors lose the opportunity to serve, for no apparent reason. The peremptory challenge appears to violate the dismissed individual's constitutional right to serve.

To be sure, rights are not absolute. Many constitutional rights, courts tell us, must yield to genuinely compelling governmental interests. As it happens, peremptory challenges do not serve an important governmental interest that justifies restricting the right to jury service. To the contrary, as indicated above, peremptory challenges denigrate the compelling interest in the jury as a body that represents the People.

Since defenders of the peremptory challenge generally reserve their strongest arguments for criminal cases, we shall focus the inquiry there. If the peremptory challenge is recognized as unconstitutional in criminal cases, it will surely collapse in civil cases where the proffered justifications for it are weaker.

THE RIGHT TO a jury trial establishes a critical bridge between the citizenry and the state. The assurance that citizens cannot be branded and punished as criminals absent the judgment of their peers protects against abusive government power. But the right to a jury trial does not by itself provide meaningful protection unless the jurors are fair. Thus, the Sixth Amendment provides the right not just to a jury, but to an "impartial" jury. If jurors are hellbent on convicting a defendant, regardless of the evidence that will come out at trial, the right to a jury trial offers small comfort. Criminal lawyers maintain that the peremptory challenge helps assure an impartial jury, by excluding jurors about whom either side has doubts.

The principal problem with this argument is that it invokes an impoverished conception of an "impartial jury." Since the jury represents the People, juries should be impartial not merely in a narrow adjudicatory sense (that is, the individual jurors are fair), but also in a political sense; the jury should represent all of the polity. The opposite of im*par*-*ti*al here is not simply partiality to one of the parties, but partisanship, more broadly: juries representing only one *part* of the community in terms of things like race, gender, or political party. (On this view, each jury ideally should represent a statistically unbiased sample of the People at large.)

This is especially important because the jury is not merely a fact-finding body. Juries also must make normative judgments. Criminal trials are unavoidably morality plays, focusing on the defendant's moral blameworthiness. And the assessment of his culpability is a task for the community, via the jury, not the judge. In a jury trial, the judge can never find a criminal defendant guilty no matter how clear his factual guilt. Thus, no man who proclaims his innocence can be condemned as guilty unless the community, via the jury, pronounces him worthy of moral condemnation. (This point is developed in Chapter 10, in connection with jury nullification.) And both civil and criminal trials frequently require juries to assess the "reasonableness" of behavior, which requires not a mere finding of historical fact, nor a scientific or legalistic assessment, but the normative judgment of ordinary citizens representing the community.

This vision finds expression in Supreme Court cases forbidding the intentional exclusion of blacks and women from the jury. More broadly, this vision underlies the oft-expressed idea that the jury pool should reflect a cross section of the community.[1] But while prospective jurors are summoned randomly in order to produce such a cross section, lawyers' peremptory challenges chisel an unrepresentative panel out of the representative pool. These challenges aggrandize the role of the lawyers at the expense of the jury and the public. By virtue of their partisan maneuvering, the parties in a case wrest control from the whole people. The deepest constitutional function of the jury is to serve the People, not the parties—to serve them in the administration of justice and the grand project of democratic self-government. Alas, over the years the short-term convenience of lawyers and litigants has won out over the long-run public function of the jury.

We must keep in mind the distinction between two types of partial juries. An individual juror may be partial in the sense of playing favorites. That is why we would not allow a relative or close friend of a party onto a jury, and why a judge may always dismiss biased jurors "for cause" (as discussed in the next chapter). But note that the Constitution speaks not of impartial *jurors*, but of an impartial *jury*. In a sense, we are all, by definition, partial. Each of us has a particular gender, race, and age, and bears many individual characteristics as well as the imprint of a set of unique life experiences. But when twelve of us from across the community come together, our individual partialities become molded into a collectively impartial (that is, representative) jury. And ideally, democratic deliberation will create a whole far greater than the sum of the parts.

The peremptory challenge defeats this vision, producing a *partial* jury derived from the *partisan* interests of the *parties*. The jury's partiality may be symmetric (with some jurors pleasing one side, some jurors the other), but it is still partial; it excludes voices and backgrounds solely to suit the preferences of the parties.

FROM THE BEGINNING, jury selection practice (like voting practice) failed to live up to the constitutional ideal. A brief review of the history provides the necessary context for fully developing the case against the peremptory challenge.

At the nation's founding, juries consisted almost exclusively of white males. Few blacks served on juries until the latter part of the nineteenth century, and women did not win widespread access until the twentieth. Even beyond these obvious outposts of discrimination, the selection system was skewed. The primary method of compiling a jury pool was the "key man" system, in which jury commissioners asked respected members of the community ("key men") for the names of persons with reputations for intelligence and integrity. The result was usually an elite-heavy group culled from the "Good Old Boy" network.

The key man system supplied the jury pool from which prospective jurors for particular cases were chosen. Individuals could then be disqualified from serving in a case in either of two ways. First, the judge could dismiss a prospective juror "for cause" if there was reason to doubt his fitness for the case, because of a conflict of interest or some other circumstance. Second, both the prosecution and defense were permitted a certain number of "peremptory challenges" whereby each could dismiss prospective jurors for any reason whatsoever without offering an explanation.

Congress abolished the federal key man system and dramatically changed federal jury selection in 1968. The Jury Selection and Service Act[2] declares it a right of all litigants in federal court to a jury "selected at random from a fair cross section of the community," and prohibits exclusion from a jury pool based on race, color, religion, sex, national origin, or economic status. It established the only criteria for jury service as age (eighteen or older), literacy, the absence of mental or physical infirmity, and the lack of a criminal record.

Seven years later, in the case of *Taylor v. Louisiana,*[3] the Supreme Court forced state courts as well to democratize jury selection, holding that the right to an impartial jury requires that the jury pool reflect the community at large. However, the random selection mandated by the 1968 Act and the *Taylor* decision applies only to the pool from which juries are chosen; neither Congress nor the Court altered the long tradition whereby members of the venire may be disqualified from a particular case either for cause or by peremptory challenge. In fact, the 1968 Act conferred on both the prosecution and the defense eight peremptory challenges in each criminal case and authorized judges to order an unlimited number of for-cause dismissals. Likewise, the *Taylor* decision did not change the tradition in state courts permitting both peremptory challenges and for-cause dismissals.

While the bases for dismissal of prospective jurors remained unchanged, the requirement of random selection of the pool did change the face of the American jury. Groups long excluded from the jury joined the pool. Most jurisdictions implemented random selection by drawing names from voter registration or motor-vehicle records—far more democratic approaches than the key man system. This remains the case today.

Thus, under the current system, jury selection occurs by weeding out members of the community at several different points. First, the original pool excludes certain people such as convicts, unregistered voters, and the homeless. The second point of elimination occurs with the random drawing of names from the master list. Once a list of prospective jurors for a particular case is established, all members are questioned by counsel or the judge (or both) to determine their fitness. During this "voir dire," with or without prompting by counsel, the judge may remove prospective jurors for cause, and each side may exercise its peremptory challenges. Finally, from those still remaining when these bases for dismissal are exhausted, a group of twelve (or fewer in some states) jurors is chosen.

While the precise methods of administration vary, this basic approach to jury selection in criminal cases is followed in most courts nationwide. Much of it is unobjectionable. Few contend that drawing the master pool from voter rolls or motor-vehicle records is a major problem. The names must be drawn from somewhere. Voter lists are a reasonable place to start, since jury service is more likely to be performed faithfully by people who take seriously their most analogous task as citizens—the vote. The random drawing of names from the master pool is even less objectionable. It is hard to imagine a fairer way of picking prospective jurors for service than random selection. The elimination of prospective jurors for cause obviously must be preserved as well. Though we argue in the next chapter that the basis of for-cause disqualification should be significantly narrowed, jurors with blatant conflicts of interest (relatives of the attorneys or parties, for example) must be excused.

Thus, the first three stages of exclusion are in principle inoffensive. The person who happens not to be called for a particular case, or who is dismissed for good cause, has no legitimate gripe. But the same cannot be said for prospective jurors who are dismissed by peremptory challenge. Citizens who take off from work or child-rearing to perform their civic duty, only to be sent home because one of the parties or lawyers dislikes them, have good grounds for complaint. And, as argued above, a jury whose composition is skewed by the idiosyncratic and partisan interests of the parties cannot be said to be impartial or representative of the People.

In part for this reason, the Supreme Court has held peremptory challenges illegitimate in certain circumstances—if, say, the dismissed person happens to be black or female and this was the reason for the dismissal. As a result of the 1986 case of *Batson v. Kentucky*,[4] and a line of cases extending *Batson*'s reach, prospective jurors may not be excluded on account of their race or gender. Whenever there is a racial or gender-based pattern in the use of peremptories, counsel must show that the dismissals were not based on race or gender.

In his concurring opinion in *Batson*, Justice Thurgood Marshall called for eliminating peremptories. Otherwise, he argued, attorneys will still make race-based peremptories provided there is no discernible pattern or as long as they can concoct an explanation. The claim of racial use of peremptories has, in fact, become a frequent argument on appeal. And the *Batson* line of cases opened the door to many moral and practical problems. As legal scholar George Fletcher argues:

> In the end, we have only two clear rules against discrimination in jury selection. Neither side may discriminate on the basis of race, and neither side may discriminate on the basis of gender. If this is all a fractured Court can do, then we will be treated to debates in the lower courts about whether for these purposes Hispanics are a race or an ethnic group and whether Jews are a race, a religion, or something else (shades of the Third Reich!). ... This is just the entry into the thicket. How do we apply the Supreme Court's teaching to gays? ... [W]e will witness the decline of a great legal system into the arbitrary allocation of protection from cultural stereotypes.[5]

Batson and its progeny do indeed leave trial courts with enormous difficulties. But the harm from peremptories cuts much deeper than their use in service of objectionable stereotypes. At least as it has evolved, the very *purpose* of the peremptory challenge—in virtually all cases, not just when used to keep blacks or women off the jury—is to create a jury favorable to one's own side rather than representative of the community. A jury engineered to be unrepresentative undermines the ideal of a public space for democratic deliberation, and is also a recipe for distorted decisionmaking. This point comes into sharper focus when we recall that juries engage not only in fact-finding but also in normative judgment. Such judgment should reflect the norms of the community at large.

Traditionally, peremptory challenges derived from bizarre stereotypes. For example, Clarence Darrow divided prospective jurors into pro-prosecution and pro-defense categories based on their religions and nationalities[6] and asserted that "cold, serious, unimaginative" persons were pro-prosecution while "alert, witty, emotional" sorts were pro-defense.[7] Similar if somewhat less strained notions became codified in assorted manuals that assisted lawyers in using their peremptory challenges. Predictably, the process eventually became more scientific. In the 1970s, groups sprung up offering to help certain defendants select a jury likely to acquit. These jury consultants conducted polls to determine correlations between a person's background (not just ethnicity and gender but occupation, income, even characteristics like reading habits) and his or her attitude with respect to matters relevant in the case. Assisted by computers, the groups compiled profiles of the kinds of jurors to be kept on or bumped off.

Throughout the 1970s, jury consultants were credited with a string of well-publicized acquittals. As a result, so-called scientific jury selection has proliferated. Today, many defense attorneys use jury consultants routinely, and some prosecutors use them as well. Jury consulting has come to include handwriting experts, who analyze prospective jurors' writing on questionnaires, and experts on body language, who observe prospective jurors during voir dire. Jury consulting has moved beyond group generalizations to highly individual predictions about prospective jurors.[8]

The harm from all this begins with its purpose: to create not an impartial jury (even in the narrow sense of that term—fair individual jurors), but one stacked in the client's favor. As eminent defense attorney Herald Price Fahringer says, "There isn't a trial lawyer in this country who wouldn't tell you—if he were being honest—'I don't want an impartial jury. I want one that's going to find in my client's favor.'"[9] Lawyers are rarely as candid as Fahringer, but in the guise of fiction Alan Dershowitz gives a revealing glimpse of the thinking behind jury selection. In the following passage from Dershowitz's novel about the criminal justice system, a jury consultant tells the attorneys representing an accused rapist what kind of jurors to seek:

> Older women. Lots of them. . . . With grandchildren. Stable families. No screwing around. No divorces. Kids who got married young. Miami Beach-in-the-winter types. Snowbirds. Italians, Irish, Jews, Greeks, maybe even some WASPs. No black women. No young women, regardless of race. And absolutely no well-educated or well-read people. Not dunces. Just not geniuses. And boring lives. No excitement. Their most adventurous trip should be a Princess cruise. No bungee jumpers, or hang gliders. They drive Chevys or Buicks. No BMWs. Boring. Boring. That's our jury. That's who we want.[10]

Needless to say, Dershowitz's "fictional" consultant aimed not for jurors likely to reach a correct decision, but rather for those likely to acquit. And the consultant's views on race and gender underscore that though the Supreme Court has outlawed peremptories based on race and gender, lawyers don't seem to care. Clever lawyers can strike a number of blacks or women and concoct a race-neutral or gender-neutral explanation.

The consultant's insistence on "absolutely no educated or well-read people" suggests a particularly perverse feature of peremptory challenges. A defense attorney representing a client he believes to be guilty (the norm in criminal defense)[11] wants a jury particularly *ill-suited* to arrive at a correct verdict. This means looking not only for jurors biased in the defendant's favor but, more generally, for the least able members of the pool. Such a jury does not represent a true cross-section of the community, nor does it represent the community well.

Incredible—and unique. Nowhere else in our system of government is virtue treated as vice. We do not try to pick the least able persons to serve in our legislatures or on our courts, or in any other capacity. No one has ever proposed subjecting voters to a reverse literacy test geared to removing the most educated or otherwise qualified.

WHY IS THE peremptory challenge necessary in the first place? The establishment of a democratically inclusive pool, random selection from that pool, and dismissal of jurors for cause appear adequate to provide a fair and able jury. Why add to this filtering process a provision for attorneys to eliminate prospective jurors for no reason? What important societal objective is advanced by the peremptory challenge?

Our analysis thus far suggests that, far from promoting a strong societal objective, peremptory challenges serve a venal purpose—to defeat rather than arrive at truth, to select partial and incompetent juries rather than impartial and able ones. Is there nevertheless a justification for peremptories that trumps citizens' right to serve and the community's expectation of a fair trial before a representative body?

Several arguments are trotted out in defense of the peremptory challenge. First is the idea of legitimacy: The parties will better respect a decision reached by a body they helped select. But what about the legitimacy of the verdict for the rest of society—who see weird juries, chosen in weird (and expensive) ways, generating weird outcomes? We do not let a defendant handpick a personalized designer legislature to determine the laws governing his conduct. Nor may the defendant pick (or veto) the prosecutor who pursues him, the grand jury that indicts him, the judge who tries him, or the appellate court that reviews his case. Yet we don't consider the legislature, grand jury, prosecutor, and appellate court illegitimate; why is the trial jury any different? The defendant is entitled to an impartial jury. Neither constitutional principles nor sound considerations of policy and morality dictate any further entitlement. Again, juries represent the People, not the parties.

Supporters of the peremptory challenge cite the common-law historian Blackstone, who maintained that a defendant ought not be "tried by any one man against whom he has conceived a prejudice, even without being able to assign a reason for such his dislike."[12] Here Blackstone erred. As noted, the defendant cannot veto a judge whom he dislikes, though the judge is more likely to affect his fate than a single juror. And if Blackstone were correct that one ought not to be tried by someone he dislikes, defendants should be permitted an unlimited number of peremptory challenges—a position no one maintains.*

A second argument marshaled on behalf of peremptories rests on our country's unbroken recognition of their place in the criminal trial. However, this history is easily exaggerated. In a scholarly article canvassing the historical records, University of Chicago law professor Albert Alschuler showed that peremptory challenges were traditionally used sparingly—"so rarely that some scholars have concluded that [during British history] challenges were simply unavailable in ordinary criminal cases."[13] Alschuler and others speculate that, in early practice, peremptories were actually used to dismiss prospective jurors who knew the parties (and thus, today, would often be dismissed for cause). Certainly, peremptories were not routinely used as a trial tactic, which is the situation today.

More importantly, while we should take seriously the claims of tradition, and exercise caution when fooling with machinery long in use, we ought not be slave to history. If peremptory challenges are a relic of an imperfect past, serving no discernible purpose warranting respect, they should not be preserved out of mere obeisance to tradition.

In addition, there are competing traditions at work. Jury selection involves not only the exclusive tradition of which the peremptory chal-

---

*That would include Blackstone who, recognizing the problem with his own position, acknowledged that "the peremptory challenge of the prisoner must however have some reasonable boundary." He maintained that thirty-five was an appropriate number. *Blackstone's Commentaries* (St. George Tucker ed., volume 5, p. 353).

lenge is part, but also the inclusive tradition embodied in several amendments to the Constitution (especially the Fifteenth, Nineteenth, Twenty-Fourth and Twenty-Sixth Amendments, respectively preventing voting discrimination against blacks, women, the poor, and the young). These glorious amendments reaffirm popular self-government and demand that all people be allowed to participate in it. By eliminating the peremptory challenge we vindicate the constitutional right to vote (which is what jurors do) free from discrimination over the more ancient *non*constitutional right to remove jurors on the basis of unarticulated prejudice.[14]

Another argument advanced in favor of peremptories is that while lawyers do not use them to obtain a sound jury, such a jury nevertheless results when each side seeks jurors favorable to it. Unfortunately, in practice no invisible hand benevolently guides jury selection. As noted, if the defense attorney knows (or at least suspects) his client is guilty— which most do most of the time—he will use his peremptories to strike those prospective jurors likely to arrive at the accurate verdict of guilty. As for prosecutors, it is true that they generally believe defendants guilty, and thus want jurors who will arrive at the truth. But suppose the prosecution has one peremptory challenge left to use on either of two remaining people. One candidate seems fair-minded, with no axe to grind. The other appears pro-prosecution, likely to convict even if the government's case proves weak (but whom the defense failed to strike, from mere oversight or lack of peremptories). Whom will the prosecution strike? Not the prospective juror likely to do the best job. Given these realities, it is hard to imagine that peremptories produce the soundest jury.

The only potentially legitimate use of peremptories is to strike those who would not approach the case with an open mind and base their decision on the evidence. But prospective jurors who fit this profile may be challenged for cause. Since there is no limit to the number of such challenges or dismissals, there appears to be no need for peremptories.*

We cannot know whether lawyers help their cases through peremp-

*We consider the interaction between peremptory challenges and for-cause challenges in detail in the next chapter.

tory challenges, because there is no reliable way to gauge the accuracy of verdicts or to determine how persons dismissed peremptorily would have voted had they served on the jury. Some experts believe jury selection makes virtually no difference. Sociologist Michael Saks, who has studied mock juries, maintains that verdicts "are far more heavily influenced by the evidence and arguments presented than by the jurors' personal characteristics."[15] We should hope so. But assuming Saks is wrong, and jury selection is as important as most lawyers believe, that means only that peremptories can help one side win a case; it does not mean they have any value to the public. Do we want a verdict to depend on whether the defense or prosecution has a better jury consultant?

Thus, in the final analysis peremptories serve either no purpose or a bad purpose. In either case, they violate the rights of those against whom they are exercised. And, in either case, they allow lawyers to narrow the range of jurors who may serve, and thus undermine the public purpose of the jury as a democratic body deliberating and learning together in an inclusive public space.

WE ARE NOT the first to argue that peremptory challenges are unconstitutional even apart from their use in service of disreputable stereotypes. Most notably, in the article cited above Professor Alschuler argues that because peremptories serve no valid purpose, they lack a "rational basis" and thus violate the Fourteenth Amendment right to "equal protection of the laws."[16]

We think an even sturdier foundation for the same conclusion is available. Yes, peremptorily dismissed jurors have been treated unequally, and for no good reason. But this fact alone fails to capture the magnitude of what is at stake. The problem with peremptories transcends the fact that they discriminate without a valid basis. More significantly, this discrimination deprives citizens of one of the most fundamental rights, duties, and responsibilities of citizenship. Peremptories violate the right of citizens to serve on juries, and deprive those who do sit of the chance to deliberate with a genuine cross-section of their fellow citizens. In the process, peremptories deprive the entire community of the kind of democratic jury to which they are entitled.

It may be responded that the peremptory challenge does not deprive persons of the right to serve—it merely makes them ineligible to serve in a particular case. However, the juror dismissed peremptorily in one case may likewise be dismissed peremptorily in another, and another (even assuming he's fortunate enough to receive several calls). Absent a right to serve in each case for which one is called, the "wait till next time" reassurance may amount to nothing.* Nor is it far-fetched to imagine a prospective juror dismissed peremptorily from several cases. People who fit certain stereotypes—for example, the well educated— tend to find their way onto lawyers' hit lists.

Moreover, and perhaps more importantly, we must consider the effect of peremptory challenges not only on the dismissed jurors but also on the resulting jury. When we take seriously the idea of the jury as a public space where deliberative self-government occurs in a body representing a cross-section of the community, we seek the realization of this ideal in *every jury*. If the jurors in Case A are a skewed sample of the citizenry rather than an impartial cross-section, they miss a special chance to engage a broad range of their fellow citizens. This omission is not cured simply because the jury in Case B is

---

*Even if the dismissed person does get to serve on another jury, she has been deprived of her rights. Imagine, by analogy, a system that gives each candidate in an election a certain number of peremptory challenges—voters who can be designated as ineligible. Would this system be acceptable because the dismissed voters can vote in other elections? Of course not. The right to vote means the right to vote in any election for which one is properly qualified, not the right to vote on one occasion or another. The right to serve on a jury should be regarded no differently. Of course, voters can vote in *every* election in their jurisdiction, whereas people obviously cannot serve on every jury. But this distinction is a matter of practicality rather than principle. People cannot serve on every jury for the simple reason that juries are restricted in size. Beyond that purely practical restriction, there is no reason to conceptualize the right to vote differently from the right to serve on a jury. The state must give a prospective voter an awfully good reason before it denies him the vote in any election. But in the case of the peremptory challenge, the dismissed juror is given no reason for his disqualification.

skewed in a different direction. Every one of Tocqueville's "public schools" should be integrated: A system that subordinates this ideal to the parties' tactical advantage lacks fidelity to our highest constitutional ideals.*

---

*Eliminating peremptory challenges may increase the difficulty of juries reaching unanimity, since lawyers will be unable to eliminate those members of the jury pool who seem most idiosyncratic or independent. As it happens, we think the time has come to reconsider the traditional requirement that verdicts in criminal cases be unanimous. At the founding, unanimity made sense in light of the composition of juries. The key man system rounded up the usual suspects, a set of relatively homogeneous citizens (no blacks, women, or poor people, for starters) more likely to reach consensus than today's more diverse juries. We should embrace that diversity, but we should also recognize that if everyone gets to serve on juries, and we eliminate the old undemocratic barriers, preserving the unanimity requirement might itself be undemocratic; it would create an extreme minority veto unknown to the Founders—one which could disempower juries by preventing many cases from reaching a verdict. However, because permitting majority verdicts could reduce the incentive for juries to deliberate, the elimination of the unanimity requirement would have to be accompanied by measures designed to ensure vigorous deliberation. See Akhil Amar, "Reinventing Juries: Ten Suggested Reforms," 28 *University of California-Davis Law Review* 1169, 1188–89 (1995).

SEVEN

Rethinking the For-Cause Dismissal

WE HAVE SAVED FOR THIS chapter one other argument advanced in favor of preserving the peremptory challenge, because analysis of this argument leads to a separate problem with the current method of jury selection. Indeed, far from rescuing peremptories, this argument actually leads to expanding the protection of prospective jurors from dismissal.

Those favoring peremptories insist that determinations of cause are an imperfect basis for removing biased prospective jurors. Counsel may suspect bias but have no provable or articulable grounds that will convince a judge. Moreover, merely requesting a for-cause dismissal, or probing the prospective juror to establish the basis for such a dismissal, could antagonize the person in question—a great risk since she may end up on the jury. In short, peremptories may help obtain a fair jury by eliminating members whose bias either side may suspect even though there exists no overt basis justifying for-cause disqualification.

This argument makes sense only to the extent that one regards it as desirable to keep off a jury anyone with any conceivable inclination or leaning. This, in fact, appears to be the prevailing perspective. Thus we have not only peremptory challenges, but also an ever-expanding notion of what justifies for-cause dismissal.

But when we focus on the desirability of a jury representative of the community engaging in democratic deliberation, as well as on each individual's constitutional right to jury service, we see the need to move in the opposite direction—not only eliminating peremptories but cutting back on the for-cause challenge as well. The overbroad for-cause dismissal, no less than the peremptory challenge, reduces the scope of community deliberation and denies the prospective juror the opportunity to engage in a key act of citizenship.

We certainly do not deny the need for some for-cause dismissals. A proper trial requires jurors who will evaluate the evidence with an open mind. As we noted earlier, relatives of the litigants obviously should not be permitted to serve on the jury. But the parameters of for-cause dismissals should be severely restricted. Voir dire should establish whether the prospective juror is a personal friend (or enemy) of any of the parties, attorneys, or witnesses. Beyond that, it should determine whether she seems willing and able to weigh the evidence and to follow the judge's instructions. Assuming satisfactory answers to these elementary lines of inquiry, she should be permitted to serve.

Under current law in many jurisdictions, for-cause dismissals cover far more ground than concrete conflicts of interest or bias. Whole categories of people are dismissed based on speculation that some circumstance in their life could unconsciously affect their impartiality. If the defendant is a businessman charged with fraud, the judge might dismiss businesspeople. If the case involves a school, bid farewell to teachers, students, and administrators. In a malpractice case, forget health-care officials. In some jurisdictions, people with lawyers in their family are bounced from all kinds of cases. One who has had conflicts with any insurance company may be dismissed from a tort case in which insurance plays a role. Anyone with stock investments might be tossed from a prosecution for insider trading.

Such people could swear under oath that they have no axe to grind in the case, but they will be dismissed on the ground that they *may* have an axe to grind of which they are not consciously aware. There is a widespread view that one must be a blank slate with respect to the facts and issues in a case in order to be an impartial juror. But the result is a partial jury—a jury that excludes certain segments of the community.

The problem with the promiscuous use of for-cause dismissals is illuminated by reference to the bicameral analogy. For some reason, we tolerate a bizarre double standard in our treatment of the two bodies in our judiciary (judges and juries)—a double standard we would never tolerate in our treatment of Senators and House members. Judges often have knowledge and opinions (and insurance policies and stock holdings), but only palpable conflicts of interest tend to be considered a basis for judicial disqualification. Why do we trust judges so much more than jurors? Indeed, juror bias may be less problematic than judge bias, because a juror is one of only twelve decision-makers—and, as discussed in the previous chapter, "partial" individual jurors may nevertheless be molded into an impartial jury. In addition, jurors must openly articulate their reasons in order to persuade their peers, whereas a biased judge can single-handedly manipulate proceedings in ways hard to detect and reverse.

In any case, the attempt to sanitize juries by removing anyone with any conceivable predisposition rests on dubious assumptions about what constitutes disqualifying "bias". No one is a blank slate. We all operate from psychological or philosophical premises—about what kind of information is credible, for example—that influence our evaluation of evidence. No selection process can eliminate this human element. Instead, we should put our trust in a body representing the entire community, expecting the group to transcend the weaknesses or idiosyncrasies of individual members through a spirited and collective deliberation of the broader body.

Even more disturbing than the dismissal of anyone with a supposed bias are dismissals of civic-minded citizens merely because they may have heard or read something about the crime or the defendant. It doesn't matter if these people have formed no concrete opinions, have no discernible bias, and consider themselves perfectly able to render an impartial verdict. They are viewed as contaminated by any acquaintance with the underlying facts or parties. In high-profile cases such as the trials of Oliver North and O.J. Simpson, this leads to a search for jurors oblivious to the world around them. In the McMartin child abuse case in California, a survey found that 97 percent of adults in the community knew about the case.[1] Seeking jurors from the remaining three percent invited an unqualified jury.

To capture the absurdity of this state of affairs, it is hard to improve on Mark Twain's characterization. In a highly publicized murder case, the judge removed all jurors familiar with the facts. The result, Twain observed, was a jury of "fools and rascals," because

> the system rigidly excludes honest men and women. . . . A minister, intelligent, esteemed, and greatly respected; a merchant of high character and known probity; a mining superintendent of intelligence and unblemished reputation; a quartz-mill owner of excellent standing, were all questioned in the same way, and all set aside. Each said the public talk and the newspaper reports had not so biased his mind but that sworn testimony would . . . enable him to render a verdict without prejudice and in accordance with the facts. But of course such men could not be trusted with the case. Ignoramuses alone could mete out unsullied justice.[2]

That Twain penned these words in 1871 suggests that rewarding ignorance in jury selection is nothing new. However, it ought not be inferred that this practice was envisioned by the Founding Fathers. They valued local juries in part because jurors would have some acquaintance with the context of the case, and some grounding in the mores and shared understanding of the community. Hence the Sixth Amendment requires that a defendant be tried by "an impartial jury" of "the State and district wherein the crime shall have been committed." The fact that the Founders required an impartial jury and a local jury in the very same sentence shows that they did not equate impartiality with ignorance.

It is folly to dismiss prospective jurors simply because they have ideas—what self-governing citizen shouldn't have ideas? We want citizens to have open minds, not empty minds. All too often, intelligent and well-informed jurors are dismissed precisely because they are intelligent and well-informed (and, as we have seen, when their intelligence does not result in a for-cause dismissal, the attorneys often exercise peremptory challenges to remove them). While we want cases tried on the evidence presented in the courtroom, not ideas or information gleaned from outside sources, it does not follow that we should strike people from a jury solely because they have heard or read a few things. We should rely more on the scalpel of strict instructions—admonishing jurors to base their verdict only on the evidence before them—and less on the sledgehammer of exclusion.

RECOGNITION THAT PEREMPTORIES violate the right to serve on a jury yields an easy remedy—abolition. The same is not the case with respect to the for-cause challenge. Clearly, such challenges must be preserved. How is it possible to ensure their vitality while preventing their overuse? Theoretically, we could allow dismissed jurors to sue the government, or allow every losing litigant to argue on appeal that the judgment should be overturned because prospective jurors were improperly dismissed for cause. In practice, either approach would flood the courts with collateral lawsuits.

But this is a case where we can protect a constitutional right even in the absence of a perfect legal remedy. All that is needed is for judges to appreciate the constitutional right of citizens to serve on juries and the virtues of cross-sectional deliberation. With these values in mind, trial judges should apply a much more exacting standard before they excuse prospective jurors for cause. The bicameral analogy suggests an obvious standard: A judge should not dismiss a juror for cause unless the judge would be willing to recuse herself from a case in a similar circumstance. (Judges should welcome such a standard, for it would facilitate jury selection and help them move their dockets along.)

It may be argued that we will not add to the actual number of persons who get to serve on juries. After all, juries eventually end up with the requisite number of members: When one person is dismissed, another ends up serving who otherwise would not have. This response misses the point. Remember, expansive use of for-cause challenges not only violates the rights of individual jurors but negatively skews the composition of the jury. Moreover, certain systematic uses of the for-cause challenge—for example, to eliminate educated people from juries—may skew the results of trials (and diminish the quality of deliberation) over a range of cases across the board. Reducing the scope of the for-cause challenge will prevent such a skewing, for each individual jury and the institution generally will more closely reflect the community at large.

In addition, we cannot measure the efficacy of a constitutional right by the number of people who exercise it. Otherwise, we could deny some people freedom of speech as long as we imported an equal number and granted them that right. Put differently, more is at stake than whether Ms. X gets to serve on a jury or Ms. Y serves instead. The notion that replacing Ms. X with Ms. Y solves the problem rests on an atomistic vision of the jury as twelve fungible individuals who happen to sit in the same room and decide a case. When the vision of the jury as a democratic institution prevails, the folly of the current expansive use of the for-cause challenge becomes obvious. Would we bar Ms. X from holding office (or voting) on the ground that she is too familiar with government, and deem her elimination acceptable because she is replaced by some Ms. Y?

Neither Ms. X nor Ms. Y should be denied her place in our democratic institutions. From the standpoint of the individual, it makes a difference whether she is never called for jury service or is called and then improperly dismissed.* From a societal standpoint, excusing prospective jurors without good reason (or, in the case of informed and educated prospective jurors, for a terrible reason) skews the jury and thwarts the function of this vital democratic institution.

*As Oliver Wendell Holmes famously remarked, "Even a dog knows the difference between being stumbled over and being kicked." Oliver Wendell Holmes, *The Common Law*, Mark DeWolfe Howe, ed. (Little Brown, 1963), p. 3. The problem of someone never serving because never called results from mere arithmetic—there are only so many trials needing so many jurors and, in certain times and places, more than enough citizens to go around. The problem of someone not serving because improperly dismissed results not from arithmetic but from the failure to appreciate the constitutional rights belonging to We the People. The latter problem should not be tolerated. The arithmetic problem could be ameliorated by expanding the size of juries. See Akhil Amar, "Reinventing Juries: Ten Suggested Reforms," 28 *U.C. Davis Law Review* 1169, 1188–89 (1995). Instead of reducing the size of juries from twelve to six (which some states have done), we should consider increasing the number of citizens involved in an important aspect of self-government and enhancing the potential for each jury to be more broadly cross-sectional, bringing citizens from all walks of life into a common conversation.

EIGHT

The Right of Young Adults
to Serve on Juries

THE SUPREME COURT HAS PROTECTED the right of blacks and women to serve on juries.[1] However, the Court and lower courts have winked at what is in some ways a more egregious exclusion. Women and blacks were dismissed from particular cases. That's bad enough, but young adults are denied the right to serve in a far more systematic fashion.

Like blacks and women, young adults have often been dismissed from a case by peremptory challenge—but that's only when they are called for jury service in the first place, which is unusual. In the past, the "key man" system weeded out young adults. The key man system has disappeared, but young adults have not reaped the benefit for two reasons. First, some states require that jurors be at least twenty-one years of age. The second problem is the infrequent refilling of the jury pool in many states and in the federal system. Federal law requires refilling the federal jury pool only every four years.[2] Some states refill it even less frequently.

The resulting exclusion of young adults is substantial. Suppose that a particular jurisdiction permits jury service for persons aged eighteen and older (which is common). Now suppose that this same jurisdiction adds new names to the pool once every four years (also common). All persons seventeen years of age at the time the pool is refilled will be ineligible to serve until they are twenty-one. All persons sixteen will be ineligible until they are twenty, and so forth. As a result, persons aged eighteen to twenty-one are vastly underrepresented on juries.

The Twenty-Sixth Amendment gives eighteen-year-olds the right to vote, and federal law makes them eligible for military service.[3] Thus, eighteen-year-olds may vote and fight, but are effectively denied the third key badge of citizenship—jury service.

In a recent article, Vikram Amar argues that the Twenty-Sixth Amendment should be construed as giving young adults the right to serve on juries.[4] As suggested in Chapter 5, this position is strong as a matter of text, history, and logic.

First, all of the voting rights amendments (the Fifteenth, Nineteenth, Twenty-Fourth, and Twenty-Sixth) confer a right to vote. That is what jurors do—they vote (after deliberation). These amendments do not, on their terms, limit the vote to the ballot box. Nor does the legislative history support such a limitation. Start with the Fifteenth Amendment, whose supporters construed it as guaranteeing blacks not only the right to vote but also the right to hold office[5]; this right, in turn, could well be construed as entailing the right to jury service since jurors do, in a way, hold office. This reading of the Fifteenth Amendment meshes with basic legal doctrine in place at the time of its adoption in 1870, sharply distinguishing between civil and political rights. Civil rights, such as the rights to own property, bring lawsuits, and make contracts, belonged to all citizens, including women. But a tight cluster of political rights— voting, holding office, jury service, and militia service—belonged only to white men. The Fourteenth Amendment extended equal civil rights to blacks. If it had been intended to extend political rights, the Fifteenth

Amendment would have been unnecessary. But the Fifteenth Amendment was necessary, lest blacks be denied political equality. It is hard to see why supporters of the Fifteenth Amendment would desire such equality only at the ballot box, ignoring the full cluster of political rights that blacks had been denied. Indeed, only a few years after the amendment was adopted, Congress passed the Civil Rights Act of 1875, affirming the right of blacks to serve on juries based precisely on the language of the Fifteenth Amendment.

At the time of passage of the Nineteenth Amendment in 1920, the linkage between women's suffrage and the right of women to serve on juries was even more clearly understood. As noted, the suffragists regarded the vote and jury service as "the twin indicia of full citizenship."[6]

This same linkage also provides a gloss on the Twenty-Sixth Amendment's protection of young adults' right to vote. As a historical matter, the amendment arose out of the perceived unfairness of young adults fighting and dying in the Vietnam War while they lacked a say in the government's policy. Was it any less unfair that young adults were frequently prosecuted for evading the draft or protesting the war while their peers did not sit on the juries that decided their fate? And if Americans over twenty-one were entitled to benefit from the views and votes of young adults on Election Day, why not in the jury room?

Moreover, supporters of the Twenty-Sixth Amendment did not limit their advocacy to the right to vote; they spoke more broadly of political participation by the young. Attorney General John Mitchell argued that people between the ages of eighteen and twenty-one deserved "to be entrusted with *all* of the responsibilities and privileges of citizenship."[7] Senator Edward Kennedy spoke of "bringing our youth into full and lasting participation in our institutions of democratic government."[8] The Senate Report on the Amendment said the Amendment aimed to give young adults "full participation in our political system."[9]

Finally, as noted in Chapter 5, the historical linkage between voting in elections and jury service has also been manifest at the state level: many state constitutions explicitly treat the two rights in tandem.

The textual and historical arguments are amply supported by logic and common sense. Of the three public institutions demanding citizen responsibility—electorate, jury, militia—the tightest two-way link is between the electorate and the jury. People who are mentally fit but physically infirm should be permitted to serve on juries and vote in elections, but ought not take up arms in the militia. No similar asymmetry exists between serving on juries and voting in elections. Not only is the ultimate act (a vote) the same in each case, but the requisite skills are similar as well. It is hard to imagine people being found fit to vote but not to serve on juries, or vice versa.* By what possible logic may people vote at the age of eighteen but not be given the opportunity to serve on juries until twenty-one or older?

It MAY BE thought that any discrimination against young adults with respect to jury service is trivial because transient—all people grow older, and when they do they become eligible to serve on a jury. But on this theory, exclusion from the ballot box would be okay too: The very laws the Twenty-Sixth Amendment overruled merely postponed the right to vote. However, this postponement meant that when young adults did get to vote, they were no longer quite so young—they might be different people with a different perspective. Thus the postponement may have deprived the electorate of a distinctive viewpoint.

The "mere postponement" argument reflects the regrettable tendency to think of constitutional rights solely in terms of individuals. We need to think of the integrity and quality of the jury as a whole, and whether something is lost when we exclude a distinctive voice. On occasion, the Court has recognized this point, observing, for example, that excluding an identifiable segment of the community "remove[s] from the jury room qualities of human nature and varieties of human experience" which "deprives the jury of a perspective on human events that may have unsuspected importance in any case that may be presented."[10] In the specific context of gender-based exclusions, the Court has noted that "the two sexes are not fungible" and "a flavor, a distinct quality is lost if ei-

*Hard, but not impossible. See page 63.

ther sex is excluded."[11] The same reasoning applies to the exclusion of the young. Especially since defendants in criminal cases are disproportionately young, it seems problematic to exclude from the jury box the distinctive flavor of young adults. And beyond the rights of defendants, we must vindicate the republican interests of other jurors and the community at large: They, too, suffer when the jury box is askew.

In 1974, the Supreme Court addressed the systematic exclusion of young adults from juries, specifically the argument that the infrequent refilling of the jury pool in the Southern District of California effectively excluded anyone younger than twenty-four.[12] The Court rejected the claim on the ground that only intentional exclusion of a group from jury service violates the Constitution. The infrequent filling of the wheel had the effect of freezing out the young, but because that was not the intention there was no constitutional problem.

That holding, however, has little continuing relevance, because the Court has since abandoned the intentional discrimination test. Also, the Court in 1974 considered the Sixth Amendment right to a jury trial and the Fifth Amendment right to equal protection, but did not consider the Twenty-Sixth Amendment. This may be because the defendants in that case had been indicted and their prosecution initiated prior to ratification of that amendment.

Under current doctrine, systematic exclusion of a group from a jury, whether intentional or not, can violate the Constitution.[13] However, a violation requires that the group be "cognizable" for Sixth Amendment purposes. While the Supreme Court has never addressed whether young people are a cognizable group, lower courts have consistently rejected such a claim.[14] That is, they have essentially rejected the notion that young people may have a certain perspective ("a flavor, a distinct quality") such that their exclusion results in a skewed jury. The courts have ignored a great deal of social-science data showing that people of different ages think (and act) differently.[15]

Of course, the same may be true of other groups as well. If we prevent jury selection practices that keep out the young, where do we stop? As the United States Court of Appeals for the First Circuit put it, "If the age classification is adopted, surely blue-collar workers, yuppies, Rotarians, Eagle Scouts, and an endless variety of other classifications will be entitled to similar treatment."[16]

However, the groups cited by the court, unlike young adults, are *not* systematically excluded from jury service.* Moreover, the idea of protecting young adults from jury discrimination is anything but arbitrary—it is rooted firmly in the Twenty-Sixth Amendment's protection of their right to vote.

Under current Supreme Court law, blacks, women, and the poor may not be systematically kept off juries. Significantly, a specific constitutional amendment ensures that each of these groups cannot be denied the right to vote. The following symmetry emerges. By virtue of the Fifteenth Amendment, blacks cannot be denied the vote in elections; by virtue of Supreme Court law, their right to serve and vote on juries is protected. By virtue of the Nineteenth Amendment, women cannot be denied the vote in elections; by virtue of Supreme Court law, their right to serve and vote on juries is protected. By virtue of the Twenty-Fourth Amendment, the poor cannot be denied (through a poll tax) the right to vote in elections; by virtue of Supreme Court law, they cannot be discriminated against in jury selection.[17]

For some reason, the symmetry breaks down where young adults are concerned. By virtue of the Twenty-Sixth Amendment, they cannot be denied the vote. However, the Court has failed to protect their right to serve on juries. Recognition of that right is all that is needed to complete an elegant tapestry weaving together voting and jury service, the two most central rights and responsibilities of citizenship.

Of course, to recognize that young adults have a right to serve on juries does not necessarily invalidate all methods of jury selection that reduce their involvement. As noted, courts have said that many rights can be overridden by a sufficiently strong state interest. But once we elevate eighteen-year-olds to the same status as blacks and women, any method of jury selection that discriminates against them (or nineteen-year-olds, or anyone else above that age) may be justified only by a compelling

*If they were, such exclusion would be unacceptable. See Chapters 6 and 7.

state interest. As a practical matter, that will sound the death knell for practices that keep people of a certain age from serving. The administrative convenience of refilling the wheel every four years, instead of every year, hardly constitutes a compelling state interest.[18] Indeed, when we focus on the link between voting and jury service, the impropriety of refilling the wheel only quadrennially becomes especially clear. Would it be acceptable to hold brief voter-registration periods only once every four years? And when we focus on the big idea behind the jury, we recognize that a compelling interest—creating truly representative juries to engage in democratic deliberation—*supports* inclusion of young adults on juries.

But there's the rub. The infirmity of jury selection has gone unnoticed because of the deeply engrained tendency to view constitutional rights through the prism of the individual. So viewed, the fact that many individuals are ineligible to serve on a jury until they are twenty or twenty-one years of age seems trivial. But when we focus on the jury's inherently public function—its crucial role in self-government—we see the impropriety of keeping a distinct perspective out of the jury box.

The (un)constitutional folly of excluding a certain voice from jury deliberation becomes even more vivid when we recognize that juries are empowered to do much more than just find facts. This is the subject of our next two chapters.

NINE

Jury Review

TODAY, CONTROVERSY SWIRLS AROUND THE issue of jury "nullification"—whether criminal juries may legitimately acquit contrary to the evidence if for any reason they believe it appropriate to do so. Many recent high-profile criminal cases (involving O.J. Simpson, Bernhard Goetz, Marion Barry, Oliver North, and Jack Kevorkian, among others) have raised the issue. In each of these cases, the defense at times seemed to invite the jury to acquit for reasons unrelated to whether the defendant had committed the acts charged by the government.

Needless to say, criminal juries have the legal *power* to nullify, since they are not expected to provide an explanation for their verdicts and their acquittals are insulated from reversal on appeal.* The controversy

---

*A criminal conviction, or any verdict in a civil case, can be overturned by either the trial judge or a court of appeals. However, even in these circumstances, the verdict is accorded great deference and vacated only if clearly unsupported by the evidence.

concerns the extent to which juries have the *right* to nullify. As a practical matter, the major issues are whether judges should instruct the jury that nullification is a legitimate weapon in its arsenal and whether lawyers may openly urge the jury to nullify.

Nullification poses a difficult question, which we directly take up in the next chapter. Unfortunately, the debate over nullification has swallowed up a closely related and equally important question—whether juries have the right to play a role in deciding some questions of constitutional law. One possible consequence of such a right would be a jury's authority to acquit a criminal defendant because it finds the law he is charged with violating to be unconstitutional. (As with nullification, the practical issues are whether the judge and the defense counsel may bring the constitutional issue to the jury's attention.) A second consequence would be a jury's right, in a civil suit against a government official, to assess whether that official violated the Constitution.

THE IDEA OF juries finding a statute unconstitutional may seem preposterous, because today we think of the jury as a mere fact-finding body. But if we approach the issue afresh, some forms of jury review (akin to "judicial review," in which judges may declare laws unconstitutional) might make good sense. After all, the Constitution belongs to We the People, not to government officials. If, as we argued at length in Chapter 1, We the People have the inalienable right to alter and amend our Constitution, mightn't the people have the lesser right to interpret it when acting in a judicial forum?*

Jury review would not mean that jurors would replace judges as the primary decision-makers responsible for constitutional interpretation. Jury review would exist in addition to, not instead of, judicial review— for example, a criminal defendant would prevail if he convinced either judge or jury that the law in question was unconstitutional. Moreover, a jury's determination would apply only in the case before it. Indeed, seen

---

*Of course, as explored more fully below, a body of twelve cannot be equated with "The People" as readily as can a national majority.

from this vantage point, it seems especially odd for criminal juries *not* to exercise individual judgment about the Constitution. If a jury votes to convict, it generally sends a person to jail. Should we ask jurors to send someone to jail for violating a law they regard as unconstitutional?

At one level, juries would seem ideally situated to enjoy the authority to apply the Constitution—in some ways they are *both* "the People" *and* agents of government. That is, they are ordinary citizens not permanent government officials, but they act in an official capacity, exercising power vested in them by the state.

Note that the power to decide questions of constitutional law does not entail jury nullification; it demands only that a jury enjoy the same authority as a judge. Judges may not ignore a law simply because they think it wrong, unjust, or silly; but they may—indeed must—do so if they regard that law as unconstitutional. Why should juries do any different? (The case for permitting them to do so becomes stronger if, as we urged in the previous chapters, the jury becomes more inclusive and less partial; a jury representing the entire community is less likely to render an idiosyncratic judgment.)

We are accustomed to the notion that only judges decide questions of constitutional law. In fact, all government officials take an oath to uphold the Constitution. Surely, when President Thomas Jefferson pardoned persons convicted under the Sedition Act of 1798 because he thought the Act unconstitutional, he acted within his constitutional authority, notwithstanding the fact that federal courts had upheld the Act in cases involving the very convicts in question. (Arguably, he was duty bound to so act.) If Jefferson could independently make a judgment call about the Constitution, in the exercise of his authority to pardon, why shouldn't a jury do the same in exercising its authority to decide a case?

In fact, the most authoritative statement in support of judicial review—Chief Justice John Marshall's famous assertion that "it is emphatically the province and duty of the judicial department to say what the law is"[1]—arguably supports jury review. Juries are part of the "judicial department." Recall the earlier analogy between the two-tiered legislature and the two-tiered judiciary. Just as both the House and Senate have to agree that a criminal bill is constitutional for it to become law, arguably both judge and jury should agree on its constitutionality before a defendant can be convicted.

Whatever one thinks of the law/fact division of labor between judges and juries that evolved during the nineteenth century, it may not resolve the question of jury review of constitutionality. As emphasized in Part I, we must distinguish between the Constitution and ordinary laws. The former is the most precious possession of the People. We the People have delegated to our servants the right to make and interpret ordinary laws. Provided that we retain clear ownership over the Constitution (which trumps ordinary laws), the government remains ours. Thus, jurors may be stuck with a law or an interpretation of a law they don't like, but should they be stuck with a Constitution that is not theirs?

Second, and related, many statutes are intricate and involve technical legalese—arcane language or subjects beyond the ken of non-lawyers. By contrast, the Constitution is neither prolix nor esoteric.[2] It was intended to be accessible to the citizenry, as well it should be since it belongs to the citizenry. It was made, and can be unmade, by We the People—citizens in special assemblies asked to listen, deliberate, and vote up or down. If ordinary citizens are competent to make constitutional judgments when signing petitions or assembling at conventions, why not in juries too? Is there not some truth in Thomas Jefferson's characterization of jury trials as "trials by the people themselves"? Why should the People's Constitution be excluded from the People's purview when they render a verdict?

While the notion of juries finding a statute unconstitutional may sound bizarre to our modern ears, it did not to those who founded our government. Quite the contrary. In his celebrated lectures on law, Founding Father James Wilson declared that "whoever would be obliged to obey a constitutional law, is justified in refusing to obey an unconstitutional act of the legislature. . . . [E]very one who is called to act, has a right to judge."[3] Though Wilson did not single out the jury by name, surely jurors are "called to act" when asked to convict a defendant of violating a law that may be unconstitutional.

At the Massachusetts convention that ratified the Constitution, Theophilus Parsons (who would eventually become Chief Justice of the state Supreme Court) was even more explicit, citing jury review as major protection against oppressive government. He noted that the brave citizen would disobey an unconstitutional law, and "only his own fellow-citizens can convict him . . . and innocent they certainly will pronounce him, if the supposed law he resisted was an act of usurpation."[4]

In the eighteenth century, the jury was not regarded as a mere fact-finding body. The expectation that it would resist unconstitutional laws (and, in some contexts, make determinations of law as well as fact) appears in the writings of the most eminent American lawyers of the age— Jefferson, Adams, and Wilson, to name just three.[5] Indeed, Georgia's constitution explicitly empowered juries to decide questions of law.

However, right from the start some turf-conscious judges resisted this doctrine. A notorious example is the 1800 case of *United States v. Callender*,[6] where a publisher was prosecuted for violating the 1798 Sedition Act, which in effect criminalized criticism of Congress or the President. When defense counsel William Wirt tried arguing to the jury that the statute was unconstitutional, the presiding judge, Justice Samuel Chase, cut him off, explaining that it is "irregular and inadmissible" to make such an argument because "it is not competent to the jury" to decide a question of constitutionality.[7]

Chase should have quit right there. His position may have been incorrect, but at least it was coherent. However, he added that "we all know that juries have the right to decide the law, as well as the fact— and the constitution is the supreme law of the land, which controls all laws which are repugnant to it."[8] Attorney Wirt pounced: "Since, then, the jury have a right to consider the law, and since the constitution is law . . . the jury have a right to consider the constitution."[9] Justice Chase replied, "A non sequitur, sir," and a frustrated Wirt sat down.[10]

Chase's closer evokes Ring Lardner's line: "'Shut up,' he explained."[11] And the non sequitur belongs to Chase—Wirt's logic was impeccable. Moreover, Chase ignored clear precedent. In 1794, a unanimous Supreme Court had stated that juries may decide questions of law.[12] The case involved a special jury presided over by the Supreme Court. In instructing the jury, Chief Justice (and Founding Father) John Jay discussed the respective roles of judge and jury. Jay stated that because judges are presumed to have greater legal expertise than juries, a judge may instruct the jury as to issues of law, and jurors should "pay that respect, which is due to the opinion of the court."[13] However, Jay told the jurors in unambiguous terms, "you have nevertheless a right to take upon yourselves to judge of both, and to determine both the law as well as the fact in controversy. . . . [B]oth objects are lawfully within your power of decision."[14]

That case was handed down just a half dozen years before Chase blithely held to the contrary in *Callender*. Not surprisingly, he was impeached for his overall handling of the *Callender* case, and for refusing to allow the defense in another criminal case to argue a point of law to the jury. Though he survived impeachment, roughly half of the Senate voted to convict. Attorney Wirt, for his part, became one of the great lawyers of his time, with the record for longest service as United States Attorney General.

Nevertheless, Chase's position, not Wirt's eventually won acceptance. The position laid down by Jay (and argued by Wirt) eroded during the nineteenth century; Chase was not the only judge to disregard or question it. In fact, an array of courts and commentators weighed in on the question of whether juries could decide questions of law (and the corollary issue of whether lawyers may argue points of law to the jury), with no consensus emerging. The issue was finally resolved by the Supreme Court in 1895, in the case of *Sparf & Hansen v. United States*.[15] The Court held that juries may not decide—and lawyers cannot argue to the jury—questions of constitutional law.

The *Sparf* opinion leaves a lot to be desired. From the Court's meandering opinion, two principal arguments emerge: permitting juries to decide questions of law would (1) lead to chaos and (2) compromise judges' power of judicial review. These superheated arguments have some force, but less than the Court suggested.

The first argument (one also suggested by Justice Chase in the *Callender* case) is that allowing juries to decide questions of law would shatter uniform national law to such a degree that "public and private safety would be in peril."[16] What underlies this extreme fear? The argument is that some juries may rule a certain way based on their interpretation of a statute, whereas others would rule otherwise in cases with the same facts. Anarchy would result.

In reality, judicial nonuniformity is hardly unique; it happens all the time that different judges reach conflicting decisions about the constitutionality of statutes. For practical reasons, the Supreme Court cannot resolve every disagreement among lower courts. Indeed, at the time of the founding the Supreme Court lacked jurisdiction to resolve many lower court conflicts. This arrangement, in place for many years, belies the notion that non-uniformity necessarily leads to anarchy.

The *Sparf* Court's second (and related) argument is that allowing juries to decide questions of law would usurp the authority of the courts, especially the Supreme Court. The *Sparf* Court asked rhetorically, "[D]oes the Constitution of the United States, which established that Supreme Court, intend that a jury may, as matter of right, revise and reverse" decisions by that Court?[17] This question is misleading. Clearly, the Constitution does not give juries the power to reverse Supreme Court decisions—those decisions bind the parties as well as the lower courts. The only issue is whether juries retain the right to vote their own opinions on the law in the cases before them. An answer in the affirmative would hardly destroy the authority of the Supreme Court.

Yet the *Sparf* Court insisted that if juries could decide questions of law, courts "would for every practical purpose be eliminated from our system of government" and ours would "cease to be a government of laws."[18] This is wild hyperbole. Juries are comprised by a group far more representative of the People than are the government officials—judges—whom the *Sparf* Court gave sole authority to interpret the law. (Ironically, in this century it has been widely argued that *judicial* review, at least as it has been exercised, undermines a government of laws.[19]) What's more, the judge in a criminal case would remain free to

acquit the defendant if the judge reads the Constitution more gener-
ously than the jury does. Thus, judges would continue to play a huge
role in protecting constitutional rights, even if *Sparf* were decided the
other way. Again, jury review supplements rather than supplants judicial review.

AND YET, DESPITE the flaws in the Court's opinion, and the arguments
in favor of jury review canvassed above, we confess to misgivings about
jury review in criminal cases. In such cases, the analogy between judicial review and jury review breaks down: Trial judges' decisions may be
reversed by a court of appeals, whereas a jury's acquittal is unreviewable. And our comparison of the People in the jury box to the People at
a constitutional convention or in a national referendum should not be
overstated. Each individual jury consists of only a dozen people. When
that small group's decision cannot be reviewed, we must be wary of empowering it to make decisions about the Constitution.

The unreviewability of acquittals takes on added significance in light
of the Reconstruction Amendments to the Constitution. These amendments did not repeal the fundamental populism of the original Constitution and Bill of Rights, but they did radically transform the respective
powers of the federal and state governments. In 1789, the Framers wor-
ried far more about an abusive federal government than about states and
localities. But the Civil War, and the treatment of blacks in the South
generally, sparked concern about local tyranny. The Thirteenth, Fourteenth, and Fifteenth Amendments altered the constitutional balance,
adding constraints on states (and private individuals, insofar as the Thirteenth Amendment outlawed slavery) and creating a more uniform country. If local bodies—juries—had the unreviewable power to decide
constitutional questions, these amendments might have become a dead
letter in places where they were unpopular. Thus, it is quite plausible to
think of these national amendments as qualifying the power of local bodies to thwart national laws. (It is not surprising that the Supreme Court
never quite made this argument in *Sparf*. In the previous two decades,

the Court *itself* systematically destroyed congressional Reconstruction through stingy statutory construction and aggressive judicial review.)

One possible response reinvokes the distinction between statutes and the Constitution. As noted, whatever confusion may result from nonuniformity of decisions already inheres to some extent in a relatively decentralized judiciary. Where ordinary laws are concerned, this nonuniformity may cause inconvenience; where the Constitution is concerned, it generally enhances liberty. This is because disagreements about constitutionality tend to work against the federal government. If any major institutional actor deems a federal law unconstitutional, that institution generally can make its objection stick—at least in criminal law, where persons' lives, liberty, and property are most vulnerable. If either house of Congress believes a bill unconstitutional, the bill cannot become law (and no one can be convicted in the absence of a law). If the President believes the bill unconstitutional, he may veto. Even if the veto is overridden, he may pardon anyone convicted of violating the law in question. So too, if judges deem the law unconstitutional, they can prevent or overturn a conviction. Jury review would add one layer of protection against unconstitutional incarceration, and thus reinforce the Constitution's liberty-conscious structure.* From this perspective, it seems odd to exempt from constitutional authority only the jury, a body of citizens representative of the People who own the government.

Though the counterargument has weight, in the end many reasonable people will reject (unreviewable) jury review in criminal cases. (Indeed, we are uncertain ourselves.) But in certain civil cases, the balance comes down in favor of jury review. In the civil context, the principal objection to jury review does not apply. In contrast to criminal cases, a civil jury's determination is reviewable—both by the trial judge, who can render a judgment notwithstanding the verdict, and the court of appeals, which can reverse the verdict. As a result, jury review would not

---

*Jury review might help acquit some defendants, but only those charged with violating laws deemed unconstitutional by a group of ordinary citizens. There is little reason to fear jurors making dubious constitutional judgments that lead them to free murderers or rapists. Trained judges, not ordinary citizens, are the ones who have given us exclusionary rules of evidence that needlessly free violent offenders.

create much risk of nonuniformity. What it would create is a healthy dialogue and collaboration between the two branches of the judiciary—judges and juries. Just as juries would have to be cognizant of the judges' view or risk seeing their verdicts undone, so judges would surely take notice if juries consistently took a certain position on a constitutional question.

The perfect scenario for jury review arises in civil suits alleging that government officials have violated citizens' constitutional rights. Keeping government officials honest was traditionally a major function of the jury. A paradigmatic case illustrating how jury review could serve this function involves the Fourth Amendment's requirement that police searches and seizures be "reasonable." Under current law, only judges determine the propriety of searches.* But the assessment of reasonableness is often a classic jury-type question, calling for the common sense and normative judgement of ordinary citizens as to whether our servants have abused their authority.

The reasonableness of a search is an example of what is sometimes called a mixed question of law and fact. The ultimate determination (whether the search violated the Constitution) is one of law, but it is inextricably linked with findings of fact (concerning the motives and judgment of the police). The case for jury review is strongest when such mixed questions are at issue. While the jury should not be seen solely as a fact-finding body, that clearly is its privileged realm.** When the jury decides that a search was or was not reasonable for Fourth Amendment purposes, we get the best of all worlds. A body of ordinary citizens plays a role in interpret-

---

*Today, the issue typically arises in the context of a criminal case, when the defendant calls for the exclusion of evidence on the ground that it was improperly obtained. In our view (and the Framers'), the more sensible remedy for a Fourth Amendment violation is a civil suit for damages against the wrongdoing government or its official(s). Unfortunately, the courts have made such suits difficult to maintain. See Akhil Amar, "Fourth Amendment First Principles," 107 *Harvard Law Review* 757 (1994).

**The Seventh Amendment makes specific reference to the jury's role as factfinder whereas neither the Sixth nor Seventh explicity refers to the jury's role in deciding questions of law. While the Framers regarded juries as competent to decide questions of law as well as fact, they considered them especially qualified with respect to the latter (and judges especially qualified with respect to the former). Chief Justice Jay provided a clear expression of this position in *Georgia v. Brailsford*, 3 U.S. (3 Dall.) 1, 4 (1794), discussed earlier.

ing the People's Constitution, and does so in a context calling for factfinding and normative judgement—the jury's bread and butter. But the decision is subject to the review of a court, which brings to bear its legal expertise while showing some deference to the jury's findings of fact.

Legislatures and judges properly lay down rules establishing the per se reasonableness or unreasonableness of certain types of searches and seizures (for example, permitting sobriety checkpoints on highways but forbidding the random search of homes). But often reasonableness calls for a contextual assessment that defies broad categorization, and a jury is well positioned to make this particularized judgment. As long as judges stand ready to reverse egregious decisions, the jury power would not unduly threaten national uniformity. At the same time, if juries consistently find certain types of searches unreasonable, the judiciary might well respect and accept this perspective from the community.

SOME WILL OBJECT that jurors simply aren't up to the task of interpreting the Constitution. However accessible the Constitution's language may be, and however much the ordinary citizen in 1800 may have been equipped to deliberate about it, times have changed. Today, most people cannot name three Supreme Court Justices, much less render constitutional opinions.

This argument, of course, echoes the argument (discussed in Part I) that the People cannot be trusted to amend the Constitution. Our answer is the same—if the premise that people are ignorant about the Constitution is correct, further distancing them from the Constitution only worsens the problem. If the People today are indeed incompetent to make decisions about our Constitution, it may be because the country has lost the powerful and once-prevailing sense that the Constitution is *the People's* law. Permitting juries to interpret the Constitution might help restore that sense, and strengthen the citizenry. In 1788, a prominent Anti-Federalist argued that if ordinary folk were lacking, jury service would uplift them: *"Give them power and they will find understanding."*[20]

Recognizing the legitimacy of jury review would raise a series of practical questions. How extensively may lawyers argue points of constitutional law to a jury? Should they be allowed to submit briefs to the jury? Should the jury be asked to identify its constitutional findings? Should the judge instruct the jury about how other juries, or courts, have found in similar cases?

For present purposes, two brief answers should suffice. First, to say that some juries have the right to consider the Constitution does not require that every case be treated as a full-fledged trial on the constitutional issue. Congress, in voting on a bill, and the president, in deciding whether to sign it, should also be sensitive to issues of constitutionality, but they need not ask for briefs or otherwise follow the kind of procedure used by an appellate court. Second, these issues of implementation need not be resolved overnight, nor by uniform rules. Different courts could treat the matter differently, much as they treat myriad matters of procedure differently, and over time we will have the benefit of observing the results of various approaches. The case for permitting some juries to consider the Constitution does not require a single, precise blueprint.

The argument for (suitably limited) jury review rests on principle, and that principle—popular sovereignty—lies at the foundation of the Constitution. Jury review represents one more means by which the People retain genuine control of our Constitution.

TEN

Jury Nullification

IT IS ONE THING FOR a criminal jury to acquit a defendant because it finds the law under which he is prosecuted to be unconstitutional. It is quite another for a jury to acquit for any reason whatsoever, notwithstanding evidence proving the defendant's guilt. The jury's right to "nullify" refers to the latter, and is a subject of great controversy.

As noted, the jury undeniably has the legal power to nullify, since acquittals are immune from reversal by a court. The issue is the extent to which the jury has the right to nullify. When is nullification proper? And should juries be instructed about nullification—and defense attorneys permitted to urge juries to indulge it?

Nullification is deeply rooted in the common law and colonial tradition. In the famous trial of John Peter Zenger, a newspaper printer charged with libeling a public official in 1735, a New York jury acquitted the defendant despite his apparent factual guilt. The widely hailed verdict was well known to the Framers who, all available evidence suggests, approved of nullification. John Adams, for one, explicitly endorsed the jury's right to reach a verdict "in their own best understanding, judgment, and conscience, though in direct opposition to the direction of the court."[1]

That the Framers regarded nullification as an appropriate weapon in the jury's arsenal is suggested by the structure of the criminal justice system. As noted, a jury's decision to acquit a defendant—unlike a conviction, or the verdict for either side in a civil case—cannot be appealed. Even if the jury verdict appears unsupported by the evidence, the verdict stands and the defendant may not be retried. Legal scholars Peter Westen and Richard Drubel persuasively argue that only one rationale accounts for immunizing acquittals from review: the desire to protect the jury's power to acquit against the evidence.[2]

Why would the Framers protect jury nullification? Because, quite simply, it represents a version of popular sovereignty—the triumph of community values over overreaching government officials. In most cases of acquittal, the jury interposes itself between the government and an accused simply by finding that the charge is false. It can be even more profoundly democratic when ordinary citizens protect a peer from the government *despite his or her factual guilt,* because they believe punishment would be wrong. Nullification bridges the potentially dangerous gap between law and justice, and between the government and the People.

Indeed, the constitutional case for nullification is so strong that nullification "opponents" rarely deny that juries have the right to nullify. More often, they argue that juries should not be told about their right. The rationale is that, if jurors are instructed about their right to acquit against the evidence, and are urged to do so by the defense, they will nullify routinely. Instead of an instrument of democracy, nullification will become a recipe for anarchy. As one court put it, in an oft-cited case rejecting a nullification instruction, "What makes for health as an occasional medicine would be disastrous as a daily diet."[3] On this view, the proper balance is reached when jurors have the power to nullify, but are given no encouragement from the bench.

This view has taken hold. Although instructions about nullification were once routinely given, today no federal court gives such instructions, and among the state courts only Indiana's and Maryland's do so. Likewise, except in these two states, defense attorneys are not permitted to argue nullification (though they sometimes subtly encourage it, urging the jury to "send a message" of one kind or another via an acquittal). The thinking is that jurors already know about their power to nullify, or will figure it out during deliberations. However, as long as they are not told about it, they will reserve this dangerous weapon for those extreme cases that clearly warrant it.

We believe this view mistaken for several reasons. For one thing, it is obviously problematic to proclaim the existence of a constitutional right while deliberately keeping those who possess the right in the dark. In some cases, jurors will feel that though a conviction would be unjust they are bound to render it. In such cases, both the defendant and the jurors are effectively denied their rights.

Indeed, though the case for nullification is often framed in terms of justice for the criminal defendant, its effect on the jurors is also important. When jurors feel constrained to reach a criminal verdict at odds with their consciences, they may not view their experience as one of *self*-government. To the contrary, they may feel like pawns who perform mechanical fact-finding at the bidding of government officials (judges). To inculcate such a perception in ordinary citizens is to reverse the empowering role that the Framers envisioned for jury service.

As a practical matter, the see-no-evil approach towards nullification fosters enormous confusion. On the one hand, jurors may hear about nullification through popular culture (and through the active campaign of some groups to convince prospective jurors that they may nullify[4]), and they get the hint when a defense attorney urges them to "send a message" or to "make sure the community's voice is heard." On the other hand, they are instructed by the court that their job is solely to find facts or, at most, to find facts and apply the law to those facts.

Such mixed signals can only confound rational decisionmaking. When jurors deliberate, in a case where they might be tempted to nullify, they are at war with themselves and one another. They may end up deliberating about whether they have the right to nullify rather than about the appropriate result in the case at hand. Legal scholars Alan Scheflin and Jon Van Dyke, prominent proponents of a nullification instruction, argue that in refusing to instruct about nullification, judges "in fact are creating the anarchy they seek to avoid."[5]

ONE REASON THE pro-instruction forces have not prevailed is that nullification has been improperly framed as an all-or-nothing proposition. Pro-nullification advocates imply that juries have the right to acquit for any reason they find appropriate. This is a dangerous and unjustified position. If we wanted jurors to have such total authority, we would empower them to make decisions about the admissibility of evidence as well—a proposition virtually no one supports.

The right of nullification rests on a kind of popular sovereignty, but popular sovereignty has built-in limits. For example, the People have the right to amend the Constitution but, as we have seen, certain amendments would be inherently improper and all amendments must undergo a proper process of deliberation. Likewise, nullification in an appropriate case is a grand expression of popular sovereignty; used improperly, it is a lawless act. To support nullification is obviously not to support a white jury's acquittal, based solely on racist solidarity, of a white man who kills a black man.

The challenge is to establish the proper boundaries of nullification. In doing so, we must pay attention to the larger place of the jury in our constitutional design. A sound approach to nullification would (1) educate and respect jurors; (2) encourage healthy deliberation in the exercise of self-government; and (3) recognize the role of normative judgment above and beyond mechanical fact-finding in jury decisionmaking. With these criteria in mind, we can explore the contours of appropriate nullification, and try to craft a workable, nonarbitrary definition of "proper nullification."

We begin by focusing on the different functions of judge and jury. We have warned against an unjustifiable double standard in the treatment of these two judicial bodies, but there *are* important structural differences between them (just as the House and Senate have somewhat particularized roles; only the Senate ratifies treaties, for example, whereas only the House may draft a bill of impeachment). For present purposes, the key distinction is that judges are expected to give written opinions or otherwise explain the grounds for their decisions. Judges literally *say* what the law is. Arguably, where they fail to do so, they violate their office. The very word "jurisdiction" combines *jus* (law) and *dicto* (speech)—speaking or pronouncing the law.[6] Doing so often involves looking for guidance from or trying to maintain consistency with past cases and, in turn, guiding judges in future cases. In short, judges, even when deciding questions of fact, resolve cases within a larger decision-making matrix.

Criminal trial juries are very different. They are expected to look at the case in front of them, and are carefully instructed to be uninfluenced by anything outside of the courtroom—which includes jury decisions in other cases. Likewise, insofar as they do not provide written opinions or formal explanation of their decisions, their verdicts are not envisioned as direct precedent in other cases. To be sure, verdicts can and should influence public policy. But that is a byproduct of a verdict, not its *raison d'être*. The structure of jury decision-making suggests that trial jurors must look neither to the past for guidance nor to the future for agenda-setting. Rather, they are to decide the case before them based on the merits of that case alone.

From this basic structure, the proper contours of jury nullification begin to emerge. Here, then, is one proposed standard: The jury may legitimately nullify when it believes that a conviction would be unjust to *the particular defendant* because of the circumstances of the case. The jury should not nullify because it dislikes the law or wishes to achieve some larger purpose such as sending a message to the government. There are ample forums for expressing disapproval of a law or government policy. The criminal jury trial is designed for a different primary purpose: to do justice in the case at hand.

This conclusion comports with the logic of democracy. For a body of just twelve people to refuse to convict merely because it dislikes a law is antidemocratic; the law-making function belongs to the public at large, either directly or through its elected representatives.* Likewise, sending a message to government is outside the province of the trial jury. The (unreviewable) criminal jury owes the People a proper determination in the case at hand, not a larger verdict about the government.

Scheflin and Van Dyke have written that the value of nullification lies in the fact that it "permits the jury to suspend the application of a *particular* law in a *particular* instance to a *particular* defendant in the interest of conscience and justice."[7] They did not italicize the word "particular," but they should have. With an emphasis on that word, they may well have hit the nail on the head: The point of nullification is to perform justice in the particular case before the jury. So understood, nullification is neither antidemocratic nor an invitation to anarchy.

This perspective can be illuminated by reference to well-known instances of apparent nullification. The infamous acquittal of Emmett Till's murderers was obviously a lawless use of the nullification power; the jurors did not seek to do justice, but to vent racial prejudice.[8] Likewise, if the O.J. Simpson jurors heeded Johnnie Cochran's call to send a message to the authorities about racist or overzealous government officials, they acted improperly.[9] Their role was to do justice with respect to Simpson. If reliable evidence established that he committed the charged murders, it would not be unjust to punish him. To the contrary, it would be unjust to acquit him.

On the other hand, the Oliver North and Marion Barry cases may have presented examples of legitimate nullification. North was acquit-

---

*On this account, the jurors who acquitted John Peter Zenger were justified, because New Yorkers at the time had no say in Parliamentary elections and thus no chance to register disapproval of the libel laws.

ted of violating the Boland Amendment forbidding assistance to the Nicaraguan *contras*. The jurors apparently concluded that he was a fall guy carrying out orders from political superiors in circumstances where obedience was justified. They may have felt that it would be unfair to punish him notwithstanding his technical violation of the law.[10] (By contrast, if the acquittal simply derived from the jurors' feelings about foreign policy, it was improper.)

Marion Barry, the mayor of the District of Columbia, was acquitted of most charges of drug possession despite overwhelming evidence of guilt. However, the case against him stemmed from an incident in which Barry, sitting in a hotel room and violating no laws, was semiseduced and practically begged to take drugs by a young woman enlisted by the government. The jury may have felt that Barry showed an understandable weakness rather than criminally culpable behavior and, in any case, the public disgrace and loss of public office he suffered were sufficient punishment.[11] Note that this is not a case of the jury objecting to the law; rather, on the very specific and unusual facts of this case, they judged that strict enforcement of the law would be unjust.

If the Barry and North juries acted in the above manner, they sought to do justice in a *particular* case to a *particular* defendant based on the *particular* circumstances. One can disagree with whether they did justice, just as one can disagree with any factual or legal determination a jury makes. But these juries were at least acting within their authority, rendering normative judgment based on the facts of the case.

In such cases, juries nullify not the law but the factual evidence of guilt. In this connection, legal scholar George Fletcher suggests that the word "nullification" is misleading. He observes that so-called nullification often involves juries "recognizing principles of justification that go beyond the written law."[12] Instead of the term *nullification*, Fletcher suggests that we think of the jurors "completing and perfecting" the law as presented to them by the court.[13] He advances this position in connection with the acquittal of Bernhard Goetz, who shot four youths who approached him in a New York subway. Fletcher speculates that the jury believed that the concept of self-defense must permit a defendant to react as Goetz did. On this interpretation, the jury sought no broader purpose than to do justice based on the very individual circumstances of that case—another instance of appropriate nullification.

Today, nullification is given a bad name by political activists who use it for partisan purposes. Pro-life groups, for example, urge jurors to acquit defendants because they disagree with current government abortion policy. Such groups should aim their advocacy at legislatures or at the People at large, who can change policy through amendments, plebiscites, or election of like-minded government officials. They should not urge a jury to do anything but justice in the case before it. But these groups do not taint the idea of nullification any more than pornographers taint the First Amendment. Likewise, cases such as the acquittal of Emmett Till's killers should stigmatize nullification no more than the election of Adolf Hitler stigmatized elections. That a good practice can be put to bad use is reason to hone rather than discard the practice.

The reforms discussed in earlier chapters would ensure that the jurors who wield the nullification weapon are more likely to represent a cross section of their community. A proper instruction on nullification would hone things further. And there is no reason to assume that it would dramatically increase the instances of nullification. Indiana and Maryland, which instruct their juries about nullification, do not appear to experience rampant use of it.[14] Indeed, common sense suggests that a sound instruction on nullification will likely increase the instances of proper nullification and decrease the instances of improper nullification. A proper instruction will provide ammunition to those jurors who resist a call for lawless nullification. Far from encouraging anarchy, it would help create the optimal atmosphere in the jury box. Everything would be on the table: Jurors would know about their right to nullify but would also understand its limits. They would not be left to guess as they are at present.

Consider, again, the case of Oliver North. Let us assume, hypothetically (but quite plausibly) that three different viewpoints emerged during deliberations. Some jurors wanted to acquit because they believed

North to be an American hero carrying out a laudable anti-Communist mission. Other jurors wanted to acquit because they believed that on the facts of this case, it would be unjust to convict someone who understandably felt compelled to carry out orders from superiors. A third group accused both groups of ignoring the judge's instructions on the law. Members of the first two groups responded that a jury has the right to nullify whenever it wishes. The third group said it didn't know anything about that, and felt compelled to stick to its task as defined by the judge.

Under the current no-instruction approach, the jurors are left to flail about in ignorance. Under our approach, the court would instruct the jury about its right to nullify to do justice, while clarifying that it may not nullify for some larger purpose—say, to express disapproval of the law or approval of the political policy carried out by the defendant. The first group, which supported nullification for any reason, and the third group, which opposed nullification for any reason, would be disarmed. And both of these groups should be open to the second group's argument for responsible nullification. Of course, members of the first and third groups might refuse to budge; obstinacy can rear its head in the jury room as it can anywhere else. But a careful instruction at least provides useful guidance. It also shows trust in the People who compose the jury. This is appropriate inasmuch as the jury system, like the doctrine of nullification, derives from trust in ordinary citizens—the very trust that undergirds self-government generally.

Critically, our proposed approach to nullification comports with the criteria we set forth above: (1) it educates jurors (by explaining their proper role in democratic self-government) and treats them with respect (by leveling with them about their rights and powers); (2) it encourages healthy deliberation (by clarifying its proper focus); and (3) it recognizes the role of normative judgment in jury decisionmaking (by authorizing nullification in appropriate cases).

In the end, our proposed instruction (emphasizing the jury's right to nullify in order to do justice in a particular case, but not to promote some larger agenda) is less important than the need for *some* instruction about nullification that comports with the criteria sketched above. It is possible to imagine nullification instructions different from what we have proposed and yet consistent with these criteria.

SOME FEAR HAS been expressed that nullification will be used to convict as well as acquit against the evidence. But jurors would never be so instructed: Under the American system, a person can be punished only because he breaks the law, not because the community disapproves of him or his actions. There is surely no reason to fear that instructing a jury about its power to acquit will encourage it to convict. Moreover, convictions, unlike acquittals, may be set aside by either a trial court or a court of appeals if unsupported by the evidence.

UNFORTUNATELY, THE NULLIFICATION debate brings out an alarming "flexibility" in some observers. Some of the same people who applauded the apparent nullification in the case of Oliver North or Marion Barry found nullification deplorable in the other case. The case for a well-defined right of nullification should not depend on political allegiance. (The Fully Informed Jury Association [FIJA], a group that lobbies nationwide for laws requiring instructions about nullification, is nonpartisan.) Nullification, properly understood, furthers no partisan agenda; it produces justice in individual cases. It rests on no political ideology, save the desire for individualized justice and the doctrine of popular sovereignty.

ELEVEN

The Public's Right to a Jury Trial

THE SIXTH AMENDMENT CONFERS ON the criminal defendant the right to a jury trial. But what if the defendant wants to waive that right, preferring to be tried by a judge in a bench trial? Does the public have a right to a jury trial? If so, the defendant has no right to avoid such a trial, for the public's right is not his to waive.

As we emphasized in Chapter 4, the jury serves purposes transcending the interest of an individual defendant—recall Tocqueville's assertion that the core interest underlying the jury trial is that of the jurors rather than the parties. And the citizenry's interest in a jury trial transcends that of the twelve jurors. The public benefits from having ordinary citizens monitor judges, the police, and prosecutors. In a 1979 case, Supreme Court Justice Harry Blackmun noted these interests, as well as the need for the public to be "educat[ed about] the manner in which criminal justice is administered."[1]

Blackmun made these observations while discussing the gallery's right to a *public* trial, but his insight would also seem to apply to the right to a *jury* trial, for every trial in which a jury sits is to that extent a public trial.* The fundamental point is simply this: The jury trial is not just by the people, but *for* them as well. If so, it is not for the defendant (or the government) to waive.

That perspective seems sound in theory. In practice, the Supreme Court has held otherwise. In the 1930 case of *Patton v. United States*,[2] the Court held that the jury trial right belongs to the defendant alone, to waive as he pleases. However, the Court's opinion does not survive scrutiny.

The precise issue before the Court was whether the defendant could waive his right to a twelve-person jury, and be tried by a smaller panel. But in the course of holding that he could, the Court declared that the entire right to a jury trial could be waived. The Court emphasized the language of the Sixth Amendment: "In all criminal prosecutions, *the accused* shall enjoy the right to . . . an impartial jury. . . ." As the Amendment explicitly frames the right to a jury trial in terms of the defendant, the Court construed it to be his right alone.

The Court's decision offers a classic illustration of the danger of viewing individual constitutional clauses in isolation. Focusing on the Sixth

---

*The ideas of a jury trial and a public trial are closely linked. Just as jurors' participation serves as an education in government affairs, so too does the public's observation from the gallery. Moreover, the public trial assures that the jurors are not the only ones monitoring government officials. Indeed, the public's very presence in the courtroom can discourage judicial misbehavior. As common law historian and judge Matthew Hale explained in his influential treatise, if a judge is biased, "his partiality and injustice will be evident to all bystanders." Matthew Hale, *The History of the Common Law of England* [6th ed., 1820] p. 344. Just as the phrase "the People" appears in five of the ten amendments that make up our Bill of Rights, we must take seriously the republican and populist overtones of its etymological cousin, "public," in a sixth—*the* Sixth—Amendment. In a system of r*epublican* government, the people rule, if not day to day at least in the long run. All governmental policy and policymakers can, in time, be lawfully replaced by the sovereign people via ordinary elections and constitutional conventions. This ultimate right of the public to change policy and policymakers creates a strong presumption that government action in all three branches will be open to public scrutiny. Thus a public trial, like a trial by the People (jurors), helps preserve popular sovereignty.

Amendment, the Court ignored the clear words of Article III: "The Trial of *all* Crimes . . . *shall* be by Jury." The debates at the state conventions to ratify the Constitution establish beyond any doubt that these words were understood as words of obligation.[3]

Nothing in the text of the Sixth Amendment repeals Article III, nor do the debates preceding the Sixth Amendment's adoption indicate any intention to do so. The Amendment does not say the defendant has a *waivable* right to a jury trial, or a right to a *nonjury* trial. Indeed, in a case four decades before *Patton,* the Supreme Court acknowledged that the Sixth Amendment was not "intended to supplant" Article III's jury clause.[4] In *Patton,* the Court ignored this precedent, ignored the plain meaning of Article III, and ignored the command of the Ninth Amendment that the expression of some rights (in this case the accused's Sixth Amendment right to a jury trial) must not be construed to deny or disparage other rights (in this case the public's Article III right to a jury trial).

One question remains: If Article III guarantees a jury trial in all cases, why did Congress bother to add the jury clause of the Sixth Amendment? It would seem superfluous. The historical answer is clear, and requires only that we read the entire clause. It gives the accused the right to an impartial jury *"of the State and district wherein the crime shall have been committed."* Article III did not specify the place from which the jury was to be drawn; the Sixth Amendment, far from giving the defendant waiver power over the jury trial, simply filled this void.

The legislative history of the Sixth Amendment overwhelmingly confirms this reading. The Anti-Federalists wanted an explicit guarantee that juries would be organized around local communities. They proposed that the Sixth Amendment guarantee a jury from "the vicinage" of the crime, and a compromise ensued.[5]

To read the Sixth Amendment as depriving the public of a jury trial requires a bizarre twist: taking a clause in the Bill of Rights designed to strengthen jury trial as evincing a desire to weaken it. Had this been the intended or even a plausible reading of the clause in 1791, the Anti-Federalists would have protested mightily. Instead, there is not a scrap of evidence that they or anyone else considered Article III's guarantee of a jury trial to be undone by the Sixth Amendment.

In *Patton*, the Supreme Court claimed that no one at the founding viewed the right to a jury trial as going beyond the protection of the accused. This represents a stunning historical revisionism that ignores the writings of Thomas Jefferson, prominent Anti-Federalists, and many others. The Framers undeniably saw the jury as serving *the public*, both in its capacity to monitor and help administer government, and in its educative role for the actual jurors.

As late as 1898, the Supreme Court was squarely on record that the defendant could not waive a jury trial.[6] In *Patton*, the Court casually dismissed the 1898 case, and failed even to mention an 1874 case whose unambiguous language squarely addressed the precise issue in *Patton:* "In a criminal case, [defendant] cannot . . . be tried in any other manner than by a jury of twelve men, although he consent in open court to be tried by a jury of eleven men."[7]

Patton was not the Court's finest hour. But there is one impressive moment in the Court opinion. While the Court got the wrong answer, it asked the right question: Is jury trial a guarantee to the accused only, or is it a component of "a tribunal as a part of the frame of government"?[8] If the latter, the Court seemed to concede, a judge acting without a jury was simply not a court capable of trying a defendant, just as the Senate acting without the House is not a legislature capable of passing laws.

Inexplicably, the Court apparently determined that the jury is not really part of the frame of government. The *Patton* opinion thus represents a classic case of the modern tendency to see constitutional rights through a purely libertarian lens. The jury trial is indeed an issue of individual right, but also (and more fundamentally) a question of government structure.* After all, a guilty defendant, looking to bribe his way

---

*Taken to its extreme, our position might seem to imply that plea bargains are unconstitutional, since they involve a criminal law determination without the presence of a jury. However, the public's right to a jury trial formally applies only if there is a trial. While we are less than enthusiastic about plea bargaining—precisely because it cuts the public out of the loop—we do not believe that the Constitution forbids it. The more reasonable position is that the accused can waive trial altogether by pleading guilty. If he does so, there is nothing to try, and hence no trial—public or otherwise. However, if he chooses to stand trial, both judge and jury must be present.

out, or pull a few strings, might well prefer a bench trial. And there is no particular reason why the defendant will concern himself with all the public benefits that flow from a jury trial. But the Framers' populist and republican vision of the jury reminds us that the jury represents the polity—the People—not the defendant.

TWELVE

Suing Our Servants

IN PREVIOUS CHAPTERS, WE HAVE seen various ways in which the Supreme Court has compromised the Framers' vision of the jury. It gets worse. For while the Framers envisioned an expansive role for juries to protect citizens from government, the Supreme Court has proclaimed an expansive role for judges to protect government from citizens. Whereas the Framers empowered juries to preserve the rightful sovereignty of the People, the Court has disarmed juries and promoted a wrongheaded sovereignty of government.

Specifically, the Court has invoked the doctrine of "sovereign immunity" to protect states from lawsuits for damages.[1] It claims to derive this doctrine from the Eleventh Amendment, but this rests on a profound misunderstanding of that amendment, and a more general lack of appreciation of the Constitution's structure.

Popular sovereignty means that ultimate control of the government resides in the hands of the People. We the People have delegated limited "sovereign" powers to various organs of government; but whenever a government entity transgresses the limits of the authority delegated to it, it ceases to act in the name of the sovereign, and surrenders any "sovereign immunity" it might otherwise possess.[2] Simply put, governments have neither "sovereignty" nor "immunity" to violate the Constitution.

When states act unconstitutionally, they must in some way undo the violation by ensuring that victims are made whole. In many cases, only government liability for damages can provide this assurance. But according to the Supreme Court, a citizen suing a state for violating her constitutional rights often cannot recover damages because the states are sovereign and therefore enjoy immunity from a suit in federal court.

This doctrine could not possibly get things more backwards. In America, *We the People* are sovereign, which is a major reason why violations of our Constitution cannot be ignored. To cite sovereignty as a basis for denying a remedy to the wronged citizen is like citing democracy as a reason for denying people the vote.

The Court's error has deep roots in its misunderstanding of the Eleventh Amendment. By all accounts, the Eleventh Amendment was passed as a response to the Supreme Court's decision in *Chisolm v. Georgia*[3] in 1793. *Chisolm* took place against the backdrop of Article III of the Constitution, which gives federal courts jurisdiction in two categories of cases: where the subject matter is of a certain kind, or the parties are of a certain status. First, federal courts may hear questions that arise under the Constitution or a federal statute, or that involve federal admiralty policy—this is known as "federal question" jurisdiction. Second, even cases raising no federal issues may be heard in federal court if the different parties have "diverse" citizenship—if, say, a suit involves a citizen of State A on one side and a citizen of State B (or State B itself) on the other side. The rationale for diversity jurisdiction is that a state court—from either State A or State B—might be biased against the out-of-state party.

Chisolm involved a breach-of-contract suit by a nonresident of Georgia against the State of Georgia. No federal or constitutional question was presented, so the case was filed in federal court solely because of the diversity of the parties. Georgia asserted its "sovereign immunity" from the lawsuit, arguing in effect that no action may ever be brought against a state. The Supreme Court rejected the contention. In response came the Eleventh Amendment, stating that "The Judicial power of the United States shall not be construed to extend to any suit in law or equity commenced or prosecuted against one of the United States by citizens of another state."

The Supreme Court has taken the position that the Eleventh Amendment affirms blanket sovereign immunity for states. As the Court sees it, *Chisolm* rejected such a claim and the Eleventh Amendment was passed to undo *Chisolm* and immunize states from lawsuits—at least those lawsuits seeking damages.

Neither the history nor the language of the Eleventh Amendment supports this position. The key to *Chisolm* is that it permitted federal court jurisdiction in suits against a state on the basis of diversity of citizenship alone, even in the absence of a constitutional or federal question. That was the holding the Eleventh Amendment sought to remedy: The Amendment in no way immunizes states from federal suits based on constitutional violations.

Thus, the Framers of the Eleventh Amendment aimed to keep out of federal court suits against states in which the only basis for federal jurisdiction was diversity—where a resident of State A sued State B. Not only does the amendment omit mention of a suit brought by a citizen against *his own* state, but it also omits mention of cases involving admiralty. The three basic categories of cases known to the Framers were law, equity, and admiralty. Yet the amendment bans only suits in "law and equity," pointedly omitting admiralty. Why this omission? Because federal admiralty policy was a *subject matter* deemed by Article III to warrant a hearing in federal court. The Eleventh Amendment plainly was designed not to oust federal jurisdiction over lawsuits brought against states on matters of federal importance—but only to keep out those cases based solely on diversity of jurisdiction.

In the end, the Court's interpretation of the Eleventh Amendment creates a curious category of cases in which the United States Congress may pass laws that operate directly on the states but that can be enforced only in state courts. As it happens, that reinstates a remedial regime (from the Articles of Confederation) that the Constitution's Framers regarded as dangerous and explicitly rejected. In empowering Congress to give the federal courts jurisdiction to hear all cases arising under federal laws, the Framers explicitly rejected the prior scheme. The Framers' idea was that, in such cases, citizens were entitled to be heard in federal courts, where life tenure of judges assured the political independence to enforce federal rights unflinchingly. Yet, under the Supreme Court's perverse reading of the Eleventh Amendment, lawsuits claiming that a state has violated the federal rights of citizens—cases where state courts can *least* be trusted to decide independently—can be brought in state court only.

This situation is even more egregious where constitutional violations are concerned. No rights are more sacred than those protected by the supreme law of the land. The Framers made a point of extending federal jurisdiction to cases arising under the Constitution itself. Again, federal judges, insulated from parochial politics, were to play a special role in safeguarding constitutional rights against state governments. The Supreme Court's Eleventh Amendment jurisprudence mocks these solemn premises: Federal jurisdiction is barred even when citizens seek relief against states that have violated the most basic constitutional rights. If this was what the Eleventh Amendment intended, it is amazing that so many Federalists supported it, willingly dismantling so much of what they had so recently worked so hard to erect.

Few propositions of law are as basic today—or were as universally embraced two hundred years ago—as the ancient legal maxim, "where there is a right, there should be a remedy." The proposition that every person should have a judicial remedy for every legal injury done him was a common provision in the state constitutions; was invoked in in *The Federalist Papers;* and was a cornerstone of John Marshall's famous opinion in *Marbury v. Madison.*[4] Yet the very existence of sovereign immunity will often drive a wedge between a legal right and an effective remedy. This is especially true today, when not only are states immune from suit but most individual government officials receive immunity from personal liability. (Such individuals will often lack the ability to make full payment in any event.) In addition, wrongdoing that enriches the state will sometimes be impossible to trace to individual officials, leaving no one to sue.

We must not lose sight of the fundamental distinction between constitutional wrongs and other legal violations. Unlike other legal rights created—and subject to qualification, modification, and limitation—by government, constitutional rights derive from a higher source than government itself. Their very purpose is to hold government to a certain standard. Thus, absent a clear statement by the People in the Constitution, the document should not be read to create gaps between rights and remedies.

Perhaps sensing as much, the Supreme Court has sought to leaven its Eleventh Amendment case law. Recognizing the problems of following general sovereign immunity of government to its logical conclusion, the Court has limited the rule through various doctrinal gymnastics and legal fictions. For example, in some cases citizens are permitted to sue a state official rather than the state itself, even though the official was plainly acting in his official capacity and a successful suit will require that payment be made out of the state treasury.[5]

If this fiction were extended to all citizen suits against states, perhaps little harm would come from the Court's interpretation of the Eleventh Amendment: It would dissolve into a technical matter of writing the officer's name instead of the state in the complaint. However, the Court has subsequently limited the remedy in these suits to prospective relief: Federal courts may not order state officials to pay money from the state treasury to make whole victims of past constitutional wrongdoing.[6] Perversely, a state government that spends money to avoid violating the Constitution ends up financially worse off than one that cynically flouts higher law until ordered to comply in the future.

In a modern Eleventh Amendment case that reaffirmed the doctrine of sovereign immunity, the Court made a startling observation: "Our Eleventh Amendment doctrine is necessary to support the view of the federal system held by the Framers of the Constitution," because they believed "strong state governments were essential to serve as a 'counterpoise' to the power of the federal government."[7] The notion that immunizing states from lawsuit supports the Framers' design turns history upside down and inside out. The statement that the Framers envisioned strong states as essential to counterbalance the federal government is true, but irrelevant when a private citizen sues a state for violating a federal right. The Framers' idea of the state and federal governments keeping each other honest was designed to promote liberty: They wouldn't have dreamed of giving states carte blanche to oppress their citizens and violate the Constitution. Consider the words of James Madison:

> Was, then, the American Revolution effected, was the American Confederacy formed, was the precious blood of thousands spilt, and the hard-earned substance of millions lavished, not that the people of America should enjoy peace, liberty, and safety, but that the governments of the individual States . . . [would have] attributes of sovereignty? . . . [A]s far as the sovereignty of the States cannot be reconciled to the happiness of the people, the voice of every good citizen must be, Let the former be sacrificed to the latter.[8]

The Supreme Court's entire Eleventh Amendment jurisprudence betrays Madison's vision.[9] This is neither the time nor the place to catalog the whole mess,[10] but the ultimate state of affairs is clear: The icon of the federal courthouse open to remedy all constitutional wrongs has given way to a burlesque image of a doctrinal obstacle course on the courthouse steps.

It bears mention that, just as the Court has misread the Eleventh Amendment to immunize states from lawsuits, it has employed general principles of sovereign immunity of mysterious origin to bar many suits against the federal government. This is equally objectionable. Under our Constitution, sovereignty belongs to the People, not to the government—be it state or federal.

As we have discussed at great length, the jury plays a leading role in preserving that sovereignty. We have noted the specific role of juries in holding government officials liable for usurping their authority. However, this protection has been eroded by the Supreme Court's vision of sovereign and official immunity.

By insulating the government from lawsuits based on constitutional violations, the Court invites government officials to abuse their authority and prevents citizens from vindicating their rights. In so doing, the Court has warped the very notion of government under law. The invocation of sovereign immunity in cases where the state plainly is not sovereign—because it has acted outside of its legitimate authority—resurrects the theory of governmental supremacy that was anathema to the Framers. In other words, the Court has transformed government sovereignty into the very tool of oppression that our revolutionary forebears wielded pen and sword to destroy. The Court's sovereign immunity doctrine puts governments above, not under, the law. It makes government officers masters, not servants, of the People.

Part Three

the Cartridge Box

THIRTEEN

National Security:
The Constitutional Design

IF ASKED ABOUT AMERICA'S DEFENSE structure, most people
would say that the country is defended by a national army of paid professionals. That's true as far as it goes, but at least as a constitutional
matter the situation is more complicated. The Constitution recognizes
two different military regimes—an army and a militia—and divides
control over one of them (the militia) between the states and the federal
government. To modern eyes, this may seem surprising. Why didn't the
Framers simply authorize the federal government to raise an army?

The Framers' vision of military matters is illuminated by analogy to
the courts. Just as the Framers refused to give permanent government
professionals (judges) a monopoly over judicial power, they refused to
give permanent government professionals (a standing army) a monopoly
over military power. To prevent potential tyranny by judges, the Framers

gave an institution composed of ordinary citizens (the jury) central responsibility in the judicial branch; to prevent potential tyranny by a standing army, they gave an institution composed of ordinary citizens (the militia) central responsibility for national security.

Why exactly did the Framers distrust a standing army? They feared that an aristocratic central government, lacking sympathy with and confidence from ordinary constituents, would prop itself up with an army of lackeys and hirelings (mercenaries, vagrants, convicts, aliens, and the like). Such hired guns, full-time soldiers who sold themselves into virtual bondage to the government, were considered the dregs of society—men without land, homes, families, or principles. Full-time service in the army further weakened their ties to civilian society, and harsh army discipline increased their servility to the government.

The Framers preferred placing national security in the hands of a militia consisting of the armed citizenry—all able-bodied white men. Militiamen were regular citizens, members of the community with civilian occupations. Though not full-time soldiers, they would be armed and trained and thus ready to respond (as they had in the War of Independence) when the need arose. The militia was far less likely to become an instrument of a federal government's tyrannical designs. Citizen-soldiers, serving alongside their families, friends, neighbors, classmates, and fellow parishioners—in short, their community—would be constantly reminded of civilized norms of conduct. They were unlikely to become uncivilized marauders or servile brutes. The constitutional principle of civilian control over the military would be internalized in the everyday mind-set of each militiaman.

But the Framers reluctantly decided not to commit themselves to a militia alone for defense of the nation. Because militia service was only part-time, with members carrying out their normal civilian business most of the time, the militia could not provide the constant vigilance that might be needed to ensure national security. As Alexander Hamilton explained in *Federalist* 8, the country might need a small permanent army, "a sufficient force to make head against a sudden descent, till the militia could have time to rally."[1]

The decision was made, therefore, to empower Congress to raise a standing army. Though the Framers hoped that the militia would prove adequate to meet the country's security needs (and thus that resort to the standing army would prove unnecessary), they hedged their bets, authorizing Congress to "raise and support Armies" and "provide and maintain a Navy."[2] But ever uneasy with this grant of power, they restricted it: Congress could raise an army, but "no Appropriation of Money to that Use shall be for a longer Term than two Years."[3]

Even as empowering Congress to raise an army solved one problem (total reliance on the militia), it raised a new problem. The possible emergence of a standing army actually increased the importance of the militia. The militia was still expected to be the primary force if the country were invaded, and it would also have to guard *against* the standing army. These two goals were in tension. For the militia to best protect against external attack, it needed to be available to the federal government. But giving the federal government control over the militia would undercut the militia's role of protecting against the federally controlled army.

Faced with this series of concerns, the Framers worked out an elaborate design. First, consider the key provisions in Article I, Section 8 of the Constitution:

> The Congress shall have Power . . .
> To declare War. . . .
> To raise and support Armies, but no Appropriation of Money to that Use shall be for a longer Term than two years;
> To provide and maintain a Navy;
> To Make Rules for the Government and Regulation of the land and naval Forces;
> To provide for calling forth the Militia to execute the Laws of the Union, suppress Insurrections and repel Invasions;
> To provide for organizing, arming, and disciplining the Militia, and for governing such Part of them as may be employed in the Service of the United States, reserving to the States respectively,

> the Appointment of the Officers, and the Authority of training
> the Militia according to the discipline prescribed by Congress.

Note the careful division of control over the militia between the states and the federal government. Because the states would train the militia and appoint its officers, militiamen would presumably remain loyal to the states. And the militia would remain under the control of the states except during certain national emergencies. Thus, states and localities were sufficiently protected should the federal government use the standing army to harass or attack. The federal government, for its part, could oversee the training of the militia (to ensure quality and uniformity) and could call it out to "execute the Laws, suppress Insurrections, and repel Invasions." This would enable the federal government to respond effectively when a foreign country invaded or when internal disorder threatened domestic tranquility.

Yet this division did not quell Anti-Federalist fears. Many pointed a suspicious finger at the language empowering Congress "to provide for organizing, arming, and disciplining the Militia." Patrick Henry and others feared that Congress would use the power granted by this provision to *dis*arm the militia.[4] The Framers confronted this concern with the Second Amendment: "A well regulated Militia, being necessary to the security of a free State, the right of the people to keep and bear Arms, shall not be infringed." The Second Amendment's preface served as a reminder that the militia, rather than the standing army, was expected to be the country's military bulwark. The substance of the Amendment helped fulfill that expectation. An armed citizenry would protect against both foreign forces and a standing army should the latter prove necessary.

The Third Amendment served a related purpose and, though now obscure, it helps illuminate the Constitution's original design. It says: "No Soldier shall, in time of peace be quartered in any house, without the consent of the Owner, nor in time of war, but in a manner to be prescribed by law." Like the Second, the Third Amendment protects civilian values against the threat of an overbearing military. No standing army in peacetime can be allowed to dominate civilian society, either openly or by subtle insinuation. The Second Amendment's militia could thwart any open military usurpation (such as a siege), but what about more insidious forms of military occupation, featuring federal soldiers cowing civilians by psychological guerrilla warfare, day by day and house by house? The Third Amendment protected against military threats too subtle and stealthy for the Second Amendment's "well-regulated militia."

To the extent that lawyers today think about the Third Amendment at all, they view it as supporting the right of individual privacy believed to inhabit the Bill of Rights.[5] To be sure, there is an important link between the Third Amendment and the Fourth (which restricts searches and seizures)—both protect "houses" from needless and dangerous intrusions by government officials. But we should not overlook the equally important linkage between the Second and Third Amendments. Both reflect a wariness of a professional military and a conscious choice to entrust national security to the People.

So too, we must keep sight of the deep connection between the militia and the jury. Both institutions directly checked the power of government officials, and also served an auxiliary benefit: promoting knowledge of and commitment to civic affairs. The militia, no less than the jury, was a public space in which people from various walks of life would come together to work on a common project critical to self-government. The militia's military function should not obscure its political character. Thus, as legal scholar David Williams observes, while the Second Amendment confers a right to bear arms, its full significance lies in the fact that it "vests that right in a body notable for its interactive and collective nature, to prevent the politics of interest and to encourage the politics of the common good."[6]

In a century in which juntas have illegitimately seized power across the world, it is understandable that people sometimes slip into thinking of the military as the antithesis of democracy. The Framers saw otherwise. They constructed a regime in which the People play such a decisive role that the military reflects, rather than conflicts with, democratic principles.

The Founders thus set up a system in which individual citizens would play a day-to-day role in all three branches of government—by voting for the legislature, by serving as the military arm of the executive, and by peopling the lower house of the judiciary. And in moments of constitutional crisis, the People would keep government officials in check and tyranny at bay through their rights of popular amendment (whenever they deemed fit), military resistance (in the event of true tyranny), and jury nullification (when just and proper).

FOURTEEN

The Constitutional Right to Serve in the Military

CURRENT SUPREME COURT DOCTRINE ON military service turns the Constitution on its head. The Court has held that citizens may be conscripted into the armed forces at any time and for any purpose; yet citizens who wish to join the armed forces have no constitutional right to do so. Such an approach might make sense in an authoritarian regime; in a regime based on popular sovereignty, it is perverse.

In Part II, we noted the unjustified distinction between the treatment of the vote (where a constitutional right is recognized) and of jury service (where it is not—at least not fully). Like jury service, military service has not been deemed a constitutional right.[1] Like jury service, it should be.

The Supreme Court has grounded the right to vote in the provision mandating elections of House members, presumably on the ground that you can't have an election without voters. As noted in Chapter 5, the inference applies equally to a right to jury service. The same holds true for military service, only more so. The Constitution makes several references to the citizen militia that was expected to be the nation's primary military force, and the Second Amendment protects the right to bear arms in order to ensure the viability of this militia. It makes little sense to imagine that the Framers protected militiamen's right to possess weapons without protecting their right to serve in the militia in the first place.

Note that Article I, Section 2's reference to the election of the House (the provision cited by the Court as implying a right to vote) speaks of election "by the People." Likewise, the Second Amendment, in protecting the vitality of the militia, protects the right of "the people" to bear arms. So too, the First Amendment speaks of the right of "the people" to assemble. These clauses refer to the same "people"—citizens acting in concert, politically or militarily, to preserve, protect, and defend self-government.

There is simply no basis for denying a right to serve in the military. Not only does military service represent a basic badge of citizenship,[2] but limiting this right prevents people from fully and equally exercising their other rights of citizenship. (This point is discussed in detail in Chapter 16, in connection with the right of women to serve in combat.)

Moreover, as with the jury box, we should not think of the right to serve in the military as helpful only to the individuals who get to serve. Rather, just as juries should reflect the entire community, our armed forces should reflect our entire society. Only such a military can be trusted; this understanding underlay the Framers' very concept of the militia. As David Williams observes, "[T]he militia would be virtuous because it was thought to include all of the citizens of the republic. By definition, this universality reflected the common good, rather than the good of a narrow slice of society."[3]

We must recognize just what the American military defends when it defends America. First and foremost, it defends an idea. No one understood this more clearly than Abraham Lincoln, who honored the soldiers at Gettysburg for fighting to protect "government of the people, by the people, for the people." Americans are not united by a common ethnicity, religion, or even language. What binds all Americans is a shared citizenship rooted in a Constitution dedicated to a transcendent idea (popular sovereignty) that makes the People paramount.

If that idea is what the military defends, how can we deny citizens—the People—the right to serve in it? If America is to be faithful to its constitutional ideal, the People, on the battlefield no less than in the jury box or at the voting booth, must enjoy the right to participate. And a military regime that excludes people without a compelling reason (like a jury or electorate that does the same) cannot be expected to act in a way fully consonant with American ideals.

Nevertheless, for two reasons, some will find the proposed right to military service less convincing than the right to vote or serve on a jury. First, because national security is at stake, we should err on the side of prudence—which may mean permitting more exclusions than we do in other areas. Second, most adults are able to perform at least passably at the ballot box and in the jury box, but many are entirely unqualified to perform martial tasks.

These objections miss the point. Yes, national security is at stake, but so is self-government—whether at the polls, in the jury room, or in the military. And recognizing a right to military service will in no way jeopardize national security, because such a right does not mean that everyone must be accepted into the armed forces. The Supreme Court has said that the right to vote belongs to "qualified citizens,"[4] and the same restriction should obviously apply to military service. The fact that more people will prove unqualified at fighting than at voting means only that more exclusions will be justified; it does not counsel against recognizing a general right to serve. Moreover, many members of the armed forces *don't* fight; they serve in various other ways.

Under current law, challenges to exclusion from the military are made under the Equal Protection Clause. As a rule, the exclusion is upheld as long as the government can point to some conceivable "rational basis" for it. This standard essentially dooms all claimants, since the government can almost always advance some explanation—morale, administrative convenience, and so on—for its exclusionary policy. By contrast, if we recognize a fundamental constitutional right to military service, the government would have to show a compelling interest that could not be achieved by a less restrictive alternative. This standard, needless to say, is much more difficult to meet. That is as it should be. The stricter standard vindicates the Framers' vision of a citizenry that defends the nation, with participation in national defense conversely helping to define the citizenry. If we keep faith with this vision, citizens should not be denied the opportunity to serve absent a very good reason.

When a homosexual (or a person who fails to meet the height requirements, or anyone excluded from the military for any reason) challenges his exclusion, his complaint is not just that he is treated less well than someone else but that he is denied the right to serve his country. The recognition of such a right is the natural starting point for an inquiry about whether the exclusion passes constitutional muster. Moreover, recognition of a constitutional right to serve in the military serves as a welcome reminder of an essential constitutional truth that has faded from view in modern times: the military, like the criminal justice system, cannot be trusted if divorced from the People.

This last point suggests another possible ground of resistance to the proposed right. We have derived the right to military service in part from the special constitutional status of a citizen-based regime: the militia. Even assuming that the Constitution established a right to serve in the militia, what relevance has that today? The "unorganized militia" still exists on the statute books, but has little practical significance. As some of the Framers envisioned, there evolved a "select militia"[5]—the state National Guards. If the right to serve in the military means only the right to serve in these part-time semicivilian units, we have indeed made much of little. For the importance of the National Guard notwithstanding, the country's primary military force today is a standing army of paid volunteers. Absent a right to serve in that institution, the citizenry has no meaningful right to military service.

But for precisely that reason, the right to serve in the military should apply to the standing army. This is a clear case of changed circumstances warranting an adaptation of constitutional understanding. In 1787, the citizens' right (and duty) to serve their country on the battlefield manifested itself in militia service. Today, with a different military structure, the citizens' connection to national security—a key principle to the Framers, as we have seen—requires recognizing their right to serve in our nation's primary fighting force.

Today we no longer depend for national security on the citizen regime envisioned by the Framers and established by the Constitution: The armed forces are organized nationally, not by state, and membership in it is fulltime. The ideal of the farmer-soldier, lawyer-soldier, doctor-soldier, or merchant-soldier, whose residence and loyalty remained in his community even when he picked up his rifle, has been largely lost. But just because we no longer rely on an eighteenth-century type militia, it hardly follows that we should sever the link between citizenship and military service. It remains the case that citizens can serve their country, and promote self-government, by taking up arms and putting on the country's uniform. And it remains the case that an inclusive military will presumably do a better job of promoting and protecting the country's ideals.

Significantly, today we no longer think of our army as a collection of misfits, as a standing army was regarded in 1787. To the contrary, as should be clear from any Marine recruiting commercial or politician's speech, our society exalts the armed forces. There was a period during and after the Vietnam War when soldiers felt disdained by civil society, but that was a fleeting phenomenon linked to a despised war. Today, military service is regarded as the Framers regarded it (albeit in the standing army rather than the militia)—as a shining badge of citizenship.

We neither help the cause of military effectiveness nor keep faith with the Framers' vision if we think of our armed forces as something apart from the citizenry. Recognizing the constitutional right of qualified citizens to serve in the military would help preserve that vital link.

FIFTEEN

Gays in the Military

IN RECENT YEARS, THE MILITARY'S policy of excluding homosexuals has become highly controversial. Largely missing from the argument has been the idea that military service is a crucial aspect of
self-government. To listen to the debate, it might as well be about homosexuals in the fire department or on the highway commission.

To be sure, opponents of gays in the military argue that national security is too important to be subject to social engineering—or even to the
demands of equality. And, yes, gay soldiers argue that they should be
allowed to serve their country. But what needs to be emphasized is that
such service is *constitutionally* privileged. We must remember that the
Constitution envisions the preservation and embodiment of self-government in terms of citizens' control of bullets as well as ballots. Most fervent anti-gay advocates would not dream of stripping gays of the vote.

Why? In large part because everyone understands that voting is a sacred right of citizenship, and that an inclusive electorate is necessary to an effective democracy. But this truth about voting also holds for military service, and this insight about an inclusive electorate also applies to an inclusive military.

The debate over gays in the military is often framed as a conflict between military concerns and civil rights.[1] This dichotomy betrays the Framers' vision: They contemplated a citizen militia as the nation's primary fighting force because they wanted national security to rest in the hands of the People. Only such a body could be trusted to put the public good ahead of partial interests, to remain faithful to the republic rather than a threat to it. As David Williams notes, "to offer these advantages, the militia had to be universal, not a subset of private persons or the state apparatus."[2]

Because the Framers had a cramped notion of universal citizenship, their militia consisted only of able-bodied white males. The "able-bodied" part makes obvious sense. The "white" part has been interred with the nation's officially racist past. The "male" part continues to fade, as women increasingly serve in the federal armed forces. Thus, even as the citizen militia has been replaced by a professional army as the country's main fighting force, our more inclusive notion of citizenship has led to a military more representative of the populace.

The modern armed forces treat only one group as pariahs: homosexuals. The policy of exclusion has a long pedigree: One military historian traces America's first expulsion of a homosexual to 1778.[3] However, the exclusionary policy was informal, and rarely implemented, until well into the twentieth century. The development of an official policy resulted largely from historical accident. Many soldiers returned from World War I suffering from shell shock. The emerging psychiatric profession offered to help the government minimize such problems in the future by screening soldiers to keep out the mentally ill or poorly adjusted. At the time, homosexuality was regarded as a mental illness, so the screening policy kept identified homosexuals out of the armed forces. An official policy of exclusion was codified in 1943.[4] Under its current variant (the so-called "don't ask, don't tell"), soldiers and prospective soldiers are not asked about their sexual orientation but may be excluded if it comes to light.[5]

The policy of excluding homosexuals from the military warrants serious reconsideration. The psychiatric community no longer regards homosexuality as an illness,[6] and gay men and lesbians have proven that they can serve with distinction.[7]

Ending the ban does not require approval of homosexuality. It only requires recognition that the Constitution does not permit different classes of citizenship. The military's exclusionary policy compromises the ideal of self-government and stamps homosexuals as second-class citizens, just as women and blacks were once stamped.* (Unsurprisingly, female soldiers are far less supportive of the ban on homosexuals than their male counterparts.[8]) And it deprives homosexuals of the chance to earn the respect of their fellow citizens and thus reinforce their claim to full citizenship.

THE MILITARY, LIKE the jury box, is a public space where diverse people work together (and learn from one another) on a project crucial to self-government. Excluding certain groups defeats the vision of a nation bound by a shared commitment rooted in mutual citizenship. As we have argued at length, a jury pool that does not fully reflect the community falls short of the constitutional ideal. The jury must engage in democratic deliberation, and excluding certain people from the process reduces the scope and quality of the deliberation. The jury no longer reflects and represents the community—it is, in other words, less democratic. The identical point applies to the military. The military represents America. When it excludes certain groups, such representation becomes incomplete. Just as a jury that bars blacks fails to

---

*It may be answered that there are no inherently superior races or genders, but many Americans still regard homosexuality as sick or sinful. The distinction fails. At the time the franchise and uniform were handed to blacks and women, belief in the inferiority of these groups still prevailed in many quarters.

represent the community, a military that bars homosexuals fails to represent America.

This may be more than a matter of appearances: A group that does not represent America might act differently from one that does. Legal scholar Ken Karst powerfully argues that the exclusion of gays from the military both reflects and reinforces a macho mind-set.[9] Such a mind-set, in turn, might contribute to an environment in which superiors abuse subordinates, men sexually harass women, and military atrocities are more likely. Obviously we cannot be sure that open acceptance of gay men and lesbians would exert a humanizing influence on the military, but one thing is certain: A more inclusive military will be more representative of American society. In a country that puts its faith in the People, we should welcome that development.

ONE DISTURBING ASPECT of the exclusion of gay men and lesbians is its selective enforcement depending on the needs of the moment. Thus, during the Vietnam War when manpower needs were acute, exclusions were rare. Gay men were allowed to fight and die for their country in an unpopular war, then kicked out when the country no longer needed them. Likewise, during the Persian Gulf War, the Pentagon adopted a "stop-loss" policy, putting the discharge of gay soldiers on hold. Gay soldiers who revealed their sexual identity during this time were told to remain in service; they'd be dealt with after the war.[10]

The notion that the country will accept service in lean times, and deny the right to serve in other times, represents a one-sided view of citizenship—as if blacks, after being freed to fight in the Civil War, were then returned to servitude after the war. It is often (and rightly) remarked that a citizen's relationship to the government should not be a one-way street in which people happily accept benefits and give back nothing in return. Surely the reverse is equally true: it is unseemly to permit people to bear the burdens of citizenship only when it suits the government's short-term purposes. In a regime of popular sovereignty, the government exists for the benefit of the People, not the other way around.

THE COURT CHALLENGES to the military's ban on gays* have been framed primarily in terms of the right to equal protection of the laws. We believe that homosexuals' claims should also be grounded in the right of qualified citizens to serve in the military. Although that would make it harder for the government to justify exclusion, the courts' inquiry would still revolve around whether a sufficiently strong governmental interest in the exclusionary policy overrides the claimed right. National security obviously cannot be ignored—we would be foolish to allow even a wholesome notion of citizenship to trump national survival. So, in the final analysis, recognition of a right to serve in the military would not assure the inclusion of homosexuals. We still need to address and assess the government's reasons for excluding homosexuals. As it happens, those reasons are not sufficiently strong to justify limiting popular sovereignty and depriving citizens of the opportunity to exercise their citizenship to the fullest.**

The government does not argue that an individual's homosexuality interferes with his or her martial potential. Few dispute that gay men and lesbians have contributed to America's military efforts, and no one maintains that sexual orientation directly impedes their ability to do so. However, it is alleged that gay soldiers interfere with the overall mili-

---

*At this writing, the policy is the notorious "don't ask don't tell"; homosexuals are not actively rooted out of the armed forces provided they don't openly acknowledge their sexual orientation. As a practical matter, the policy has led to more discharges of gay soldiers than preceded its adoption. The policy, vulnerable on assorted grounds (including the First Amendment), is under challenge in courts around the country.

**Even under equal protection doctrine, the government must show a compelling interest if its policy discriminates against certain "suspect classes"—groups afforded special protection. If homosexuals are deemed a suspect class, the military's exclusionary policy would almost certainly fall. The key factors that qualify a class as "suspect" are: a history of discrimination; the group's distinguishing trait bearing no relation to the group's contribution to society; the trait's immutability; and the group's relative powerlessness to protect itself in the political arena. In *Watkins v. United States Army*, 847 F.2d 1329 (9th Cir. 1988), the United States Court of Appeals for the Ninth Circuit persuasively argued that, based on these criteria, homosexuals are a paradigmatic suspect class. (Other aspects of *Watkins* are discussed below in the text.) Sitting en banc, the Ninth Circuit vacated this holding. 875 F.2d 699 (9th Cir. 1989) (en banc), cert. denied, 111 S.Ct. 384 (1990). The Supreme Court has not addressed whether gays are a suspect class. For a cogent analysis of the issue, see Kenji Yoshino, "Suspect Symbols: The Literary Argument for Heightened Scrutiny for Gays," 96 *Columbia Law Review* 1753 (1996).

tary effort; their presence allegedly causes problems because of the attitudes of heterosexual soldiers towards them. The contempt for homosexuals felt by some of their comrades-in-arms creates dissension, and may even damage the army's self-esteem and recruiting efforts.

In the case of *Watkins v. United States Army*,[11] the United States Court of Appeals for the Ninth Circuit demolished this cluster of concerns, noting that excluding homosexuals on this basis "illegitimately cater[s] to private biases."[12] As the court noted, the very same arguments were once used to segregate our armed forces along racial lines, something that came to be regarded as a constitutional slap in the face of fellow citizens.

Surely the fact that some heterosexual jurors might not wish to associate with gays could not justify excluding gays from the jury room; indeed, a key function of the jury is to bring together diverse Americans who might not otherwise associate. So too, the military is a place where Americans learn to work together despite their differences. As the racial integration of the armed forces has shown, the best way for the military to deal with private prejudice is not to yield to it, but to work to overcome it.

As the *Watkins* court also noted, the government sometimes argues not simply that heterosexuals' prejudices create problems, but that such prejudices are justified. In short, the army accepts the view that homosexuality is immoral, and does not wish to be tainted by association. But while there is disagreement in the legal community as to the legitimacy of legislation based solely on moral views,[13] surely there must be limits. Even if legislation may be premised solely on moral disapproval, something much stronger is needed when legislation denies a critical right and responsibility of citizenship.

We are talking about an *army*, whose job is to defend the nation, not the Boy Scouts or some other organization whose job is largely to present a particular image. Unfortunately, the armed forces is sometimes treated as a club, with its membership policy changing according to the image of the club leader. For example, Perry Watkins, though openly gay, was welcomed into the army in 1967, given superior performance reviews repeatedly, and permitted to reenlist several times. Then, in 1981, he was discharged on the basis of his sexual orientation. What happened between 1967 and 1981? One difference was the presence of a new administration in Washington. (Another difference, alluded to above, was the change in the military's manpower needs. Watkins was not the only gay soldier considered acceptable during the Vietnam War but unwelcome when less needed.) The extent of the enforcement of the military's ban on gays has varied according to the political ideology of the moment. This is no more tolerable than if the right to vote, or serve on a jury, were expanded or contracted depending on the views of the regime in power.

Significantly, a future administration with a different ideology or facing different manpower needs would not hesitate to recruit the likes of Watkins. And imagine an unpopular war—in which homosexuals seek *exemption* from military service. They would surely be assailed as shirkers and cowards. Is it appropriate, then, to turn them away when they wish to exercise their civic responsibilities?

THE ARMY ALSO argues that the presence of open homosexuals could give rise to distracting sexual relationships or tensions. But, as the *Watkins* court emphasized, this problem arises in a purely heterosexual context as well, yet the army does not exclude women. The goal of preventing sexual distractions "would be advanced much more directly by a ban on all sexual contact between members of the same unit, whether between persons of the same or opposite sex."[14]

The army further argues that the privacy of its soldiers will be compromised by the presence of homosexuals. Soldiers eat, sleep, and shower in close proximity. Is it fair to heterosexual soldiers that men potentially attracted to them share their cramped quarters? This argument proves much too much. Should homosexuals also be banned from high school, college, and professional sports teams on the same ground? In many sports, athletes not only share locker rooms but come into close physical contact in practice and during competition. If a sex-based squeamishness justifies exclusion, why stop at the military? Moreover, when the armed forces became integrated, many white soldiers objected to sharing close quarters with blacks. But the democratic idea of equal citizenship properly overcame that privacy concern, and the same should hold true for gays. (In general, the debate over gays in the military eerily echoes the debate over blacks in the military.)

Yet another argument is that homosexuals pose a security risk. Because of the stigma attached to their sexual orientation, they are allegedly susceptible to blackmail. Of course, this argument applies only to *closeted* homosexuals, not to those who openly proclaim their homosexuality. Yet the military has never adopted a policy of permitting open homosexuals to serve. The reverse is often the case, especially under the government's new "Don't ask, don't tell" policy; clandestine homosexuals may serve while open homosexuals may not.

In the final analysis, the military's exclusionary policy should fail because: (1) the government's interest is relatively weak, much of it based on the simple fact that some soldiers and military authorities dislike homosexuality; (2) military service is a major aspect of citizenship, a key responsibility of the People; and (3) homosexuals are no less citizens than anyone else, and no less able to assist the cause of national security. Only the strongest government interest justifies denying qualified citizens the right to serve in the military. As gay men and lesbians (as a class) have proven themselves qualified to serve, they should be kept out only by dint of some compelling reason. The proferred government interests are far from compelling, and the government interest in democratic control over our major institutions cuts against the exclusionary policy.

ONE POSSIBLE COUNTERARGUMENT maintains that homosexuals are *not* full citizens, since many states have virtually defined them as criminals. In the 1986 case of *Bowers v. Hardwick*[15] the Supreme Court upheld a statute criminalizing sodomy. Armed with the idea that the Constitution permits the criminalization of an activity central to gay identity, other courts readily reject the claims of homosexuals in various areas—including the military.[16]

Hardwick was decided by a five–four vote, and Justice Powell, who voted with the majority, subsequently recanted[17] (but only after he had retired). In any case, while lower courts are bound to follow *Hardwick*, commentators like us are wholly free to criticize it. We believe the decision flawed,* and hope the Court will reconsider its holding.[18]

In any case, the Court held only that sodomy statutes do not violate the right to privacy. The Court declined to address the claim that such statutes violate the right to equal protection, leaving that question for another day. Still less did the Court concern itself with the context of the military. Whatever one thinks of homosexual sodomy, we should be extremely reluctant to restrict service in the military on that basis.** It would be nice if the next Court to address the military's exclusionary policy would begin its opinion as follows: "This case is not about homosexuality; it's about citizenship and self-government."

That is, the issue comes down to a highly speculative threat to military effectiveness competing with the inescapable fact that exclusion from service renders certain persons second-class citizens and makes our military less democratic. As a practical matter, some citizens must be denied the opportunity to fight for their country (or serve on juries)

---

*While the challenged Georgia statute prohibits heterosexual as well as homosexual sodomy, the majority chose to analyze only the latter. And the Court held only that such a provision does not offend due process; it refused to consider whether a statute permitting heterosexual sodomy but prohibiting homosexual sodomy violates equal protection. Thus, the Court's opinion is dubious. After all, either male-female sodomy can be criminalized or it cannot. If it can, then *Bowers* seems at odds with Court cases protecting sexual privacy of heterosexual couples. (Moreover, *Bowers* would turn out to be not antihomosexual but antisodomy, in which case it bears less significance for gays in the military.) If, on the other hand, heterosexual sodomy cannot be criminalized, we have what seems like clearly unconstitutional sex discrimination—sodomy between man and woman is protected, but between man and man can be criminal. Accordingly, Mary can engage in sodomy with John, but Bill cannot—solely because Bill is a man. This is not the only problem with *Bowers*, but should suffice to show that opposition to gays in the military should not rest on the unstable foundation of this case.

**We also note that there are many forms of same-sex conduct other than sodomy—kissing, petting, hand-holding, saying "I love you," and so forth. Surely, *Bowers* does not extend to all these forms of conduct.

because they lack the ability to do so adequately. Such people are simply unable to perform certain acts of citizenship. That is a far cry from denying people the full fruits of citizenship just because others dislike them. The former is a practical necessity; the latter, a departure from the American way. And a country defended by something less than the People dramatically departs from the constitutional design.

IT IS SOMETIMES asserted that only people with military experience can legitimately judge the need for the exclusionary policy. This perspective has two ramifications. It disqualifies people who have not served in the military from deriding the proferred government interests; and, more importantly, it calls upon the courts to defer to the officials who make the policy.

The argument is not frivolous. As a general proposition, experience creates expertise and expertise deserves respect. But we must be wary of going too far down this road. Few people would or should recuse themselves from every issue about which they lack personal experience. Otherwise, men would be disqualified from the debate on abortion, and only lawyers could shape the justice system. In the latter case, that has more or less happened, and with unpleasant results. This is not surprising. Direct involvement can produce myopia, whereas distance provides perspective. If we had adopted a policy of total deference to the military, President Truman would not have ordered its racial integration.

As for the courts, they cannot wholly defer to the military without abandoning their responsibility to interpret the Constitution and protect the rights of citizens. The courts traditionally defer to the military, but fortunately they have never given it carte blanche. Left to its own devices, the military has done some untoward things, such as exposing unwitting citizens to LSD and nuclear radiation. To defer in such cases, or when the military excludes people without a valid basis, gives the military too much respect and the Constitution too little. In addition, deference is less justifiable when the military fails to reflect the People. To the extent that the institution is undemocratic, more (not less) searching scrutiny of its decisions becomes necessary.

The irony is that today the military is one of the few areas in which homosexuals face official discrimination from the United States government. It should have been one of the first places discrimination was eliminated, not the last. The oft-cited notion that discrimination should be permitted in the military because of its special status gets things backwards. It is one thing to forbid persons the right to be clerks or postal workers, quite another to refuse their offer to take up arms to defend their country. The profound constitutional connection between military service and citizenship should make us especially reluctant to embrace a nonrepresentative regime that denies the claims of citizens to defend their country.

As it happens, the racial integration of America's military facilitated integration throughout American civil society. This development conformed to the Framers' vision of militia (and jury) service bringing people together and fostering a sense of community. To permit homosexuals to serve in the military is to make America more democratic, and more faithful to our constitutional ideals.

Absent the most compelling reason, we should not deny people the honor and opportunity to serve. We must remember that when they do so they are more than warriors; they are citizens protecting and participating in our constitutional democracy.

SIXTEEN

Women in Combat

MUCH OF THE FOREGOING ARGUMENT applies to the right of women to serve in the military. However, that right is significantly strengthened by a further consideration—the Nineteenth Amendment, prohibiting voting discrimination on the basis of sex. On its face, this might seem a peculiar claim. What does the right to vote have to do with the right to fight? In fact, as we have argued at various points, the two rights are closely related. The Constitution establishes each as a political right and responsibility crucial to self-government. To deny someone either is to stamp her a second-class citizen. As noted, more specific connections between the rights to vote and to serve in the military (as well as to serve on juries) assert themselves at every turn in American history. For example, women were finally granted the franchise, in part, in recognition of their contribution in World War I. More recently, eighteen-to-twenty-one-year-olds were granted the vote in recognition of their military service in Vietnam.

In the latter case, it was recognized that people at risk of dying for the country cannot fairly be deprived of an electoral voice. The converse applies with equal force: When we give people a say in their government, we cannot legitimately withhold from them a crucial aspect of their other political rights and thereby diminish their ability to exercise that say.

That is why the Nineteenth Amendment, while ostensibly dealing only with voting, should erase any doubt about whether women can be excluded from the armed forces. At the nation's inception, women were denied all three of the major badges of citizenship: the vote, jury service, and militia service. Once the Nineteenth Amendment was adopted, guaranteeing women the right to vote, did it make any sense to permit their exclusion from juries or the militia?

Of course, the words "jury" and "militia" appear nowhere in the Nineteenth Amendment, but by the same token the word "male" appears nowhere in the earlier references to these institutions. What remains constant across time is the underlying understanding that jury and militia service are political rights and duties closely linked to suffrage. Once suffrage rights are extended, corresponding and coextensive changes in juries and militias must follow.

Another way to see this point is through the prism of the Second Amendment. In order to preserve a well-regulated militia, it protects the right of "the people" to bear arms. In 1787, that reference to "the people" meant white males, the only fully empowered political participants (voters, jurors, militiamen). But the Nineteenth Amendment, like the Fifteenth, essentially expands the meaning of "the people," and thus should be read to broaden eligibility for Second Amendment protection. To put the point another way, the Second Amendment basically says that those who vote should bear arms too. Thus, when the Nineteenth Amendment made women voters, it implicitly made them part of the arms-bearing community (the militia in 1787, the army today).*

To see the matter still more clearly, let us ask if a law making women ineligible for political office could be reconciled with the Nineteenth Amendment. Most people would say no, even though the Amendment makes no mention of holding office. The link between the right to vote and the right to hold office is sufficiently clear that one appears to entail the other. Once we recognize the tight links between suffrage and military service, the same reasoning applies: If women are allowed to vote, they should be allowed to serve.

A quirky hypothetical question helps clarify the point. Consider whether the Constitution permits a woman to be President. If we're narrow about it, we look at Article II and find that the Constitution makes repeated reference to "he" (and never "she") when describing the President. And at the founding, presidents were always analogized to kings and never to queens. But however plausible the argument that the president must be male might have been under the original Constitution, it makes no sense after the passage of the Nineteenth Amendment, even though that Amendment does not explicitly modify Article II. The fundamental point is that the Nineteenth Amendment does not simply confer the right to pull a lever; it is about women's equal political participation.

Nevertheless, it took the Supreme Court until 1975 to strike down sex discrimination in juries,[1] and in 1981 the Court upheld sex discrimination in draft registration.[2] In neither case did the Court so much as mention the Nineteenth Amendment. The Court instead treated the Constitution in a "clause-bound" fashion, ignoring its elegant tapestry.

WITH WOMEN ALREADY in the military, is there any practical significance to recognizing their right to serve? The answer is yes. First,

---

*See Chapter 14. The Nineteenth Amendment does not directly say that women may vote. Rather, it says the right to vote may not be denied "on the basis of sex." Arguably, the Nineteenth Amendment supports yet another argument prohibiting the exclusion of gays from the military, since anti-gay discrimination can be seen as sex-based. See first note on bottom of page 148.

recognition of this right casts doubt upon the Supreme Court decision upholding male-only draft registration. Rights entail obligations. As Justice Thurgood Marshall put it in dissent in the draft registration case, the Court's decision "categorically excludes women from a fundamental civic obligation."[3]

In addition, recognizing women's constitutional right to serve sets the stage for the larger claim that they may not be systematically excluded from any positions for which they are qualified. Women were traditionally excluded from all combat roles. In 1993, then-Secretary of Defense Les Aspin lifted the ban on women serving as pilots of combat aircraft and on warships. However, women are still banned from ground combat.[4] The justifications are manifold: (1) women are not qualified for combat because of their physical and psychological limitations; (2) the presence of women will disrupt cohesion, because of sex, jealousy, interference with bonding, or the risk that male soldiers will be overly protective of female colleagues or emotionally disturbed by injuries to them; and (3) women are too vulnerable to gross mistreatment, including rape, when held as prisoners of war.

These premises are shaky. Unqualified women, after all, will be kept out by gender-neutral tests of capability. Needless to say, the tests should correlate closely with the ability to fight, lest sham tests be used to stack the deck against women. For example, the requirement that a would-be soldier bench-press 250 pounds would effectively exclude women. But because of the technological sophistication of the modern military, hand-to-hand combat and other activities requiring brute strength are on the wane (and this fact, in turn, undercuts a major rationale for the exclusionary policy).[5]

As for the series of "cohesion" concerns, they were used to justify wholesale exclusion of women from military service and were traditionally used to keep women out of the firehouse and off the police force. In each of these instances, the feared consequences have not resulted—at least not enough to destroy the effectiveness of the institution. Unproven, highly speculative assertions ought not be the basis for denying full citizenship to willing would-be warriors.

Concern about their treatment at the hands of the enemy is the weakest argument for excluding women from combat. After all, male prisoners too are subject to rape, torture, and murder. The kind of paternalism that deems mistreatment of women more serious than mistreatment of men hardly qualifies as grounds for denying the ostensibly protected group an important right.

As argued in the previous chapter, an army that looks more like America is more apt to reflect America's ideals. As Elaine Scarry reminds us, the Framers made the militia the nation's primary fighting force because they "envisioned military responsibility dispersed across the entire population."[6] The militia no longer fights our wars, but it remains the case that war is too important to be left to institutions that don't truly represent the country.

Analogy to the jury box illuminates this point. The rules governing jury selection strongly militate against an all-male or all-female jury, because we recognize that such a jury does not adequately represent the community. The identical point applies in the context of the military. Soldiers do not render verdicts, but they do perform crucial acts in the public arena. It behooves us to have our armed forces be more representative of our society and therefore more likely to represent us well.*

As for the women excluded from combat, much more is at stake than the opportunity to fight. Because they cannot participate in combat, women cannot rise as fast or as high in the military hierarchy. As a practical matter, the exclusion from combat entails an exclusion from influential policymaking decisions in the armed forces. As long as women cannot show their stuff on the battlefield, we will not see female members of the Joint Chiefs of Staff.

Even more importantly, the exclusion from combat makes it harder

---

*Thus, one commentator misses the point when he asks, rhetorically, "What kind of society are we when similar opportunity in killing is the standard for equality?" Colman McCarthy, "Women at War, A Foolish First," *Washington Post*, January 14, 1990, p. F2. By this reasoning, we should exclude women from juries in death-penalty cases on the ground that such jurors may engage in killing. In the armed forces, as in the jury, the real opportunity is for full citizenship. And giving women this opportunity benefits us all by making our institutions conform to the constitutional principle of popular sovereignty.

for women to play leadership roles in *civilian* political life.* As one legal scholar cogently argues, the exclusion of women from combat positions

> supports many barriers, erected by government itself, to women's participation in government and political life. . . . Because of the exclusion, only men can be military heroes. Women political candidates cannot boast of combat service, which voters regard as a credential for public office. Women within legislative bodies are regarded as having less authority on military matters than their male colleagues because they have not "been there"; they are regarded as less qualified to serve on military oversight committees and as having less authority if on such committees. . . . They, unlike Senator Kerrey, cannot oppose a military action with the authority of a recipient of the Congressional Medal of Honor who has lost a leg in combat.[7]

Indeed, Senator Bob Kerrey, along with colleagues Bob Dole, John Kerry, and John McCain, have been among the most respected members of the United States Senate, owing largely to their achievements in combat. While these Bobs and Johns present themselves as credentialed to speak on military matters, someone like Congresswomen Patricia Schroeder is told to shut up because she hasn't been there. There has been no woman Secretary of Defense. There has been no woman who, like Colin Powell, was catapulted into presidential consideration (and in Dwight D. Eisenhower's case** the presidency) primarily on the basis of her military achievements.

In short, denying women the right to serve their country on the front

---

*Some states give veterans preference in government employment. See *Massachusetts Personnel Administrator v. Feeney*, 442 U.S. 256 (1979) (upholding a state policy giving veterans a preference in civil service hiring even though 98 percent of veterans were male). As a result of a similar policy at the federal level in the hiring of administrative-law judges, 95 percent of such judges are male.

**To say nothing of George Washington or Andrew Jackson or William Henry Harrison or Zachary Taylor or Ulysses S. Grant or Rutherford B. Hayes or Theodore Roosevelt or John F. Kennedy.

lines effectively denies them the right to be equal participants in government and public affairs as well. The Nineteenth Amendment forbids such discrimination. And again, the failure to recognize as much hurts not just women but society generally. How can we expect self-government to thrive when we reduce the selves that can play a full role, when we keep half the population from realizing its potential contribution to our democracy?

The Framers were so committed to self-government that they placed even national security in the hands of the People. Regrettably, though understandably, they had an eighteenth-century notion of who constituted the People. Regrettably, if less understandably, we are taking too long to fully correct that defect.

OPPONENTS OF GAYS in the military and women in combat often accuse the other side of "social engineering." The military, they argue, is not the place for such a thing. This argument (which was also used in opposition to racial integration of the armed forces) is ironic. Those who exclude or restrict homosexuals and women are themselves doing social engineering. Based on assumptions about esprit de corps, or moral judgments about lifestyles, they would deny people the right to serve their country and thus would reduce the scope of popular sovereignty. But the Constitution (especially as amended) contemplates a different kind of social engineering, in which inclusive public institutions promote a democratic character and maintain a democratic culture.*

---

*Legal scholar Kenneth Karst nicely captures this point: "No one thinks of the armed services as democratic in the sense that the private's opinion carries as much weight as the captain's. But surely there is strong appeal in the idea that the services are broadly inclusive of all Americans. Our popular culture repeatedly confirms our attachment to this democratic, unifying ideal. Consider the typical war movie, in which the soldiers' faces tacitly represent our ethnic diversity. . . . The services themselves reinforce the same ideal in television advertisements. . . . The ads picture the services at work, and they portray the. . . presence of women and a good ethnic mix. The implicit message, not just to potential recruits but to all of us, is that the armed forces are integrated; that America is a nation of equal citizens; and that these two conclusions reinforce each other. The full promise of this message deserves to be fulfilled. To that end, we need to deploy the resources of our law." Kenneth Karst, "The Pursuit of Manhood and the Desegregation of the Armed Forces," 38 *U.C.L.A. Law Review* 499, 501 (1991).

SEVENTEEN

The Unconstitutionality of a National Draft (?)

IS IT POSSIBLE THAT, NOTWITHSTANDING their careful design concerning the military, the Framers left unanswered the most obvious question: whether Congress may institute a draft? Actually, the status of a military draft is rather clear from the Constitution's text. Nevertheless, throughout the nineteenth century the federal government's power to conscript soldiers was a matter of bitter controversy. And when the issue was finally resolved by a unanimous Supreme Court in 1918, the Court's opinion turned the Framers' scheme upside down.[1]

During the War of 1812, when a draft was first proposed, heated debates over its constitutionality ensued. However, the war ended with the issue unresolved. During the Civil War, both the Union and the Confederacy did in fact conscript soldiers. Supreme Court Chief Justice Roger Taney argued in a private manuscript that conscription was unconstitutional,[2] but the issue never reached the Court. Many lower courts in both the Union and Confederacy upheld conscription, though the Pennsylvania Supreme Court held conscription unconstitutional.[3] However, when one judge in the majority retired and was replaced, the Pennsylvania Court reversed its holding.[4]

Finally, in the 1918 *Selective Draft Law Cases*,[5] the Supreme Court decisively upheld the constitutionality of World War I conscription.[6] The court opined that the power to conscript derives directly from Article I, Section 8, Clause 12, which authorizes Congress "to raise and support Armies." Though the Court went on at some length, the (il)logic of its opinion comes down to a single sentence: "As the mind cannot conceive an army without the men to compose it, on the face of the Constitution the objection that it does not give power to provide for such men would seem to be too frivolous for further notice."[7]

Stunningly, the Court apparently failed to consider that the power to raise an army need not entail conscription; Congress can instead resort to paying people to induce them to join the armed forces. Indeed, as suggested in Chapter 13, the Framers generally used the term "army" to refer to a mercenary force. In his *Sentiments on a Peace Establishment*, George Washington pointedly contrasted the citizen "militia" with "mercenary armies."[8] Similarly, *Federalist* 24 describes the two potential military forces as "the militia" and a "permanent corps in the pay of the government," and refers to the latter as an "army."[9] Eighteenth-century dictionaries confirm this usage as conventional.[10]

The eighteenth-century meaning of "army" alone rebuts the notion that the power to raise armies entails the power to conscript. But the full case against conscription requires looking at the Army Clause in conjunction with Article I, Section 8, Clause 15, which gives the federal government power to call out the militia "to execute the Laws of the Union, suppress Insurrections and repel Invasions." Notice that Clause 15 *does* authorize a draft of sorts. Because at the time of the founding the militia consisted of all able-bodied adult white males,* Clause 15 gave the federal government power to draft the whole eligible citi-

---

*Today, the nomenclature is somewhat more complicated. By statute, there are two militias—the "unorganized militia," consisting of all able-bodied men, and the organized militia consisting of each state's trained National Guard (10 U.S.C. Sec. 311).

zenry—but only *in certain specified national emergencies and pursuant to certain specified procedures.*

There, clear as the words on a page, is the Founders' scheme with respect to military service: The federal government may call out the citizenry (militia) when national security directly requires; in other circumstances, it may, if it chooses, raise a force of volunteers (an army).

One may respond that the Clause 12 power to "raise armies" gives Congress the power *both* to raise a mercenary standing army *and* to draft soldiers. However, such a reading does violence to the constitutional scheme (quite apart from the fact that the word army connoted mercenaries, not draftees). For if the Clause 12 power to raise armies authorizes a general draft at any time, for any reason, then Clause 15 is meaningless. Why would the Framers give Congress an all-purpose power to draft citizens and then, just a few clauses later, give Congress the power to draft citizens on three specific occasions? It makes as much sense as if the Framers, several clauses after empowering Congress to regulate commerce with all foreign nations, separately empowered Congress to regulate commerce with European nations.

We owe it to the Framers to presume, albeit subject to rebuttal, that they did not author a pointless Clause 15. In the words of the great Chief Justice John Marshall, "[I]t cannot be presumed that any clause in the Constitution is intended to be without effect; and therefore such a construction is inadmissible, unless the words require it."[11] The words of Clauses 12 and 15 do not require the bizarre conclusion that the power to call out the militia in certain circumstances is a wholly subsumed subset of the power to raise armies. Rather, read properly (using the words the way the Framers did), the two clauses complement each other: Clause 12 authorizes Congress to raise a permanent army of mercenaries, while Clause 15 authorizes conscription of the citizenry in the event of national emergency.

History buttresses the textual and structural evidence. It is clear why the Framers created two military forces and divided power over them as they did. As we saw in Chapter 13, their careful design protected states from the federal government—the states trained the militia and retained control over it except in case of national emergency. But when the power to raise an army is construed to include the power to conscript the citizenry, this protection amounts to nothing. If Congress can draft the entire citizenry into a federal army, what is left of the state militias? The states could be left defenseless should the federal army seek to intimidate, harass, or invade. As Justice Taney succinctly put it "[If the draft] can be maintained, all of the [militia] clauses in the Constitution . . . are abrogated. There is no longer any militia—it is absorbed in the Army."[12] Taney went on to say that the federal power to conscript would entail the power to destroy the infrastructure of the state, drafting not only many citizens but the governor and civil authorities as well.[13]

The two-tiered military structure protected not only the states, but individual citizens as well. Wretches miserable enough to volunteer as hired guns might deserve whatever treatment they got at the hands of army officers, but people wrenched by conscription from their land, homes, and families deserved better. They were entitled to be placed in units with fellow citizens from their own locality, and officered by local leaders—men chosen by state governments closest to them and most representative of them, men of standing in the community, whom they were likely to know from civilian society and who were likely to know them. The ordinary harshness of military discipline would be tempered by the many social, economic, and political linkages that preceded military service, and that would be reestablished thereafter.* Officers would know that, in a variety of ways, they could be called to account back home after the fighting was over.

---

*Several historians have depicted the friendly and intimate nature of the militia. See Robert Gross, *The Minutemen and Their World* (1976), p. 71 ("The muster was almost a family reunion. Fathers and sons, uncles and nephews, brothers, cousins and in-laws often enlisted in the same units."); Gordon Wood, *The Radicalism Of The American Revolution* (1992), p. 45 ("The Minutemen of the towns were held together less by chains of command than by familial loyalties. . . . Over one-quarter of the Lexington militiamen mustered by Captain John Parker on April 19, 1775 were related to him by blood or marriage.") The social aspects of militia service are nicely captured by the following account of a typical militia muster in late seventeenth-century Massachusetts: "[A] town's militia company generally assembled on public grounds, held roll call and prayer, practiced the manual of arms and close order drill, and passed under review and inspection by the militia officers and other public officials. There might also be target practice and sham battles followed in the afternoon—when times were not too perilous—by refreshments, games, and socializing." Russel Weigley, *History of the United States Army* (1967), p. 6.

Finally, note how the Third Amendment reinforces the argument against a national draft. Since the Third Amendment flatly forbids Congress to conscript civilians as involuntary innkeepers and roommates of soldiers in peacetime, what sense does it make to read the Army Clause as giving Congress peacetime power to exercise even more drastic coercion by conscripting civilians into the army itself?* It would be awfully odd to say that Congress has virtually no peacetime power to force soldiers upon civilians, but total peacetime power to force civilians into soldiers.

THE FACT THAT all of this has gone unrecognized is ironic. Conservatives trumpet the cause of federalism (states' rights), and lament the erosion of this basic constitutional principle.[14] They relish the Tenth Amendment's reminder that the federal government has only those powers delegated to it, with all other powers reserved to the states (and "the people," though this part of the Amendment usually gets overlooked). While worshipping the Tenth Amendment's general declaration, conservatives ignore the Constitution's very specific commitment to federalism—the placing of the armed citizenry under control of the states except in three enumerated emergency situations. Conversely, liberals champion many individual rights, but pay little attention to the right against blanket national conscription. While often expressing distrust of a national military-industrial complex that can run amok, they ignore a very specific protection against that threat.

Inasmuch as the Constitution established a military federalism in large part to protect the states from the federal government, conservatives should question the notion that the federal government can con-

---

*We stress "peacetime" to drive home the distinction between the Army Clause and the Militia Clause. The Army Clause makes no distinction between war and peace; therefore, if the clause authorizes wartime conscription, it presumably also authorizes peacetime conscription. The Militia Clause, by contrast, limits Congress's power to conscript the militia to specified national emergencies—just as the Third Amendment limits Congress's quartering power to wartime. The significance of the peacetime/wartime distinction is developed in the text below.

script citizens whenever it wishes. Likewise liberals, who prize individual freedom, should not ignore the way the Militia Clause protects liberty. And our argument should be taken seriously by anyone dedicated to the proposition that constitutional text, structure, and history matter.

To be sure, the argument that conscription destroys the constitutional design can be plausibly countered by an argument based on changed circumstances. The thinking that underlay the Framers' adoption of military federalism may be outdated. Today, an argument against conscription based on the notion that the states must deter or defend against attack by a federal army seems farfetched. For one thing, there is no longer an "armed citizenry" in the eighteenth-century sense. While many people possess guns, few receive military training. And though there remains a state militia of sorts—each state's National Guard, consisting of citizen soldiers who serve the states except when called into federal service—these organizations need not be eviscerated by a draft. Rather, National Guard units could be exempt from a federal draft (as was the case during the Vietnam War, to the benefit of Dan Quayle and many others), and the state military would remain intact. Even a draft that included some or most of a state's National Guard would arguably pose no threat to the security of that state. This assessment rests largely on the faith that the federal government will not attack any state—a faith generally redeemed by American history.[15]

Thus, the primary reason for the Framers' rejection of conscription—protection of the states—has lost much of its relevance. However, the Framers' military design rested on another principle besides federalism: libertarianism. We have lamented that modern constitutional analysis is skewed by the tendency to view constitutional rights solely as protecting individuals from majorities, overlooking the document's populist underpinnings (specifically, its protection of the citizenry at large from a self-dealing or unrepresentative government). But libertarianism and populism are not mutually exclusive, and federalism sometimes operates at the intersection of the two. That is, a major rationale behind states' rights is that powerful states serve as buffers between their citizens and the federal government.

All of which directly applies to the Framers' approach to national security. Note that service in the militia, which was compulsory at the time of the founding, was limited—the militia would be called out by the federal government only in the event of national emergency. By contrast, the "army," which consisted of volunteers, could be raised for any purpose whatever, including in peacetime or to fight in foreign wars. In addition, service in the militia was part-time and local. By contrast, Congress could raise a full-time army and send its members anywhere—not only during times of obvious need but for as long as it pleased. Thus, the Framers' two-tiered structure ensured that those compelled to military service (militiamen) would stay close to home and serve only part-time, except in the event of national emergency. Potentially more onerous or disagreeable service—full-time, in non-emergencies, away from one's community, and risking one's life in combat not involving defense of the homeland—was reserved for those who volunteered. This design respected and protected the liberty of the citizenry.*

Libertarian concerns were manifest in the debates over control of the militia. Luther Martin, one of the few delegates at the Constitutional Convention who opposed the Constitution, expressed concern that Congress could "march the *whole* militia of Maryland to the *remotest* part of the Union and keep them in service as long as they think proper."[16] The answer to Martin and others who voiced similar fears was that Congress could call out the militia only in one of the specified national emergencies.[17] Such an answer would have been unavailable if Congress could conscript citizens for any purpose, any time.

The Framers were painfully aware of the British experience, where militiamen strenuously objected to being forced to fight foreign wars. Indeed, the British enacted legislation proscribing conscription for foreign service.[18] And when the issue of a draft first emerged in this country, during the War of 1812, a chorus of voices swelled in opposition.

---

*Of course, the Framers were not extreme libertarians. For example, they did not limit the occasions on which *states* could call out their militia—say, for disaster relief. Once again, an image arises of citizens working together on a common project.

Daniel Webster eloquently argued that the Framers had limited the calling out of the militia to national emergencies precisely because they believed it wrong to compel citizens to fight when their homeland was not threatened:

> Nor is it, Sir, for the defense of his own house & home, that he
> who is the subject of military draft is to perform the task allotted
> to him. You will put him upon a service equally foreign to his interests & abhorrent to his feelings. . . . [H]e is forced from home
> against right, not to contend for the defense of his country . . . &
> [if] in that strife he fall, 'tis murder.[19]

For this reason, Webster maintained, citizens (as militiamen) can be called out only "for the emergencies mentioned in the Constitution." They cannot be called out "for long periods, & for the general objects of war." Therefore, no law "compelling a service in the regular army . . . can be carried into effect."[20]

Webster recognized that libertarianism and federalism intertwined here. Limiting conscription to the calling forth of the militia established the states as buffers between the federal government and the citizenry. If the government tried to call out the militia even when the conditions specified in the Constitution were not met, governors could jump in and instruct draftees to stay put (for the governor is commander-in-chief of the militia except when it is called out *in those circumstances* specified by the Constitution). As Webster put it, "It will be the solemn duty of the State Governments to protect their own authority over their own Militia, & to interpose between their citizens & arbitrary power."[21]

Prudential concerns reinforce Webster's argument. As the Framers recognized, conscription in peacetime or for a foreign war may be futile or dangerous. In *Federalist* 24, Alexander Hamilton argued that the federal government must be empowered to raise an army of paid volunteers precisely because citizen-soldiers "would not long, if at all, submit to be dragged from their occupations and families to perform . . . disagreeable duty in times of profound peace."[22] Likewise, in *Federalist* 29 he cautioned that if citizens are sent too far from their homes for purposes distant from their immediate interests, they will revolt.[23]

Here, as so often was the case, the Framers proved prescient. During the Vietnam War, our government officials drafted citizens and sent them abroad to fight when the homeland was not directly threatened. The result? Precisely what Hamilton predicted would occur in such a case— terrible dissent in the country at large and an ineffective military effort.

The phrase "No more Vietnams" is often heard these days, connoting different (and contradictory) things to different people.[24] Perhaps one important meaning is that government officials should hesitate to conscript citizens to fight except in the circumstances specified in the Constitution and using the procedures required by it.

Admittedly, in today's "smaller world," events on foreign soil are far more likely to implicate national security than was the case in 1787. So too, threats to national security can develop faster today than they did back then. For these reasons, the conditions justifying the federal government in conscripting citizens (to repel invasion, suppress insurrection, and execute the laws) should be interpreted flexibly. Thus, for example, conscription during World War II would have been justified, even had America not been invaded at Pearl Harbor. (Of course, our experience in Vietnam cautions against *too* flexible an interpretation.)

Apart from the question of *when* the federal government may conscript citizens is the question of *how*. If we follow the Framers' Constitution, the government must navigate the channels laid down in Article I. Thus, if the federal government wants to conscript citizens, it should federalize the militia—not the National Guards, but the "unorganized militia" consisting of all adult citizens capable of defending the country.[25] Such a call must go through the states, allowing governors to determine—at least in the first instance—whether sufficiently exigent circumstances are at hand. If a governor thinks not, he might try to interpose himself between the federal government and his citizens (his unorganized militia). During the Vietnam War, the federal government conscripted soldiers directly, rather than through the states, eliminating the kind of useful governmental friction contemplated by the Constitution.

It may be objected that permitting governors to resist a draft they regard as unconstitutional will produce chaos.[26] This is a quite understandable concern, but perhaps the state/federal friction would instead produce something distinctly American: lawsuits requiring the courts to resolve a constitutional dispute.[27] Once again, we see the Framers' elaborate constitutional design: If the federal government wished to do something as severely coercive as military conscription, the states could play a role, with the judiciary (perhaps) waiting in the wings to resolve any clash.* Both separation of powers and federalism would be at work, with the delicate system of checks and balances ensuring that one tyrannical person or institution cannot wantonly abuse the citizenry.

Note the parallel between the criminal justice system and the military structure. We saw earlier that the Framers dispersed power so that a person could not be punished as a criminal without concurrence by Congress, the President, the courts, and a jury. Because a person's life and liberty were at stake, each of these branches of government could intervene to offer protection. The same concerns led the Framers to disperse the authority to compel people to risk their lives in combat. The President and Congress had to declare that a national emergency was present, and even then state governors and perhaps the courts could weigh in if they disagreed.

But the Framers' nuanced architecture has crumbled over the last two centuries, and its deep foundations have eroded. The founders' militia does not really exist today; the resort to a wholly national draft has cut the states out of the loop; and the courts have generally declined to address whether the use of military force conforms to the Constitution.[28] All of which calls to mind the remark attributed to Benjamin Franklin following the Constitutional Convention. Asked what form of government the convention had come up with, Franklin replied: "A republic, if you can keep it."[29] The Framers gave us a military structure

---

*To be sure, a court might well refuse to get involved, leaving the clash to be resolved through the political process.

that safeguarded against oppression. However, over the course of American history, this structure has been allowed to collapse.

It may well be that we cannot (and should not try to) turn back the clock: Because control of the military today lies almost exclusively in federal hands, Congress must be permitted to conscript citizens directly. And, as a practical matter, it is far from clear that courts could properly adjudicate the constitutional issues during a military emergency rather than after the fact (in, say, damage suits brought by conscripts or their survivors). But Daniel Webster's argument may still ring true for many: Involving states in the conscription process provides citizens an extra layer of protection.

Perhaps the "changed circumstances" argument should win out in the end. But we should not acquiesce in a national military draft without at least recognizing that the Founders forbade such a draft, and did so for good reason.

EIGHTEEN

The Right to Bear Arms

THE RIGHT TO BEAR ARMS, affirmed by the Second Amendment, represents the ultimate decentralization of military power. Desiring the citizenry at large to play the central role in preserving national security, the Framers established not just military federalism but military self-government.

Yet not everyone agrees that the Second Amendment confers a right to bear arms. The controversy over this putative right has occasioned a bizarre reversal. Many conservatives, who frown upon a broad reading of other constitutional rights, smile upon the right to bear arms. By contrast, many liberals, who embrace other constitutional rights, shun this one.

We agree with the few scholars who in recent years have urged liberals to take the Second Amendment seriously.[1] At the same time, we disagree with those conservatives who believe that the Second Amendment prohibits any and all gun control.

The Second Amendment says: "A well-regulated Militia being necessary to the security of a free state, the right of the people to keep and bear Arms shall not be infringed." Conservatives focus on the second part of this provision—the unequivocal declaration of a right to bear arms. Liberals focus on the prefatory part of the amendment—the declaration that the amendment was designed to preserve a "well-regulated militia." Since the modern militia is the National Guard, liberals insist that the Second Amendment merely prevents the federal government from disarming the state National Guards; it in no way protects an individual's right to his or her firearm.*

The issue is usually framed as whether the Second Amendment confers a "personal" right or a "collective" right, a right to "private" use or to "military" use. This gets the debate off track for two reasons. First, there is no necessary contradiction between the two perspectives: Private, personal gun ownership may serve a collective, military purpose. It bears noting that the Constitution authorizes the calling out of the militia to "suppress insurrections" and to "execute the laws of the United States." The Framers envisioned that if bands of outlaws and rogues took to the streets and acted lawlessly, an armed citizenry would put them down. Enabling individual homeowners to protect against individual outlaws and rogues is arguably not all that different.

Second, and more importantly, the animating spirit of the Second Amendment was not permanently fixed in 1791—the Reconstruction period altered it.[2] Appreciating both of these points requires recapturing the historical context of the Second Amendment.

We recall that the Framers' militia was not an elite fighting force but the entire citizenry of the time: all able-bodied adult white males. Since the Second Amendment explicitly declares that its purpose is to pre-

---

*Each side also makes various linquistic arguments that fail to resolve the issue. For example, both sides cite the "keep and bear arms" language for support. To "bear" arms has a military connotation. One bears arms in combat; the pistol one carries for self-protection is not usually spoken of in this way. Conversely, though, the notion of a right to "keep" arms suggests individual ownership transcending service in the militia.

serve a well-regulated militia, the right to bear arms was universal in scope. The vision animating the amendment was nothing less than popular sovereignty—applied in the military realm. The Framers recognized that self-government requires the People's access to bullets as well as ballots. The armed citizenry (militia) was expected to protect against not only foreign enemies, but also a potentially tyrannical federal government. In short, the right to bear arms was intended to ensure that our government remained in the hands of the People.

The Framers saw true self-government as dependent on the transcendent right of the people to alter or abolish their government. Whenever self-interested government actors abused their powers or shirked their duties, the People could assemble in conventions and reassert their sovereignty. As Edmund Pendleton, President of Virginia's ratifying Convention, triumphantly put it, "Who shall dare to resist the people?"[3] But to many opponents of the Constitution, the answer seemed both obvious and ominous. An aristocratic federal government, lacking sympathy with and confidence from ordinary constituents, might dare to resist the people—especially if that government were supported by a standing army. Only an armed populace could deter such an awful spectacle; hence the need to bar Congress from disarming the citizenry.

The word "people" in the Second Amendment conjures up the Constitution's bedrock principle of popular sovereignty. In John Locke's influential treatise, the people's right to alter or abolish tyrannous government invariably required a popular appeal to arms.[4] To Americans at the time of the founding, this was not merely speculative theory, but the lived experience of the age. In their lifetimes, Americans had seen the Lockean words of our Declaration of Independence made flesh (and blood) in a Revolution wrought by arms.

To be sure, following our successful armed revolution, Americans domesticated and defused the idea of violent revolution by channeling it into the instrument of the peaceful convention. Yet, as the Second Amendment reminds us, even the new legal institutions that resulted ultimately rested on force—force that ideally would never need to be invoked, yet whose latent existence would deter threats.

This, then, was the context in which the Second Amendment was adopted. The amendment clearly served a large *public* purpose. To see it as primarily concerned with an individual's right to hunt is akin to viewing the heart of the First Amendment's speech and assembly clauses as the right of persons to meet to play bridge or have sex.

However, caution is in order. The Framers' intent includes the vision not only of the original Framers but also of those who crafted later amendments. In this case, the Reconstruction period modified the Founding vision of the Second Amendment.

The original spirit of the Second Amendment might be summed up as follows: "When guns are outlawed, only the federal government will have guns!" But things changed. The leaders who framed the Fourteenth Amendment (strengthening the hand of the federal government vis-à-vis the states) did not oppose a federal standing army; they needed such an army to "reconstruct" oppressive state governments in the South. In the post–Civil War climate, a different vision of arms-bearing emerged. All law-abiding people, even those who were not militiamen (for example, women and blacks), needed guns to protect against private thuggery. It was especially important for blacks to own guns to protect their homes against attacks by the Ku Klux Klan.

The National Rifle Association (NRA), founded by ex–Union Army Officers, emerged after the Civil War. Its slogan today—"When guns are outlawed, only outlaws will have guns"—reflects its Reconstruction roots, emphasizing private rather than public (militia) arms-bearing to protect against private violence rather than public tyranny.

We need not choose between the original and the Reconstruction visions of the Second Amendment. We can embrace both. Notwithstanding our vastly reduced fear of the federal army,* we ought not to dismiss

*Why is the standing army feared so much less than it was two centuries ago? This is partly a function of its track record; while the army has committed atrocities abroad, it has rarely been used against American citizens. Also, the army is no longer viewed as an "outsider" force, consisting of aliens, convicts, and other misfits. In some ways it has come to resemble the eighteenth-century militia, comprising ordinary Americans from all walks of life. Of course, as discussed in Chapters 15 and 16, the army is still not as broadly inclusive as it should be. To the extent it moves in that direction, there will be even less reason for Americans to fear it.

the value of an armed citizenry as part, parcel, and protector of popular sovereignty. That the armed citizenry is no longer part of a "well-regulated militia" assures that the country needs another vehicle (a standing army) to deter and fight foreign foes. It does not mean that citizens can no longer play a role in protecting against their own government.

Of course, times have changed. Today, we see little eagerness by the federal government to use the standing army to tyrannize the citizenry and, given the army's ultra-sophisticated weaponry, it is unclear how much resistance an armed citizenry could muster in any case. Thus, many liberals feel contempt for the right to bear arms. The Constitution protects wholesome things like speech, privacy, and equality . . . but *guns?* In fact, there is nothing embarrassing about a self-governing people arming themselves to preserve their sovereignty. (Note that the Second Amendment speaks of "arms," not "guns.[5]") If the Framers wanted the People armed to protect against a government led by the likes of Presidents Washington, Adams, Jefferson, and Madison, we need not feel shame in retaining arms to protect our sovereignty. As for the futility of guns against the awesome machinery of today's state, law professor Sanford Levinson has argued that

> It is simply silly to respond that small arms are irrelevant against nuclear-armed states: Witness contemporary Northern Ireland and the territories occupied by Israel, where the sophisticated weaponry of Great Britain and Israel have proved almost totally beside the point. The fact that these may not be pleasant examples does not affect the principal point, that a state facing a totally disarmed population is in a far better position, for good or for ill, to suppress popular demonstrations and uprisings than one that must calculate the possibilities of its soldiers and officials being injured or killed.[6]

Levinson's argument met with a spirited rebuttal from many liberals. One gun control activist's response warrants special attention because it is provocative and challenging—but fundamentally flawed. Dissecting

Dennis Henigan's critique of Levinson will further clarify the Framers' vision of popular sovereignty.[7]

Henigan notes that the militia clauses empower the federal government to call out the militia to "suppress insurrections." In his view, this alone refutes the notion that the Framers envisioned an armed militia as protection against the government: "The Constitution cannot view the militia *both* as a means by which government can suppress insurrection and as an instrument for insurrection against the government".[8] In fact, the Framers did envision the militia playing precisely this double role. Therein lies the beauty of self-government in the military realm: Ultimate power resides with the People both to enforce the Constitution and to prevent its improper enforcement. If wanton bands rage out of control, the federal government can call on the People at large to restore order. At the same time, if the government itself—backed by the professional standing army—becomes tyrannical and utterly lawless, the People at large can resist.

Thus, Henigan errs profoundly when he cites the militia clauses as proof "that the Framers understood the militia to be an instrument of governmental authority"[9] *rather than* a source of resistance to such authority. The Framers did not choose between the two.[10] A central mission of the Constitution is to bridge the gap between the People and the government. Fearing that this gap could open too wide, the Framers provided the citizens with ways of closing it: amending the Constitution, exercising the power to nullify in a criminal case, and, yes, taking up arms. Indeed, the militia's dual role almost perfectly mirrors the dual role of the jury—assisting the government in protecting the community from private misconduct (by convicting criminals) while also guarding against an oppressive government (in criminal cases through nullification and in civil cases by holding government officials liable when they overstep their bounds).*

---

*This parallel highlights the tight link between the militia and the jury. As noted in Chapter 13, the militia was seen as a political body, not solely a military regime. It essentially consisted of armed voters (and jurors). In the militia, as in the jury, members of the community engaged in collective acts of citizenship both reflecting and protecting a government by the People.

Henigan condemns an "insurrectionist theory" resting on the "startling assertion of a generalized constitutional right of all citizens to engage in armed insurrection against their government."[11] The ability of an armed citizenry to resist an oppressive government is not a theory, but a fact. Fresh from their own revolutionary experience, the last thing the Framers would have done is to deny the People the means of armed insurrection. Indeed, as suggested above, the Declaration of Independence appealed to a Lockean right of violent revolution, triggered when government turned tyrannical and violated fundamental rights. Nearly a century later, Abraham Lincoln acknowledged the People's right to take up arms against the government.[12]

But—and here we must be very clear—the Framers regarded this right as a last resort arising only when the government forfeits its legitimacy by violating its authority and closing all political and judicial avenues for redress. That was the view of John Locke,[13] whose work on the right to revolt was second nature to the Framers, and there is no reason to ascribe to them a more radical position. Indeed, the main purpose of the Declaration of Independence was to make the case for violent revolution by piling on example after example of acts of oppression, evincing a "design to reduce [Americans] under absolute Despotism." And we must remember that Americans could not simply vote the (British) bums out of power, because George III and his Parliament never deigned to place their names on an American ballot. Under *these* circumstances, armed revolt was justified.

The Constitution did change matters. Unlike the King and Parliament, the President and Congress could be tossed out on Election Day. And, as we saw in Part I, the Constitution derived from and endorsed a new kind of revolution, a peaceful means of altering or abolishing the government. By ballots rather than bullets, the People retain the right to change their government—not only when it becomes "destructive of [its] ends" by violating inalienable rights (the claim made in the Declaration), but whenever the People see fit, by majority vote, to amend the Constitution. But there is no evidence that the Framers intended this new ballot right to popular amendment to repeal the older bullet right to armed revolt. Suppose, for example, that a paranoid president on the eve of impeachment tried to dissolve the legislature, close the courts, and impose martial law. It is hard to imagine that the Framers would have considered armed revolt off limits under these circumstances.*

Still, it may be a mistake to think of the right to armed revolt as a "constitutional" right:[14] The right arises precisely because the government has lost all legitimacy by suspending the proper forms of constitutional government—free elections, open courts, and so on. Thus, describing the People's two means of altering an unpopular government, Lincoln pointedly contrasted their "constitutional right of amending it" with their "revolutionary right to dismember or overthrow it."[15]

Henigan calls the notion of an armed citizenry entitled to take up arms "profoundly dangerous"[16] and surely he is right. But is the (worst-case scenario) alternative—a citizenry at the mercy of a wholly lawless government backed by a professional army—less dangerous? Henigan opines that if the Second Amendment is construed to protect the right to bear arms, it "may prove to be a weapon of destruction aimed at the rest of the Bill of Rights."[17] That is conceivable, but the same could be said of the First Amendment. Indeed, some people insist that the First Amendment damages America, and seek to limit its scope.[18] The conservative First Amendment alarmists and liberal Second Amendment alarmists both overreact: The country has survived two centuries of free speech and armed citizens. The mere possibility that a free people could misuse and thereby destroy its freedom is hardly grounds for withholding freedom in the first place.

NEEDLESS TO SAY, circumstances today are very different from those of 1789. We do not have an armed citizenry, since many people opt not to purchase guns. And while we should be wary of denying some people

---

*It is vital to distinguish between a generally democratic and law-abiding regime, and one that is neither. Today's extremist groups, including self-styled "militias," ignore this. For all the imperfections of American democracy today, elections are essentially free and courts are always open. Under these circumstances, those who wage war against their government and their countrymen are not following the Declaration of Independence; they are desecrating it.

a right on the ground that others do not avail themselves of it (just as large-scale failure to vote would hardly justify denying the right to vote to those who wish to exercise it), we should take seriously an argument based on changed circumstances. Insofar as we lack the armed citizenry envisioned by the Framers, and are experiencing substantial gun-related violence not envisioned by them, we ought to ask whether the benefits of the right to bear arms are overridden by its manifest harm.

But if the answer is yes, the best solution would be to repeal (rather than ignore) the Second Amendment. This we should not do without at least considering the vision underlying this maligned amendment. As Elaine Scarry puts it, "the Second Amendment is a very great amendment, and coming to know it through criminals and the endlessly disputed claims of gun clubs seems the equivalent of our coming to know the First Amendment only through pornography."[19]

Many liberals seem prone to precisely what Scarry warns against—seeing the Second Amendment through the eyes of the criminal. In a provocative piece of legal scholarship, Wendy Brown argues that whatever sense the Second Amendment made in the virtuous world of 1789, it makes none in brutish modern America.[20] She claims that the Second Amendment rests on the notion of a citizenry with a shared commitment to the public good, and today's citizenry "bears a shared commitment to almost nothing, least of all a common good."[21]

Thus, we again hear the argument that confronts us at every turn: the American people lack the virtue necessary for true self-government. The People cannot be trusted to amend the Constitution or to make laws by plebiscite because they will tyrannize minorities. They cannot be trusted (on juries) to decide questions of constitutional law because they are ignorant. And they cannot be trusted with guns because they will use them to shoot one another rather than for legitimate purposes. Once again, our answer begins with a partial confession. In some obvious respects, the American citizenry has not lived up to Thomas Jefferson's highest hopes. The solution, however, is not to further distance ourselves from self-rule but rather to embrace it. We will not build a virtuous citizenry by denying citizens the right to self-government.

Ms. Brown, a pacifist, is understandably skittish about guns. But again, the Second Amendment is about much more than guns just as the First Amendment is about much more than pornography.* Both of these amendments are about the conditions necessary to sustain self-government. Thus the preface to the Second Amendment declares the Amendment's purpose as protecting "the security of a free state." As noted, the substance of the Amendment speaks not of guns (for hunters) but of "arms" (for "the People"). The text and the spirit of the Second Amendment invite us to inquire how, in today's world, the American citizenry must be armed in order to protect our security and freedom. It may be that we must be armed with information and technology (such as access to the Internet) more than with guns. In 1991, the Russian people resisted a coup without firing a single bullet. They could not have prevailed, however, had faxes not been fired back and forth between Moscow and Washington.

WHILE THE SECOND Amendment may protect more than guns, it does not protect all guns or render all gun-control measures unconstitutional. The Constitution permits reasonable regulation—even the militia is explicitly described as "well-regulated." Such regulation probably includes permit requirements, registration, waiting periods, and mandatory education in gun use and responsibility. (The Framers *required* training in the use of weaponry. Today, such training could help reduce accidental shootings. Those who favor educating school children in responsible sex surely should welcome educating adults in responsible gun use.)

Thus, we reject the notion that the Second Amendment guarantees unrestricted access to any kind of firearm for any purpose—essentially the position of the NRA. True, the Second Amendment says the right to bear arms shall not be "infringed." However, the First Amendment says that the right to free speech shall not be "abridged"; the absolutist lan-

---

*If indeed it is about pornography at all. Sexually titillating pictures are very far from core First Amendment concerns.

guage notwithstanding, the Supreme Court has always maintained that reasonable restrictions on speech must be permitted. Surely the same is true of the Second Amendment. Indeed, restrictions on guns are easier to justify, as even gun enthusiasts readily admit in certain contexts.[22] Few people disagree that the state may prohibit the sale of guns to people convicted of violent crimes. We would not, however, tolerate a law preventing ex-convicts from buying a printing press or exercising their right to speak.

The dangers of arms-bearing can be reduced without compromising the Second Amendment's animating purpose. The legitimate purposes of arms-bearing are not defeated, for example, by a waiting period enabling gun sellers to ensure that would-be buyers are not convicted criminals. And as guns are increasingly used for purposes less germane to the Second Amendment's animating spirit, such as hunting, or wholly illegitimate purposes, such as street violence, the case for restrictions becomes easier to justify. By analogy, the Supreme Court has consistently held that commercial speech is entitled to less protection than political speech, since the latter more directly serves the primary purpose of the First Amendment.[23]

Also, not all guns are created equal. Because a handgun can be easily concealed, it may be more a weapon of aggression than deterrence. So, too, we can place restrictions on quantities of ammunition and weapons of mass aggression (like Uzis) without fear that we are unduly impeding the legitimate use of firearms by law-abiding citizens. Indeed, to permit anyone to purchase any type of weapon, no matter how dangerous and unnecessary, would itself threaten the "security of a free state."

While restrictions on guns are permissible, wholesale confiscation is not. The latter would eviscerate the purpose and language of the Second Amendment. There may be a gray area, where a legislative measure short of confiscation severely reduces the right to bear arms. Of course, gray areas are hardly unique in constitutional law, and often call for nuanced judgment rather than retreat to an absolutist position.

The modern Supreme Court has heard only one case concerning gun control.[24] This 1939 case involved a Second Amendment challenge to a congressional statute prohibiting possession of a sawed-off shotgun. The Court upheld the statute, noting that the Second Amendment was designed "to assure the continuation and render possible the effectiveness" of the militia, and that the defendant failed to offer "any evidence tending to show that possession or use of [a sawed-off shotgun] at this time has some reasonable relationship to the preservation or efficiency of a well-regulated militia."[25]

On its face, the Court opinion was not necessarily pro-gun control, inasmuch as it arguably implied that there is a right to own the kind of arms used by militias. However, lower courts have embraced the "collective" vision of the Second Amendment—the suggestion that the Amendment was about a militia, not individually armed citizens. As a result, they have adopted the corollary that there is no individual right to bear arms, and have upheld all kinds of gun-control measures.

This is probably the right result for the wrong reason. Most gun-control measures do not deprive people of the opportunity to own arms and thus to defend both themselves and, if necessary, their community. As long as the restrictions are measured, they should be permitted. But we should not pretend that the Second Amendment is a dead letter; it is, if nothing else, a powerful reminder that self-government takes many forms.

Part Four

the Lunch Box

NINETEEN

Forty Acres and a Mule

IN PARTS I, II, AND III, we argued for various constitutional rights that give life to the grand idea of popular sovereignty—government of the people, by the people, and for the people. In this concluding part, we argue, more tentatively, for one more set of rights to complete the package.

Over the years, several prominent left-of-center legal scholars—including Harvard law professor Frank Michelman, former Yale law professors Charles Black and Charles Reich, and Georgetown law professor Peter Edelman—have argued that the Constitution confers on citizens the entitlement to a minimal level of material well-being.[1] But right-of-center critics have found this argument implausible as a matter of constitutional law.

The putative right is usually located in the Due Process Clause of the

Fifth and Fourteenth Amendments or the Equal Protection Clause of the Fourteenth. Professor Black also emphasizes the Declaration of Independence's endorsement of the pursuit of happiness. Perhaps scholars have been looking for the right right in the wrong places.

The Due Process Clause speaks of *process,* requiring appropriate procedures before benefits can be denied or punishment imposed, but does not seem to grant *substantive* rights. True, the Supreme Court has cited it as the basis of some rights,[2] but the Court's odd-sounding doctrine of "substantive due process" has been widely ridiculed and largely abandoned (at least outside the context of abortion). Moreover, the clause arguably only limits government's ability to *deprive* rather than obliging government to *provide.* In other words, due process seems to involve more of a "negative" right (government may not take away what you have) than a "positive" right (government must give you what you lack). Likewise, the Equal Protection Clause seems an unpromising refuge for a right to minimal entitlements. It speaks of *equal* protection, yet virtually no one today argues that the state must equalize wealth. Here too, the wording of the clause seems mismatched to the issue at hand. As for the Declaration of Independence, while relevant for ascertaining the mind-set of the Framers, it is not the Constitution.*

As a result of all this, conservatives have long assailed the argument for minimal entitlements as a politically motivated attempt to constitutionalize the welfare state. (President Clinton's plan to nominate Edelman for a federal judgeship was scuttled in large part because of attacks on Edelman's work in this area.[3]) Robert Bork's response to one of Michelman's pieces is typical. Bork insisted that Michelman's argument derived from "social and political sympathies" and amounted to an effort to "create rights by argument from

---

*Professor Black also cites the Preamble's reference to the general welfare. We applaud efforts to take the Preamble seriously, as we ourselves tried to do in Part I. Given that the Preamble's "big idea"—popular sovereignty—foreshadows the big idea behind Article IV's Republican Form of Government Clause, our discussion of that clause later in this chapter can perhaps be seen as extending Professor Black's insight.

moral philosophy rather than from constitutional text, history, and structure."[4]

In approaching the question from a constitutional perspective, we must transcend the "individual rights" conception of the Constitution. If we focus on the collective enterprise choreographed by the Constitution, a stronger basis for the right to minimal entitlements comes into view. That is, the question is not simply what we can do for the poor, but what the poor can do for us. Or, more precisely, what they cannot do for us if they are deprived of even a minimal standard of living: they cannot fulfill the constitutional responsibilities of citizens.

We should never lose sight of the Constitution's animating principle of popular sovereignty. Does not the principle of rule by the People entail realization of the conditions necessary to make such rule possible? The Constitution demands much from the citizenry—it expects them to choose the government's officials, to protect the nation's security, and to help administer the justice system. Can it reasonably make such demands without providing the means to meet them? Is it plausible to depend on citizen voters (an electorate), a citizen military regime (the militia), and citizen judges (juries) without an expectation that citizens will be able to perform these functions? And can these functions be performed by the homeless or hungry?

Some may say that this line of inquiry was implicitly rejected by the Framers. If they regarded minimal material well-being as a necessary condition for the functions expected of citizens, why didn't they directly establish such a right?

But this question is misleading to the extent that it conflates the Framers' principles and their practices. They preached popular sovereignty, but as a practical matter only white males voted, sat on juries, and served in the militia. Over time, America's notion of citizenship has expanded, thus redeeming the promise of true popular sovereignty. Today, we have a far more inclusive sense of who may vote and serve on juries. The question thus arises whether we must supply the conditions that make such a contribution possible. Just as the Constitution protected people's guns so as to ensure an effective militia, so too might it implicitly require government to ensure the material conditions that make the discharge of civic responsibilities possible?* The preface to the Second Amendment declared the militia "necessary to the security of a free State." Could not the same be said of a functioning citizenry generally?

Because people lacking the means of subsistence must devote all of their resources to physical survival, they lack the time, energy, and even will to vote, fight, or judge. Thus, there is a tradition deep in American constitutional history—call it the "Republican Tradition"— recognizing that in order for one truly to be a citizen in a democracy and participate in the democratic process, one needs a minimum amount of independence. Economic independence is necessary if the citizen is to be able to deliberate on the common good, the *res publica* or "thing public."[5]

According to this tradition, the problem with poor people as citizens is that they don't really have wills of their own. We can give them the right to vote, but they will alienate it—selling it to rich people or foreign tyrants or simply staying at home.[6] If they do vote, their ballot is unlikely to reflect anything but naked self-interest (and perhaps not even that, since their landlord's interests may necessarily take precedence); they lack that minimal stake in society sufficient to connect their personal interests with a larger public interest. Because they have no stake in the common venture, only a demagogue like Huey Long, waging a most unrepublican

---

*While the Second Amendment protected only against government confiscation of guns, rather than requiring government to give out guns, in 1789 that was a distinction without a difference; most families owned arms as a matter of course. Indeed, in some states citizens were not simply permitted to carry arms, but legally required to do so. And a Virginia law passed in 1779 (written by Thomas Jefferson) not only required ownership of various weapons, but added that if anyone were too poor to purchase these arms, they would be "procured at the expense of the public." North Carolina and New Hampshire had similar laws. See Stephen P. Halbrook, *A Right To Bear Arms* 30, 56, 74 (Greenwood Press, 1980).

brand of class warfare, is likely to inspire in them a concern about
public affairs.

There are essentially two ways to deal with the fact that in order for a
democracy to work people must have a stake in society. The first way is
the dark side—the exclusionary side—of the republican vision. This
was largely the original American solution: enslave people, ruthlessly
disenfranchise those who lack property, adopt poll taxes and property
qualifications so that only the propertied can vote or serve on juries.[7] Indeed, human slavery was protected by a host of provisions in the original Constitution.[8]

That is not to say that the Framers were of one mind on this point.
After all, Article IV, Section 4 guarantees each state a "Republican
Form of Government," and some Framers, including James Madison,
recognized the tension between republican government and slavery. In
Federalist 43 he notes the problematic status of "those whom the constitution of the State has not admitted to the rights of suffrage"[9] and
leaves no doubt that he is talking about slaves: "an unhappy species
of population abounding in some of the States, who . . . are sunk below
the level of men."[10] As Madison recognized, not just slavery, but also
gross inequality of power among voters, compromises the ideal of republican government. In *Federalist* 39, he observes that the essence of
republican government is "that it be derived from the great body of the
society, not from an inconsiderable portion or a favored class of it."[11]

It is only a short jump from this uncontroversial proposition to recognition that in a stable and healthy republic, economic power should
broadly correspond with the distribution of formal political power. Voters need not possess mathematically identical wealth shares, even as
they possess exactly equal votes, but wild extremes of wealth and
poverty are unrepublican, and should be discouraged. (Madison believed this strongly, and Thomas Jefferson even more so.[12]) This is especially the case for the lower end of the economic spectrum, where
extreme poverty makes it virtually impossible for people to participate
in self-government.

The precise wording of Article IV, Section 4's guarantee of a republican form of government is also suggestive.* This clause does not merely create negative rights against government but imposes an affirmative obligation on it—the United States "*shall* guarantee to every State. . . ." Such a guarantee is arguably unfulfilled when some citizens are too destitute to participate in self-government.

But assuming the original Constitution falls short of protecting a right to minimal income, the situation changed significantly with adoption of the Thirteenth Amendment ("Neither slavery nor involuntary servitude, except as a punishment for crime whereof the party shall have been duly convicted, shall exist within the United States, or any place subject to their jurisdiction"), which abolished slavery. This Amendment explicitly rejects an exclusionary version of republicanism. The solution to the problem of people lacking the independence to be good citizens was no longer to enslave and exclude them from our political processes but to free and include them. The Thirteenth Amendment

---

*Regrettably, today's legal community thinks of Article IV, Section IV as "non-justiciable"—not a basis for action by the courts. This view stems largely from a misreading of the Supreme Court case of *Luther v. Borden*, 48 U.S. (7 How.) 1 (1849). After Dorr's rebellion, a splinter government emerged in Rhode Island, with its own Constitution and claim to legitimacy. The Court was called upon, under the Republican Form of Government Clause, to decide which of the two regimes was the lawful government of Rhode Island. The Court declined, and its ruling has come to stand for the broad proposition that Article IV, Section 4 is non-justiciable. But a narrower reading of the holding makes more sense. Arguably, both regimes met minimal conditions of democratic legitimacy—each was republican. Thus, the real question was akin to the international question of "recognition"—which of the two contending regimes should be recognized as the government? This is precisely the sort of question that should be (and was) left to the political branches, especially since the Senate had to decide which regime's senators to seat. But this does not mean that courts should never decide a case under the Republican Form of Government Clause. Another reason for neglect of this clause stems from post-Civil War politics. In refusing to readmit states that continued to disenfranchise now-free black men following the Civil War, Congress pointed to *Luther* and the Republican Form of Government Clause. President Andrew Johnson's challenge to this exercise of authority helped lead to his impeachment. Seeing what happened to a president who rejected Congress' theory of the Republican Form of Government Clause, the Supreme Court took pains to avoid a showdown of its own with Congress. For in-depth analysis of how both the overly broad reading of *Luther* and the Reconstruction experience have made the clause a non-justiciable hot potato, see Akhil Amar, "The Central Meaning of Republican Government: Popular Sovereignty, Majority Rule, and the Denominator Problem," 65 *Colorado Law Review* 749, pp. 774–76 (1994).

proclaims that We the People will not allow a degraded caste of people in our society. It provides people with inalienable rights in their own persons—the *sine qua non* of the independent citizen expected to contribute to the republic.

It is perhaps here, in the Thirteenth Amendment (building on the Republican Form of Government Clause), not in the Equal Protection or Due Process Clauses, that one locates the strongest source of an entitlement to sustenance and shelter. For it is here that We the People did more than protect all citizens from government deprivation; we affirmatively insisted that government ensure people's freedom even from private enslavement. Under that amendment, certain forms of degradation and deprivation *"shall not exist"* even if they come about purely by means of private forces. Over the years, the vision behind the Thirteenth Amendment has become deradicalized. We have lost sight of the fact that the nation fought a war over slavery, and that the Thirteenth Amendment radically changed the social and economic structure of our society. In going beyond the Constitution's more typical restraints on government action, it pointed the way to an inclusive notion of citizenship.

We need to ask exactly what it means to prohibit slavery. And here we benefit from the fact that the People in the Reconstruction period did not stop at the Thirteenth Amendment. The Fourteenth Amendment straightforwardly declared that all persons born in America—black and white—"are citizens of the United States." This provision, like the Thirteenth Amendment (but unlike the Due Process and Equal Protection Clauses of the Fourteenth Amendment) does not apply only in the face of "state action." Rather, just as the Thirteenth Amendment insists that all Americans be free, the Citizenship Clause of the Fourteenth asserts their status as citizens.[13] This provision, and the Fifteenth Amendment protecting the newly-freed slaves' right to vote, put a new gloss on the Thirteenth Amendment. When the Reconstruction Amendments are viewed as a triptych, a radically different vision of society emerges— one in which former slaves are expected to be full citizens. That recognition sheds light on just what it is the Thirteenth Amendment does when it abolishes slavery. Unless we interpret the amendment to guarantee each American a certain stake in society, have we really set all of our people free—free to be citizens under the Fourteenth Amendment and voters under the Fifteenth?

In saying this, we seek to recapture a nineteenth-century vision, not to impose a twentieth-century vision. Without guaranteeing independence, it would have been futile and dangerous under republican principles to have extended the rights of equal citizenship and equal votes to freed slaves. This is why the Reconstruction reformers did not stop at the Thirteenth Amendment, nor even the Fourteenth and Fifteenth. Thaddeus Stevens and his allies vigorously promoted policies of land redistribution in the South ("forty acres and a mule") and homesteading in the West.

As noted, one could plausibly argue that, even before the Reconstruction Amendments, the theme of popular sovereignty embedded in the Constitution (and exemplified by the Republican Form of Government Clause) required something like forty acres and a mule. How could the citizenry be charged with the task of self-government absent a guarantee that people not live in a state of total deprivation? Following the adoption of the Thirteenth, Fourteenth, and Fifteenth Amendments, this argument achieves a good deal of momentum. The vision underlying these amendments is an inclusive citizenry and an expansive notion of citizenship.

The need to carry out this vision lives on. We have far too many citizens who have no stake in our society. Within walking distance of the White House and the Capitol, where the day-to-day business of the federal government is carried out by our servants, scores of people sleep on grates and panhandle for pennies. These people, and many like them across the country, are citizens in name only. They do not vote, do not serve on juries, do not take up arms to defend their country, and feel no connection to the democracy which technically includes them among its rulers.

Professors Black, Michelman, Reich, and Edelman passionately argue that leaving fellow citizens in such straits is a cruel denial of their dignity and personhood. Equally important, this condition of total dependence contradicts the spirit of the Thirteenth Amendment. The issue transcends cruelty versus compassion. It implicates what our Constitution expects of the citizenry, and the promise to make those expectations realistic.

This conclusion may seem fanciful because economic deprivation bears little resemblance to the chattel slavery of the nineteenth century. After all, if the person who lacks food and shelter is a slave, who is the slaveholder? And even if the government allows people to languish in a condition that mocks the notion that they are citizens, what has government actually done to enslave them? But as the Supreme Court explained in an early Thirteenth Amendment case, "The amendment is not a mere prohibition of state laws establishing or upholding slavery, but an absolute declaration that slavery or involuntary servitude shall not exist in any part of the United States."[14] Or, as the Court put it in a later case, the Thirteenth Amendment "denounces a status or condition, irrespective of the manner or authority by which it is created."[15] The time has come to emancipate the Thirteenth Amendment from the confining paradigm of chattel slavery. Both the letter and spirit of the amendment transcend its initial mission.

Rejecting Michelman's argument favoring a right to minimal entitlements, Judge Bork insisted that recognition of constitutional rights must be "in accordance with an inference whose underlying premise is fairly discoverable in the Constitution itself."[16] We agree. But it may be wrong to suggest that the right to minimal entitlements cannot be inferred from a premise discoverable in the Constitution. We should not overlook the Thirteenth Amendment.

A FEW CLARIFICATIONS are in order. First, ours is not a socialist vision. A regime in which the state controls all resources threatens both individual liberty and true democracy. Quite literally, in such a socialist society, the citizen has no ground of her own on which to stand, to define herself, to participate in self-government, and to resist tyranny.

But an unfettered capitalist system (that fails to require any redistribution, even to those with nothing) also compromises democracy. In that society too, some people lack the independence necessary to make them worthy of the name *citizen*. Yet, the Reconstruction Amendments tell us that they *are* citizens, full citizens. Unless they are entitled to a plot of their own, they arguably remain slaves by another name.

Just as the vision of forty acres and a mule is not socialist, the minimal entitlement is not a dole. It evokes workfare more than welfare. Forty acres and a mule do not yield a harvest without labor, and in the process of laboring, citizens can gain self-respect and the respect of others. Whereas many current welfare programs have created a cycle of dependency, we advocate the minimal level of well-being necessary to promote *independence* and therefore make good citizenship possible. Since land is no longer as plentiful as it was in 1865, a modern translation of forty acres and a mule might be a job-training program or an employment voucher (rather than a something-for-nothing payment).

There are two things, however, that a modern-day version of forty acres and a mule does *not* mean. We are certainly not suggesting that everyone should have an equal amount of material goods. Ours is a vision of Thirteenth Amendment freedom, not Fourteenth Amendment equality. We argue that freedom under the Thirteenth Amendment implies a notion of minimal entitlement, not that equality under the Fourteenth implies equal income or property.

Second, we do not argue that this Thirteenth Amendment vision of forty acres and a mule is enforceable by the courts. Institutional limitations may make the courts unsuited to the task of enforcing a right to minimal entitlements. If a right to a minimal level of income were recognized, how would courts decide the appropriate level? Other determinations would have to be made as well, such as the form of payments, the level of government at which they would be administered, and how the tax burden would be distributed. As Professor Lawrence Sager has observed, these determinations involve "immensely complex questions of social strategy . . . linked to an intricate web of social services, taxes, and economic circumstances."[17] He concludes that courts are ill-equipped to wrestle with such issues, and that giving them the power to do so would usurp the function of the political branches of government.

However, it is wrong to conclude that because X is not enforceable by courts then X cannot be a protected constitutional right. The judiciary is not the only branch of government that must concern itself with constitutional rights. Under the Supremacy Clause, all the branches take oaths to support the Constitution. This point is important, since some resistance to the recognition of a right to minimal entitlements comes from the idea that legislatures, not courts, should be determining issues of this kind.[18]

At the same time, it may be a mistake to think that courts can never compel government to provide certain services. Even under the status quo the government is sometimes required to provide affirmative goods and services, such as counsel and a jury trial to indigent defendants, and food and shelter for prisoners.[19] It may be responded that by arresting and prosecuting an individual, or imprisoning him, the government creates the condition in which the individual finds himself. But this distinction is hardly decisive. The government prosecutes someone and thus forces him to defend himself, so it must provide him with the conditions—a lawyer—that enable him to do so (if he is too poor to afford one). Is that principle more sacred than the notion that the government requires a citizenry that votes and serves on juries, so it must provide the circumstances that enable a citizen to do so (if he is too poor)? Moreover, it is not only prisoners and defendants on whose behalf the government must make expenditures. The Constitution explicitly requires the government to conduct a census and elections, to replenish jury pools, and to take whatever action is necessary to preserve a republican form of government in every state. The Constitution clearly does require the government to take affirmative action (which includes the expenditure of funds) to ensure democracy and promote self-government.

Be all that as it may, we have conceded that the courts may be inadequate to the task of enforcing the vision of forty acres and a mule for every citizen. But it must be remembered that the Thirteenth Amendment does more than declare that slavery and involuntary servitude shall not exist: Section 2 explicitly empowers Congress to enforce the ban.

Perhaps the obligation to eradicate slavery extends beyond government and to the citizenry itself. Unlike virtually every other constitutional provision, the Thirteenth Amendment creates rights against, and thus imposes duties on, private citizens. Even if courts cannot enforce these duties, and even if the legislature chooses not to do so, each of us may have an obligation to help assure our fellow citizens minimal entitlements. We might discharge this obligation in any of a number of ways: for example, by giving our time and money to private programs and intermediate associations (churches, charities, and so on) that seek to provide resources to our fellow citizens. This obligation to be "points of light" is arguably not merely moral but constitutional as well.

The Thirteenth Amendment forced slave-owners to part with their labor force, often their means to prosperity. So too, it may ask us all to pay a price. The price is comparatively small, but the point is much the same: The Thirteenth Amendment commands that all Americans must be free, notwithstanding the need for some sacrifice by those who are already free.

FINALLY, LEST ANYONE claim that we are forcing a twentieth-century vision of a welfare state on an eighteenth-century document (without amending the Constitution to bring it up to speed), we note that the idea of an affirmative government obligation to provide for the welfare of its citizens is not of recent vintage. Passages in the writings of Montesquieu and Rousseau—whose works plainly influenced the Framers—suggest that a republic cannot endure unless citizens are guaranteed material subsistence. Indeed, Thomas Jefferson proposed that his home state of Virginia give each citizen fifty acres of land.[20]

While the original Framers did not explicitly declare an obligation by government to make such provision, the Thirteenth Amendment may have changed the picture. Though on the surface this amendment speaks only of freedom, not of bread, we must look beyond its words to the circumstances and vision underlying it. The Reconstruction amendments sought to make the newly-freed slaves full political citizens in the public realm. Yet given the fact that they owned nothing—not even themselves or the clothes on their back—that meant more than taking away their master's key.

While the Thirteenth Amendment was not a part of the Framers' Constitution, it is very much a part of ours. Today, many Americans, like the newly-freed slaves, own nothing and as a result cannot be true citizens. More than a century after its adoption, we have failed to make good on the vision of the Thirteenth Amendment.

A STRONG CASE can be made that the vision of forty acres and a mule also encompasses a minimal level of education. Beyond doubt, the Framers recognized the connection between self-government and education. Thomas Jefferson, insisting on the link between education and democracy, envisioned massive public education supported by state funding. Both he and James Madison labored mightily to found the University of Virginia, and the first six Presidents all urged the formation of a federal university. And as we have seen in Parts II and III, both the jury and the militia were understood as educational institutions, teaching Americans to be citizens in the process of bringing them together.

This vision did not die with the original Framers. A century later, Thaddeus Stevens, who helped shepherd the Fourteenth Amendment into the constitutional fold, championed public education. In our own century, the Supreme Court in *Brown v. Board of Education* proclaimed that education is "the very foundation of good citizenship."[21]

The American people share this mindset. In 1987, a poll found 84 percent agreeing that the federal government should "require state and local school districts to meet minimum education standards."[22] Most state constitutions require free public schools for every child. And the Supreme Court has acknowledged the role of education in enabling citizens to meet their constitutional responsibilities, noting that "education is necessary to prepare citizens to participate effectively and intelligently in our open political system."[23] Indeed, the Court has acknowledged the "importance of education in maintaining our basic institutions."[24]

However, the Court has been unwilling to translate its rhetoric into a right. In *San Antonio Independent School District v. Rodriguez*,[25] the Court denied the existence of a fundamental right to education. In response to plaintiff's contention that without education the rights to free speech and the vote would necessarily be unfulfilled, the Court said that "we have never presumed to possess either the ability or the authority to guarantee to the citizenry the most effective speech or the most informed electoral choice."[26] But, of course, we are not proposing the *most* effective or the *most* anything—only the minimal level of education that makes real citizenship possible.

The Court did, in fact, make a point of leaving open the possibility of a right to "some identifiable quantum of education" needed to provide "basic minimal skills" necessary for citizens' "full participation in the political process."[27] The Court added that the absolute denial of education might be unconstitutional.

Thus the Court clearly glimpsed the relationship of education to the constitutional scheme and was hesitant—indeed unwilling—to assert that government lacks an obligation to ensure at least minimal education.[28] Why not take the plunge and recognize a right to education? The Court suggested that one good right might deserve another, and where would it all end? Why, after all, stop at education? Why not a right to food and shelter? To which, we reply: why not indeed?

The Court also emphasized the lack of a specific textual basis in the Constitution for the right to education, and added, "[N]or do we find any basis for saying it is implicitly so protected."[29] In dissent, Justice Brennan tried to meet the challenge of finding implicit protection, arguing that "education is inextricably linked to the right to participate in the electoral process and to the rights of free speech and association guaranteed by the First Amendment."[30] As this excerpt suggests, Brennan shied away from arguing for a constitutional right to education *per se,* instead speaking of a fundamental "interest" he finds "linked" to specific constitutional rights. In this respect, he may have shown unnecessary diffidence, resulting from his failure to recognize the Thirteenth Amendment's relevance in the case.

Similarly, one legal scholar who recently argued for recognition of a right to education cited clauses all over the Constitution as the sources of that right, including the Due Process and Privileges and Immunities Clauses of the Fourteenth Amendment, the First Amendment, Ninth Amendment, and International Human Rights Law.[31] As exponents of a holistic reading of the Constitution, we are untroubled by references to multiple clauses as germane to the right to education—the Preamble merits mention as well. But it is a big mistake to neglect the most relevant provisions: the Republican Form of Government Clause, the Thirteenth Amendment, and the Citizenship Clause of the Fourteenth Amendment.

In his dissent in *Rodriguez,* Justice Thurgood Marshall lamented the majority's "unsupportable acquiescence in a system which deprives children . . . of the chance to reach their full potential as citizens."[32] We concur in the sentiment, and would add that it is grounded in the Constitution. The failure to recognize a right to education involves acquiescence in a system that is unrepublican (defying Article IV, Section 4's guarantee of republican government), and that condemns Americans to non-citizenship (contradicting the spirit, if not the letter of the Thirteenth Amendment and the Fourteenth Amendment's Citizenship Clause).

Today, millions of illiterate people need an education, and the rest of us need for them to receive one. John F. Kennedy's famous call that citizens ask not what their country can do for them but what they can do for the country implies a false dichotomy. We need to ask what the country must do for citizens so as to make it possible for the citizenry to run the country. While those championing education for the downtrodden often emphasize the significance of education to a person's economic opportunities, we must not lose sight of the republican side of education: an uneducated citizenry will not prove effective at self-government.[33]

Indeed, our youth must learn not only the "three R's" but "the big C"—Citizenship. Throughout, we have emphasized the interactive nature of American democracy. Plebiscites, juries, and the military all bring together citizens from every corner into a common space to work toward a common goal. Public schools are the ideal place to cultivate the commitment and ability to carry out our collective responsibilities. As the Supreme Court has recognized, in our schools "diverse and conflicting elements in our society are brought together on a broad but common ground . . . inculcating fundamental values necessary to the maintenance of a democratic political system."[34]

In short, our schools must teach students to be sovereign, responsible citizens in a heterogeneous democracy.* This may involve shifting away from individual assignments resulting in individual grades and making greater use of model United Nations, mock juries, and other simulations of democratic deliberation. We do not create better citizens simply by instilling knowledge. We must, in addition, nurture a culture of democracy, and nourish a keen sense that together we own our government and only by acting together can we preserve it.

The "together" part means working collectively, but it also means leaving no one behind. For this reason, recognizing a right to education affirms a commitment to popular sovereignty. *All* the People are supposed to own our government, but that is a mere bromide if some of the People fail to receive an education. Recognizing a right to education would empower the federal government to intervene when states effectively deny the right. (This is not necessarily to oppose the proposed devolution of control of education from the federal government to the states, only to preserve one possible re-

---

*Ironically, this quest underlies the strongest arguments both in favor of and against affirmative action in a university setting. Affirmative action brings young adults from diverse backgrounds together into a dialogue where they learn from one another, enabling the university to serve as a better breeding ground for deliberative democracy. Conversely, race-conscious policies arguably encourage identity politics and thus may actually hinder the long-term prospects of democratic deliberation. In keeping with our overall theme, we think the constitutional debate about affirmative action should focus on these respective claims (in other words, on the effect of affirmative action on self-government) rather than dealing exclusively with competing claims of individual rights.

medial source when local authorities fail to meet their constitutional obligation.)

Again, the goal of making people full citizens is rooted not merely in morality and policy but also in the Constitution, especially in the Republican Form of Government Clause, the Thirteenth Amendment, and the Citizenship Clause of the Fourteenth Amendment, as well as the various clauses empowering the People to vote in elections and serve on juries. And let's not forget the Second Amendment, which prefaces the right to bear arms by declaring it "necessary to the security of a free State." Where preserving a free state is concerned, military hardware is no more important than republican software; citizens need guns less than they need to be armed with some command of history, science, math, and language (as well as skill in deliberating with fellow citizens).

Conclusion

WE ARGUED IN THE INTRODUCTION that individual constitutional clauses should not be analyzed in isolation, because the Constitution is an elegant tapestry rather than a mere hodgepodge of rules. So viewed, many clauses take on an unsuspected significance. The Republican Form of Government Clause and the Thirteenth Amendment are clear examples, but not the only ones. Once we see the Constitution as a carefully woven fabric, even an obscure strand like the Third Amendment can assist our understanding.

We have tried to trace major threads in the constitutional tapestry by showing connections among clauses that are rarely discussed together. Whether or not readers agree with all our claims about particular rights, and long after they have forgotten many of them, we hope they will remember some of the important connections:

- The connection among voters, jurors, and militiamen, each given a direct role in restraining government officials. These roles also involve more specific linkages. For example, participation in elections and jury service both involve the same ultimate act (a vote), and the jury and the military both serve as public spaces where a range of citizens work together on projects crucial to self-government.
- The parallel between the Congress, with its two-tiered structure (House and Senate), and the judiciary, with its two-tiered structure (judge and jury).
- The comparison between the two branches of the judiciary (judge and jury) to illuminate questions about jury selection and the scope of a jury's authority.
- The connections among the Fifteenth, Nineteenth, Twenty-Fourth, and Twenty-Sixth Amendments, each explicitly expanding voting rights and implicitly protecting the right to full political participation.
- The connection between the First Amendment's ban on prior restraints, the Fourth Amendment's provisions governing searches, and the Eighth Amendment's prohibition against unreasonable bail and cruel and unusual punishments, each implying the special role of the jury in restraining government officials.
- The relationship between the Army Clause (conferring a broad national power to raise and use a volunteer force) and the Militia Clause (permitting a far narrower power to conscript citizens through the states).
- The links among the Thirteenth, Fourteenth, and Fifteenth Amendments, the Reconstruction triptych that deepened the Constitution's commitment to popular sovereignty.

There are, of course, many other connections. Some of these we touched on briefly (for example, the Third Amendment's separate ties to both the Second and Fourth Amendments) while others were not relevant to our particular focus. But all of the threads, mentioned and unmentioned, pale next to the brightest and strongest thread in the constitutional tapestry.

We have in mind the word "People," which begins the Constitution and then decorates the Bill of Rights literally from top (in the First Amendment) to bottom (in the Tenth). We have tried to show that this is no linguistic coincidence. Rather, the People who ordained and established the Constitution (in the Preamble) are the same People who may assemble at conventions (First Amendment) and take up arms to protect the nation (Second Amendment). So too, they are the People who enjoy rights other than those named in the document (Ninth and Tenth Amendments).

We take seriously each of the conclusions advanced in this book— the right of the People to amend the Constitution by majority vote, the right to make state law by plebiscite, the right to jury service and its various applications to jury selection, the rights of jury review and nullification, the public's right to a jury trial, the right to sue the state for constitutional violations, the right to military service and its specific application to gays and women, the right to be free from national conscription (absent special or changed circumstances), the right to bear arms, and the rights to property and education. We think these rights deserve respect, and the country is poorer when they are denied. At the same time, we recognize that we could be mistaken with respect to some of these claims.

Thus we consider this book an invitation to readers to continue the conversation that we have tried to nudge forward. But however much our fellow citizens may disagree with some of our specific points, we hope that everyone will agree on the most important point: the Constitution belongs to all of us.

THE CONSTITUTION OF THE
UNITED STATES OF AMERICA

We the People of the United States, in Order to form a more perfect Union, establish Justice, insure domestic Tranquility, provide for the common defence, promote the general Welfare, and secure the Blessings of Liberty to ourselves and our Posterity, do ordain and establish this Constitution for the United States of America.

ARTICLE I

SECTION 1. All legislative Powers herein granted shall be vested in a Congress of the United States, which shall consist of a Senate and House of Representatives.

SECTION 2. The House of Representatives shall be composed of Members chosen every second Year by the People of the several States, and the Electors in each State shall have the Qualifications requisite for Electors of the most numerous Branch of the State Legislature.

No person shall be a Representative who shall not have attained to the Age of twenty-five Years, and been seven Years a Citizen of the United States, and who shall not, when elected, be an Inhabitant of that State in which he shall be chosen.

Representatives and direct Taxes shall be apportioned among the several States which may be included within this Union, according to their respective Numbers which shall be determined by adding to the whole Number of free Persons, including those bound to Service for a Term of Years, and excluding Indians not taxed, three fifths of all other Persons. The actual Enumeration shall be made within three Years after the first Meeting of the Congress of the United States, and within every subsequent Term ten Years, in such Manner as they shall by Law direct. The Number of Representatives shall not exceed one for every thirty Thousand, but each State shall have at Least one Representative; and until such enumeration shall bemade, the State of New Hampshire shall be entitled to chuse three. Massachusetts eight. Rhode-Island and Providence Plantations one, Connecticut five, New-York six, New Jersey four, Pennsylvania eight, Delaware one, Maryland six, Virginia ten, North Carolina five, South Carolina five, and Georgia three.

When vacancies happen in the Representation from any State, the Executive Authority thereof shall issue Writs of Election to fill such Vacancies.

The House of Representatives shall chuse their speaker and other Officers: and shall have the sole Power of Impeachment.

SECTION 3. The Senate of the United States shall be composed of two Senators from each State chosen by the Legislature thereof, for six Years: and each Senator shall have one Vote.

Immediately after they shall be assembled in Consequence of the first Election, they shall be divided as equally as may be into three Classes. The Seats of the Senators of the first Class shall be vacated at the Expiration of the second year, of the second Class at the Expiration of the fourth Year, and of the third Class at the Expiration of the sixth Year, so that one third may be chosen every second Year and if Vacancies happen by Resignation, or otherwise, during the Recess of the Legislature of any State, the Executive thereof may make temporary Appointments until the next Meeting of the Legislature, which shall then fill such Vacancies.

No Person shall be a Senator who shall not have attained to the Age of thirty Years, and been nine Years a Citizen of the United States, and who shall not, when elected, be an Inhabitant of that State for which he shall be chosen.

The Vice President of the United States shall be President of the Senate, but shall have no Vote, unless they be equally divided.

The Senate shall chuse their other Officers, and also a President pro tempore, in the Absence of the Vice President, or when he shall exercise the Office of President of the United States.

The Senate shall have the sole Power to try all Impeachments. When sitting for that Purpose, they shall be on Oath or Affirmation. When the President of the United States is tried, the Chief Justice shall preside: And no Person shall be convicted without the Concurrence of two thirds of the Members present.

Judgment in Cases of Impeachment shall not extend further than to removal from Office, and disqualification to hold and enjoy any Office of honor. Trust or Profit under the United States; but the Party convicted shall nevertheless be liable and subject to Indictment, Trial, Judgment and Punishment, according to Law.

SECTION 4. The Times, Places and Manner of holding Elections for Senators and Representatives, shall be prescribed in each State by the Legislature thereof; but the Congress may at any time by law make or alter such Regulations, except as to the Places of chusing Senators.

The Congress shall assemble at least once in every Year, and such Meeting shall be on the first Monday in December, unless they shall by Law appoint a different Day.

SECTION 5. Each House shall be the Judge of the Elections, Returns and Qualifications of its own Members, and a Majority of each shall constitute a Quorum to do Business; but a smaller Number may adjourn from day to day, and may be authorized to compel the Attendance of absent Members, in such Manner, and under such Penalties as each House may provide.

Each House may determine the Rules of its Proceedings, punish its Members for disorderly Behaviour, and with the Concurrence of two thirds, expel a Member.

Each House shall keep a journal of its Proceedings, and from time to time publish the same, excepting such Parts as may in their judgment require Secrecy; and the Yeas and Nays of the Members of either House on any question shall, at the Desire of one fifth of those present, be entered on the Journal.

Neither House, during the Session of Congress, shall, without the Consent of the other, adjourn for more than three days, nor to any other Place than that in which the two Houses shall be sitting.

SECTION 6. The Senators and Representatives shall receive a Compensation for their Services, to be ascertained by Law, and paid out of the Treasury of the United States. They shall in all Cases, except Treason, Felony and Breach of the Peace, be privileged from Arrest during their Attendance at the Session of their respective Houses, and in going to and returning from the same; and for any Speech or Debate in either House, they shall not be questioned in any other Place.

No Senator or Representative shall, during the Time for which he was elected, be appointed to any civil Office under the Authority of the United States, which shall have been created, or the Emoluments whereof shall have been increased during such time; and no Person holding any Office under the United States, shall be a Member of either House during his Continuance in Office.

SECTION 7. All Bills for raising Revenue shall originate in the House of Representatives; but the Senate may propose or concur with Amendments as on other Bills.

Every Bill which shall have passed the House of Representatives and the Senate, shall, before it become a Law, be presented to the President of the United States; if he approves he shall sign it, but if not he shall return it, with his Objections to that House in which it shall have originated, who shall enter the Objections at large on their journal, and proceed to reconsider it. If after such Reconsideration two thirds of that House shall agree to pass the Bill, it shall be sent, together with the Objections, to the other House, by which it shall likewise be reconsidered, and if approved by two thirds of that House, it shall become a Law. But in all such Cases the Votes of both Houses shall be determined by yeas and Nays, and the Names of the Persons voting for and against the Bill shall be entered on the Journal of each House respectively. If any Bill shall not be returned by the President within ten Days (Sundays excepted) after it shall have been presented to him, the Same shall be a Law, in like Manner as if he had signed it, unless the Congress by their Adjournment prevent its Return, in which Case it shall not be a Law.

Every Order, Resolution, or Vote to which the Concurrence of the Senate and House of Representatives may be necessary (except on a question of Adjournment) shall be presented to the President of the United States; and before the Same shall take Effect, shall be approved by him, or being disapproved by him, shall be repassed by two thirds of the Senate and House of Representatives, according to the Rules and Limitations prescribed in the Case of a Bill.

SECTION 8. The Congress shall have Power To lay and collect Taxes, Duties, Imposts and Excises, to pay the Debts and provide for the common Defense and general Welfare of the United States; but all Duties, Imposts and Excises shall be uniform throughout the United States:

To borrow Money on the credit of the United States:

To regulate Commerce with foreign Nations, and among the several States, and with the Indian Tribes;

To establish a uniform Rule of Naturalization, and uniform Laws on the subject of Bankruptcies throughout the United States;

To coin Money, regulate the Value thereof, and of foreign Coin, and fix the Standard of Weights and Measures;

To provide for the Punishment of counterfeiting the Securities and current Coin of the United States;

To establish Post Offices and post Roads;

To promote the Progress of Science and useful Arts, by securing for limited Times to Authors and Inventors the exclusive Right to their respective Writings and Discoveries;

To constitute Tribunals inferior to the supreme Court;

To define and punish Piracies and Felonies committed on the high Seas, and Offences against the Law of Nations;

To declare War, grant Letters of Marque and Reprisal, and make Rules concerning Captures on Land and Water;

To raise and support Armies, but no Appropriation of Money to that Use shall be for a longer Term than two Years;

To provide and maintain a Navy;

To make Rules for the Government and Regulation of the land and naval Forces;

To provide for calling forth the Militia to execute the Laws of the Union, suppress Insurrections and repel Invasions;

To provide for organizing, arming, and disciplining, the Militia, and for governing such Part of them as may be employed in the Service of the United States, reserving to the States respectively, the Appointment of the Officers, and the Authority of training the Militia according to the discipline prescribed by Congress;

To exercise exclusive Legislation in all Cases whatsoever, over such District (not exceeding ten Miles square) as may, by Cession of particular States, and the Acceptance of Congress, become the Seat of the Government of the United States, and to exercise like Authority over all Places purchased by the Consent of the Legislature of the State in which the Same shall be for the Erection of Forts, Magazines, Arsenals, dock-Yards, and other needful Buildings;—And

To make all Laws which shall be necessary and proper for carrying into Execution the foregoing Powers, and all other Powers vested by this Constitution in the Government of the United States, or in any Department or Officer thereof.

SECTION 9. The Migration or Importation of such Persons as any of the States now existing shall think proper to admit, shall not be prohibited by the Congress prior to the Year one thousand eight hundred and eight, but a Tax or duty may be imposed on such Importation, not exceeding ten dollars for each Person.

The Privilege of the Writ of Habeas Corpus shall not be suspended, unless when in Cases of Rebellion or Invasion the public Safety may require it.

No Bill of Attainder or ex post facto Law shall be passed.

No Capitation, or other direct, Tax shall be laid, unless in Proportion to the Census or Enumeration herein before directed to be taken.

No Tax or Duty shall be laid on Articles exported from any State.

No Preference shall be given by any Regulation of Commerce or Revenue to the Ports of one State over those of another; nor shall Vessels bound to, or from, one State, be obliged to enter, clear, or pay Duties in another.

No Money shall be drawn from the Treasury, but in Consequence of Appropriations made by Law; and a regular Statement and Account of the Receipts and Expenditures of all public Money shall be published from time to time.

No Title of Nobility shall be granted by the United States: And no Person holding any Office of Profit or Trust under them, shall, without the Consent of the Congress, accept of any present, Emolument, Office, or Title, of any kind whatever, from any King, Prince, or foreign State.

SECTION 10. No state shall enter into any Treaty, Alliance, or Confederation; grant Letters of Marque and Reprisal; coin Money; emit Bills of Credit; make any Thing but gold and silver Coin a Tender in Payment of Debts; pass any Bill of Attainder, ex post facto Law, or Law impairing the Obligation of Contracts, or grant any Title of Nobility.

No State shall, without the Consent of the Congress, lay any Imposts or Duties on Imports or Exports, except what may be absolutely necessary for executing its inspection Laws: and the net Produce of all Duties and Imposts, laid by any State on Imports or Exports, shall be for the Use of the Treasury of the United States, and all such Laws shall be subject to the Revision and Controul of the Congress.

No State shall, without the Consent of Congress, lay any Duty of Tonnage, keep Troops, or Ships of War in time of Peace, enter into any Agreement or Compact with another State, or with a foreign Power, or engage in War, unless actually invaded, or in such imminent Danger as will not admit of delay.

ARTICLE II

SECTION 1. The executive Power shall be vested in a President of the United States of America. He shall hold his Office during the Term of four Years, and, together with the Vice President, chosen for the same Term, be elected as follows.

Each State shall appoint, in such Manner as the Legislature thereof may direct, a Number of Electors, equal to the whole Number of Senators and Representatives to which the State may be entitled in the Congress; but no Senator or Representative, or Person holding an Office of Trust of Profit under the United States, shall be appointed an Elector.

The Electors shall meet in their respective States, and vote by Ballot for two Persons, of whom one at least shall not be an Inhabitant of the same State with themselves. And they shall make a List of all the Persons voted for, and, of the Number of Votes for each; which List they shall sign and certify, and transmit sealed to the Seat of the Government of the United States, directed to the President of the Senate. The President of the Senate shall, in the Presence of the Senate and House of Representatives, open all the Certificates, and the Votes shall then be counted. The Person having the greatest Number of Votes shall be the President, if such Number be a Majority of the whole Number of Electors appointed; and if there be more than one who have such Majority, and have an equal Number of Votes, then the House of Representatives shall immediately chuse by Ballot one of them for President; and if no Person have a Majority, then from the five highest on the List the said House shall in like Manner chuse the President. But in chusing the President, the Votes shall be taken by States, the Representation from each State having one Vote; A quorum for this Purpose shall consist of a Member or Members from two thirds of the States, and a Majority of all the States shall be necessary to a Choice. In every Case, after the Choice of the President, the Person having the greatest Number of Votes of the Electors shall be the Vice President. But if there should remain two or more who have equal Votes, the Senate shall chuse from them by Ballot the Vice President.

The Congress may determine the Time of chusing the Electors, and the Day on which they shall give their Votes; which Day shall be the same throughout the United States.

No Person except a natural born Citizen, or a Citizen of the United States, at the time of the Adoption of this Constitution, shall be eligible to the Office of President; neither shall any Person be eligible to that Office who shall not have attained to the Age of thirty five Years, and been fourteen Years a Resident within the United States.

In Case of the Removal of the President from Office, or of his Death, Resignation, or Inability to discharge the Powers and Duties of the said Office, the Same shall devolve on the Vice President, and the Congress may by Law provide for the Case of Removal, Death, Resignation or Inability, both of the President and Vice President, declaring what Officer shall then act as President, and such Officer shall act accordingly, until the Disability be removed, or a President shall be elected.

The President shall, at stated Times, receive for his Services, a Compensation, which shall neither be encreased nor diminished during the Period for which he shall have been elected, and he shall not receive within that Period any other Emolument from the United States, or any of them.

Before he enter on the Execution of his Office, he shall take the following Oath or Affirmation—"I do solemnly swear (or affirm) that I will faithfully execute the Office of President of the United States, and will to the best of my Ability, preserve, protect and defend the Constitution of the United States."

SECTION 2. The President shall be Commander in Chief of the Army, and Navy of the United States, and of the Militia of the several States, when called into the actual Service of the United States; he may require the Opinion, in writing, of the principal Officer in each of the executive Departments, upon any Subject relating to the Duties of their respective Offices, and he shall have Power to grant Reprieves and Pardons for Offences against the United States, except in Cases of Impeachment.

He shall have Power, by and with the Advice and Consent of the Senate, to make Treaties, provided two thirds of the Senators present concur; and he shall nominate, and by and with the Advice and Consent of the Senate, shall appoint Ambassadors, other public Ministers and Consuls, Judges of the supreme Court, and all other Officers of the United States, whose Appointments are not herein otherwise provided for, and which shall be established by Law: but the Congress may by Law vest the Appointment of such inferior Officers, as they think proper, in the President alone, in the Courts of Law, or in the Heads of Departments.

The President shall have Power to fill up all Vacancies that may happen during the Recess of the Senate, by granting Commissions which shall expire at the end of their next Session.

SECTION 3. He shall from time to time give to the Congress Information of the State of the Union, and recommend to their Consideration such Measures as he shall judge necessary and expedient; he may, on extraordinary Occasions, convene both Houses, or either of them, and in Case of Disagreement between them, with Respect to the Time of Adjournment, he may adjourn them to such Time as he shall think proper; he shall receive Ambassadors and other public Ministers; he shall take Care that the Laws be faithfully executed, and shall Commission all the Officers of the United States.

SECTION 4. The President Vice President and all civil Officers of the United States, shall be removed from Office on Impeachment for, and Conviction of, Treason, Bribery, or other high Crimes and Misdemeanors.

ARTICLE III

SECTION 1. The judicial Power of the United States, shall be vested in one supreme Court, and in such inferior Courts as the Congress may from time to time ordain and establish. The Judges, both of the supreme and inferior Courts, shall hold their Offices during good Behaviour, and shall, at stated Times, receive for their Services, a Compensation, which shall not be diminished during their Continuance in Office.

SECTION 2. The judicial Power shall extend to all Cases, in Law and Equity, arising under this Constitution, the Laws of the United States, and Treaties made, or which shall be made, under their Authority;—to all Cases affecting Ambassadors, other public Ministers and Consuls;—to all Cases of admiralty and maritime Jurisdiction;—to Controversies to which the United States shall be a Party;—to Controversies between two or more States;—between a State and Citizens of another State;—between Citizens of different States,—between Citizens of the same State claiming Lands under Grants of different States,—and between a State, or the Citizens thereof, and foreign States, Citizens of Subjects.

In all Cases affecting Ambassadors, other public Ministers and Consuls, and those in which a State shall be Party, the supreme Court shall have original Jurisdiction. In all the other Cases before mentioned, the supreme Court shall have appellate Jurisdiction, both as to Law and Fact, with such Exceptions, and under such Regulations as the Congress shall make.

The Trial of all Crimes, except in Cases of Impeachment, shall be by Jury; and such Trial shall be held in the State where the said Crimes shall have been committed; but when not committed within any State, the Trial shall be at such Place or Places as the Congress may by Law have directed.

SECTION 3. Treason against the United States, shall consist only in levying War against them, or in adhering to their Enemies, giving them Aid and Comfort. No Person shall be convicted of Treason unless on the Testimony of two Witnesses to the same overt Act, or on Confession in open Court.

The Congress shall have Power to declare the Punishment of Treason, but no Attainder of Treason shall work Corruption of Blood, or Forfeiture except during the Life of the Person attainted.

ARTICLE IV

SECTION 1. Full Faith and Credit shall be given in each State to the public Acts, Records, and judicial Proceedings of every other State. And the

Congress may by general Laws prescribe the Manner in which such Acts, Records and Proceedings shall be proved, and the Effect thereof.

SECTION 2. The Citizens of each State shall be entitled to all Privileges and Immunities of Citizens in the several States.

A Person charged in any State with Treason, Felony, or other Crime, who shall flee from Justice, and be found in another State, shall on Demand of the executive Authority of the State from which he fled, be delivered up, to be removed to the State having Jurisdiction of the Crime.

No Person held to Service or Labour in one State under the Laws thereof, escaping into another, shall, in Consequence of any Law or Regulation therein, be discharged from such Service or Labour, but shall be delivered up on Claim of the Party to whom such Service or Labour may be due.

SECTION 3. New States may be admitted by the Congress into this Union; but no new State shall be formed or erected within the Jurisdiction of any other State; nor any State be formed by the Junction of two or more States, or Parts of States, without the Consent of the Legislatures of the States concerned as well as of the Congress.

The Congress shall have Power to dispose of and make all needful Rules and Regulations respecting the Territory or other Property belonging to the United States; and nothing in this Constitution shall be so construed as to Prejudice any Claims of the United States, or of any particular State.

SECTION 4. The United States shall guarantee to every State in this Union a Republican Form of Government, and shall protect each of them against Invasion, and on Application of the Legislature, or of the Executive (when the Legislature cannot be convened) against domestic Violence.

ARTICLE V

The Congress, whenever two thirds of both Houses shall deem it necessary, shall propose Amendments to this Constitution, or, on the

Application of the Legislatures of two thirds of the several States, shall call a Convention for proposing Amendments, which, in either Case, shall be valid to all Intents and Purposes, as Part of this Constitution, when ratified by the Legislatures of three fourths of the several States, or by Conventions in three fourths thereof, as the one or the other Mode of Ratification may be proposed by the Congress; Provided that no Amendment which may be made prior to the Year One thousand eight hundred and eight shall in any Manner affect the first and fourth Clauses in the Ninth Section of the first Article; and that no State, without its Consent, shall be deprived of its equal Suffrage in the Senate.

ARTICLE VI

All Debts contracted and Engagements entered into, before the Adoption of this Constitution, shall be as valid against the United States under this Constitution, as under the Confederation.

This Constitution, and the laws of the United States which shall be made in Pursuance thereof; and all Treaties made, or which shall be made, under the Authority of the United States, shall be the supreme Law of the Land; and the Judges in every State shall be bound thereby, any Thing in the Constitution or Laws of any State to the Contrary notwithstanding.

The Senators and Representatives before mentioned, and the Members of the several State Legislatures, and all executive and judicial Officers, both of the United States and of the several States, shall be bound by Oath or Affirmation, to support this Constitution; but no religious Test shall ever be required as a Qualification to any Office or public Trust under the United States.

ARTICLE VII

The Ratification of the Conventions of nine States, shall be sufficient for the Establishment of this Constitution between the States so ratifying the Same.

Done in Convention by the Unanimous Consent of the States present the Seventeenth Day of September in the Year of our Lord one thousand seven hundred and Eighty seven and of the Independence of the United States of America the Twelfth, in witness whereof we have hereunto subscribed our Names.

Geo. Washington
Presid't. and deputy from Virginia

Attest
WILLIAM JACKSON
Secretary

DELAWARE
Geo. Read
Gunning Bedford jun
John Dickinson
Richard Bassett
Jaco. Brom

MASSACHUSETTS
Nathaniel Gorham
Rufus King

CONNECTICUT
Wm. Saml. Johnson
Roger Sherman

NEW YORK
Alexander Hamilton

NEW JERSEY
Wil. Livingston
David Brearley
Wm. Paterson
Jona. Dayton

PENNSYLVANIA
B Franklin
Thomas Mifflin
Robt. Morris
Geo. Clymer
Thos. FitzSimons
Jared Ingersoll
James Wilson
Gouv Morris

NEW HAMPSHIRE
John Langdon
Nicholas Gilman

MARYLAND
James McHenry
Dan of St. Thos. Jenifer
Danl. Carroll

VIRGINIA
John Blair
James Madison Jr.

NORTH CAROLINA
Wm. Blount
Richd. Dobbs Spaight
Hu Williamson

SOUTH CAROLINA
J. Rutledge
Charles Cotesworth Pinckney
Charles Pinckney
Pierce Butler

GEORGIA
William Few
Abr Baldwin

Articles in addition to, and amendment of the Constitution of the United States of America, proposed by Congress and ratified by the Legislatures of the several states, pursuant to the Fifth Article of the original Constitution.

(The first ten amendments were passed by Congress on September 25, 1789, and were ratified on December 15, 1791.)

Amendment I

Congress shall make no law respecting an establishment of religion, or prohibiting the free exercise thereof; or abridging the freedom of speech, or of the press; or the right of the people peaceably to assemble, and to petition the Government for a redress of grievances.

Amendment II

A well regulated Militia, being necessary to the security of a free State, the right of the people to keep and bear Arms, shall not be infringed.

Amendment III

No Soldier shall, in time of peace be quartered in any house, without the consent of the Owner, nor in time of war, but in a manner to be prescribed by law.

Amendment IV

The right of the people to be secure in their persons, houses, papers, and effects, against unreasonable searches and seizures, shall not be violated, and no warrants shall issue, but upon probable cause, supported by Oath or affirmation, and particularly describing the place to be searched, and the persons or things to be seized.

Amendment V

No person shall be held to answer for a capital, or otherwise infamous crime, unless on a presentment or indictment of a Grand Jury, except in cases arising in the land or naval forces, or in the Militia, when in actual service in time of War or public danger; nor shall any person be subject for the same offence to be twice put in jeopardy of life or limb; nor shall be compelled in any criminal case to be a witness against himself, nor be deprived of life, liberty, or property, without due process of law; nor shall private property be taken for public use, without just compensation.

Amendment VI

In all criminal prosecutions, the accused shall enjoy the right to a speedy and public trial, by an impartial jury of the State and district wherein the crime shall have been committed, which district shall have been previously ascertained by law, and to be informed of the nature and cause of the accusation; to be confronted with the witnesses against him; to have compulsory process for obtaining witnesses in his favor, and to have the assistance of counsel for his defence.

Amendment VII

In Suits at common law, where the value in controversy shall exceed twenty dollars, the right of trial by jury shall be preserved, and no fact tried by a jury, shall be otherwise re-examined in any Court of the United States, than according to the rules of the common law.

Amendment VIII

Excessive bail shall not be required, nor excessive fines imposed, nor cruel and unusual punishments inflicted.

Amendment IX

The enumeration in the Constitution, of certain rights, shall not be construed to deny or disparage others retained by the people.

Amendment X

The powers not delegated to the United States by the Constitution, nor prohibited by it to the States, are reserved to the States respectively, or to the people.

Amendment XI *(Ratified on February 7, 1795)*

The Judicial power of the United States shall not be construed to extend to any suit in law or equity, commenced or prosecuted against one of the United States by Citizens of another State, or by Citizens or Subjects of any Foreign State.

Amendment XII *(Ratified on June 15, 1804)*

The Electors shall meet in their respective states, and vote by ballot for President and Vice-President, one of whom, at least, shall not be an inhabitant of the same state with themselves; they shall name in their ballots the person voted for as President, and in distinct ballots the person voted for as Vice-President, and they shall make distinct lists of all persons voted for as President, and of all persons voted for as Vice-President, and of the number of votes for each, which lists they shall sign and certify, and transmit sealed to the seat of the government of the United States, directed to the President of the Senate;—The President of the Senate shall, in the presence of the Senate and House of Representatives, open all the certificates and the votes shall then be counted;—The person having the greatest number of votes for President, shall be the President, if such number be a majority of the whole number of Electors appointed; and if no person have such majority; then from the persons having the highest numbers not exceeding three on the list of those voted for as President, the House of Representatives shall choose immediately, by ballot, the President. But in choosing the President, the votes shall be taken by states, the representation from each state having one vote; a quorum for this purpose shall consist of a member or members from two-thirds of the states, and a majority of all the states shall be necessary to a choice. And if the House of Representatives shall not choose a President whenever the right of choice shall devolve upon them, before the fourth day of March next following, then the Vice-President shall act as President, as in the case of the death or other constitutional disability of the President.—The person having the greatest number of votes as Vice-President, shall be the Vice-President, if such number be a majority of the whole number of Electors appointed, and if no person have a majority, then from the two highest numbers on the list, the Senate shall choose the Vice-President; a quorum for the purpose shall consist of two-thirds of the whole number of Senators, and a majority of the whole number shall be necessary to a choice. But no person constitutionally ineligible to the office of President shall be eligible to that of Vice-President of the United States.

Amendment XIII *(Ratified on December 6, 1865)*
Section 1. Neither slavery nor involuntary servitude, except as a punishment for crime whereof the party shall have been duly convicted, shall exist within the United States, or any place subject to their jurisdiction.

Section 2. Congress shall have power to enforce this article by appropriate legislation.

Amendment XIV *(Ratified on July 9, 1868)*
Section 1. All persons born or naturalized in the United States, and subject to the jurisdiction thereof, are citizens of the United States and of the State wherein they reside. No State shall make or enforce any law which shall abridge the privileges or immunities of citizens of the United States: nor shall any State deprive any person of life, liberty, or property, without due process of law; nor deny to any person within its jurisdiction the equal protection of the laws.

Section 2. Representatives shall be apportioned among the several States according to their respective numbers, counting the whole number of persons in each State, excluding Indians not taxed. But when the right to vote at any election for the choice of electors for President and Vice President of the United States, Representatives in Congress, the Executive and Judicial officers of a State, or the members of the Legislature thereof, is denied to any of the male inhabitants of such State, being twenty-one years of age, and citizens of the United States, or in any way abridged, except for participation in rebellion, or other crime, the basis of representation therein shall be reduced in the proportion which the number of such male citizens shall bear to the whole number of male citizens twenty-one years of age in such State.

Section 3. No person shall be a Senator or Representative in Congress, or elector of President and Vice President, or hold any office, civil or military, under the United States, or under any State, who, having previously taken an oath, as a member of Congress, or as an officer of the United States, or as a member of any State legislature, or as an executive or judicial officer of any State, to support the Constitution of the United States, shall have engaged in insurrection or rebellion against the same, or given aid or comfort to the enemies thereof. But Congress may by a vote of two-thirds of each House, remove such disability.

Section 4. The validity of the public debt of the United States, authorized by law, including debts incurred for payment of pensions and bounties for services in suppressing insurrection or rebellion, shall not be questioned. But neither the United States nor any State shall assume or pay any debt or obligation incurred in aid of insurrection or rebellion against the United States, or any claim for the loss or emancipation of any slave, but all such debts, obligations and claims shall be held illegal and void.

Section 5. The Congress shall have power to enforce, by appropriate legislation, the provisions of this article.

Amendment XV *(Ratified on February 3, 1870)*
Section 1. The right of citizens of the United States to vote shall not be denied or abridged by the United States or by any State on account of race, color, or previous condition of servitude.

Section 2. The Congress shall have power to enforce this article by appropriate legislation.

Amendment XVI *(Ratified on February 3, 1913)*
The Congress shall have power to lay and collect taxes on incomes, from whatever source derived, without apportionment among the several States, and without regard to any census or enumeration.

Amendment XVII *(Ratified on April 8, 1913)*

The Senate of the United States shall be composed of two Senators from each State, elected by the people thereof, for six years; and each Senator shall have one vote. The electors in each State shall have the qualifications requisite for electors of the most numerous branch of the State legislatures.

When vacancies happen in the representation of any State in the Senate, the executive authority of such State shall issue writs of election to fill such vacancies: *Provided,* That the legislature of any State may empower the executive thereof to make temporary appointments until the people fill the vacancies by election as the legislature may direct.

This amendment shall not be so construed as to affect the election or term of any Senator chosen before it becomes valid as part of the Constitution.

Amendment XVIII *(Ratified on January 16, 1919)*

Section 1. After one year from the ratification of this article the manufacture, sale, or transportation of intoxicating liquors within, the importation thereof into, or the exportation thereof from the United States and all territory subject to the jurisdiction thereof for beverage purposes is hereby prohibited.

Section 2. The Congress and the several States shall have concurrent power to enforce this article by appropriate legislation.

Section 3. This article shall be inoperative unless it shall have been ratified as an amendment to the Constitution by the legislatures of the several States, as provided in the Constitution, within seven years from the date of the submission hereof to the States by the Congress.

Amendment XIX *(Ratified on August 18, 1920)*

The right of citizens of the United States to vote shall not be denied or abridged by the United States or by any State on account of sex.

Congress shall have power to enforce this article by appropriate legislation.

Amendment XX *(Ratified on February 6, 1933)*

Section 1. The terms of the President and Vice President shall end at noon on the 20th day of January, and the terms of Senators and Representatives at noon on the 3d day of January, of the years in which such terms would have ended if this article had not been ratified; and the terms of their successors shall then begin.

Section 2. The Congress shall assemble at least once in every year, and such meeting shall begin at noon on the 3d day of January, unless they shall by law appoint a different day.

Section 3. If, at the time fixed for the beginning of the term of the President, the President elect shall have died, the Vice President elect shall become President. If a President shall not have been chosen before the time fixed for the beginning of his term, or if the President elect shall have failed to qualify, then the Vice President elect shall act as President until a President shall have qualified; and the Congress may by law provide for the case wherein neither a President elect nor a Vice President elect shall have qualified, declaring who shall then act as President, or the manner in which one who is to act shall be selected, and such person shall act accordingly until a President or Vice President shall have qualified.

Section 4. The Congress may by law provide for the case of the death of any of the persons from whom the House of Representatives may choose a President whenever the rights of choice shall have devolved upon them, and for the case of the death of any of the persons from whom the Senate may choose a Vice President whenever the right of choice shall have devolved upon them.

Section 5. Sections 1 and 2 shall take effect on the 15th day of October following the ratification of this article.

Section 6. This article shall be inoperative unless it shall have been ratified as an amendment to the Constitution by the legislatures of three-fourths of the several States within seven years from the date of its submission.

Amendment XXI *(Ratified on December 5, 1933)*

Section 1. The eighteenth article of amendment to the Constitution of the United States is hereby repealed.

Section 2. The transportation or importation into any State, Territory, or possession of the United States for delivery or use therein of intoxicating liquors, in violation of the laws thereof, is hereby prohibited.

Section 3. This article shall be inoperative unless it shall have been ratified as an amendment to the Constitution by conventions in the several States, as provided in the Constitution, within seven years from the date of the submission hereof to the States by the Congress.

Amendment XXII *(Ratified on February 27, 1951)*

No person shall be elected to the office of the President more than twice, and no person who has held the office of President, or acted as President, for more than two years of a term to which some other person was elected President shall be elected to the office of the President more than once. But this Article shall not apply to any person holding the office of President when this Article was proposed by the Congress, and shall not prevent any person who may be holding the office of President, or acting as President, during the term within which this Article becomes operative from holding the office of President or acting as President during the remainder of such term.

Amendment XXIII *(Ratified on March 29, 1961)*

Section 1. The District constituting the seat of Government of the United States shall appoint in such manner as the Congress may direct:

A number of electors of President and Vice President equal to the whole number of Senators and Representatives in Congress to which the District would be entitled if it were a State, but in no event more than the least populous State; they shall be in addition to those appointed by the States, but they shall be considered, for the purposes of the election of President and Vice President, to be electors appointed by a State; and they shall meet in the District and perform such duties as provided by the twelfth article of amendment.

Section 2. The Congress shall have power to enforce this article by appropriate legislation.

Amendment XXIV *(Ratified on January 23, 1964)*

Section 1. The right of citizens of the United States to vote in any primary or other election for President or Vice President, for electors for President or Vice President, or for Senator or Representative in Congress, shall not be denied or abridged by the United States or any State by reason of failure to pay any poll tax or other tax.

Section 2. The Congress shall have power to enforce this article by appropriate legislation.

Amendment XXV *(Ratified on February 10, 1967)*

Section 1. In case of the removal of the President from office or of his death or resignation, the Vice President shall become President.

Section 2. Whenever there is a vacancy in the office of the Vice President, the President shall nominate a Vice President who shall take office upon confirmation by a majority vote of both Houses of Congress.

Section 3. Whenever the President transmits to the President pro tempore of the Senate and the Speaker of the House of Representatives his written declaration that he is unable to discharge the powers and duties of his office, and until he transmits to them a written declaration to the contrary, such powers and duties shall be discharged by the Vice President as Acting President.

Section 4. Whenever the Vice President and a majority of either the principal officers of the executive departments or of such other body as Congress may by law provide, transmit to the President pro tempore of the Senate and the Speaker of the House of Representatives their written declaration that the President is unable to discharge the powers and duties of his office, the Vice President shall immediately assume the powers and duties of the office as Acting President.

Thereafter, when the President transmits to the President pro tempore of the Senate and the Speaker of the House of Representatives his written declaration that no inability exists, he shall resume the powers and duties of his office unless the Vice President and a majority of either the principal officers of the executive department or of such other body as Congress may by law provide, transmit within four days to the President pro tempore of the Senate and the Speaker of the House of Representatives their written declaration that the President is unable to discharge the powers and duties of his office. Thereupon Congress shall decide the issue, assembling within forty-eight hours for that purpose if not in session. If the Congress, within twenty-one days after receipt of the latter written declaration, or, if Congress is not in session, within twenty-one days after Congress is required to assemble, determines by two-thirds vote of both Houses that the President is unable to discharge the powers and duties of his office, the Vice President shall continue to discharge the same as Acting President; otherwise, the President shall resume the powers and duties of his office.

Amendment XXVI *(Ratified on July 1, 1971)*
Section 1. The right of citizens of the United States, who are eighteen years of age or older, to vote shall not be denied or abridged by the United States or by any State on account of age.

Section 2. The Congress shall have power to enforce this article by appropriate legislation.

Amendment XXVII *(Ratified on May 7, 1992)*
No law varying the compensation for the services of Senators and Representatives shall take effect until an election of Representatives shall have intervened.

Endnotes

INTRODUCTION

1. In a *Washington Post*-ABC poll in the summer of 1994, 83 percent of respondents claimed that most members of Congress care more about special interests than about ordinary constituents. Eighty-three percent also said that members of Congress care more about keeping power than about the best interests of the nation, and 78 percent opined that newly-elected members of Congress quickly lose touch with the people. See *The Hotline* (available on Nexis), July 5, 1994.

2. *The Federalist Papers* No. 51, p. 323 (Clinton Rossiter, ed., New American Library, 1961).

3. *Selective Draft Law Cases*, 245 U.S. 366 (1918).

4. *United States v. Butler*, 297 U.S. 1, 62 (1936).

5. We do not wish to overstate our intended contribution. We stand on

the shoulders of giants, especially former Yale Law School professor Charles Black. In a classic work on constitutional interpretation, Black argued that some constitutional issues can best be resolved by looking not at individual clauses but at the structure of the Constitution and the government it creates—the relationship of parts to one another and to the whole. See Charles L. Black, Jr. *Structure and Relationship in Constitutional Law* (Louisiana State University Press, 1969).

6.   Thus, for example, leading conservative theorist Robert Bork believes that discerning the Framers' intent is the decisive task in most cases involving the Constitution, whereas leading liberal theorist Ronald Dworkin considers Framers' intent irrelevant in many cases. See Robert Bork, *The Tempting of America* (The Free Press, 1990); Ronald Dworkin, *Freedom's Law* (Harvard University Press, 1996). By and large, Bork is revered by conservatives and reviled by liberals, with Dworkin eliciting the opposite response.

CHAPTER 1

1.   For example, a Harris Poll conducted in 1987 showed that 75 percent of Americans favored the proposed Equal Rights Amendment. See Ellen Creager, "ERA is Back," *Chicago Tribune*, March 5, 1989, p. C8. The amendment was proposed by the requisite two houses of Congress, but was not ratified by the requisite three-fourths of the states.

2.   Max Farrand, ed., *The Records of the Federal Convention of 1787* (Yale University Press, 1937), volume 2, p. 476.

3.   *The Federalist Papers* No. 78, p. 469 (Clinton Rossiter ed., New American Library, 1961).

4.   Jonathan Elliot, *The Debates in the Several State Conventions on the Adoption of the Federal Constitution* (J.B. Lippincott & Co., 1881), volume 2, p. 434.

5.   Ibid., pp. 434–35 (emphasis in original).

6.   See Elliot, *Debates*, volume 4, pp. 9, 230 (remarks of Iredell).

7.   See Elliot, *Debates*, volume 3, p. 37 (remarks of Pendleton).

8.   See Bernard Schwartz, *The Bill of Rights: A Documentary History* (Chelsea House, 1971), p. 1026.

9.   Ibid. at p. 1072 (remarks of James Jackson of Georgia).

10.   Elliot, *Debates*, volume 1, p. 327.

11.   For examples, see Akhil Amar, "The Consent of the Governed: Constitutional Amendment Outside Article V," 94 *Columbia Law Review* 457, 492–93 (1994).

12.   Schwartz, *The Bill of Rights*, volume 2, p. 1118 (remarks of Thomas Tudor Tucker).

13.   Merrill D. Peterson, ed., *The Portable Thomas Jefferson* (Viking, 1975), p. 432.

14.   Paul Leicester Ford, ed., *The Writings of Thomas Jefferson* (G.P. Putnam's Sons, 1899), volume 10, p. 89 (1817 letter to Baron F.H. Alexander von Humboldt).

15.   Joseph Story, *Commentaries on the Constitution of the United States* (Hilliard, Gray, & Co. 1833), volume 1, sec. 330.

16.   Gordon S. Wood, *The Creation of the American Republic, 1776–1787* (University of North Carolina Press, 1969).

17.   Robert McCloskey, ed., *The Works of James Wilson* (Harvard University Press, 1967), volume 1, p. 304.

18.   Ibid.

19.   See George Will, "Hands Off Madison's Document," *Washington Post*, June 30, 1989, p. A23.

CHAPTER 2

1.   410 U.S. 113 (1973).

2.   381 U.S. 479 (1965).

3.   See, for example, Joseph Zimmerman, *Participatory Democracy* (Praeger, 1986), p. 70.

4.   See, for example, Tom Wicker, "Justice or Hypocrisy," *New York Times*, August 15, 1991, p. A23 (dismissing opposition to affirmative action because "polls also show Americans opposed to many elements of the Bill of Rights").

5.   *The Federalist Papers* No. 55, p. 346 (Clinton Rossiter ed., New American Library, 1961).

6.   Ibid.

7.   *The Federalist* No. 1, p. 33 (emphasis added).

8.   See, for example, Peter Odegard, *Pressure Politics: The Story of the Anti-Saloon League* (Columbia University Press, 1928), p. 173.

9.   See Chapter 1, note 1.

10.   See "Social Security Poses Senate Stumbling Block On Budget Amendment," *National Journal's Congress Daily,* February 3, 1995 (reporting a poll of 1,200 people finding that roughly four-fifths support a balanced-budget amendment).

11.   410 U.S. 113 (1973).

12.   For example, a 1994 Gallup Poll found that only 13 percent of Americans favored a ban on abortion. See William Schneider, "Reopening the Debate Over Abortion," *National Law Journal,* February 18, 1995.

13.   See Robert Bork, *The Tempting of America* (The Free Press, 1990), p. 127.

14.   See Robert Bork, "Neutral Principles and Some First Amendment Problems," 47 *Indiana Law Journal* 1 (1971) (arguing that the First Amendment protects political speech only); Letter, "Judge Bork Replies," *American Bar Association Journal* (February 1984) p. 132 (recanting earlier position on First Amendment).

15.   Henry Steele Commager, *Majority Rule and Minority Rights* (Oxford University Press, 1943), p. 18, quoting letter from Jefferson to William Jarvis of September 28, 1820.

16.   Ibid., p. 16 (quoting letter from Jefferson to James Madison of December 20, 1987).

CHAPTER 3

1.   See Thomas E. Cronin, *Direct Democracy* (Harvard University Press, 1989), pp. 78–79.

2.   *James v. Valtierra,* 402 U.S. 137, 141 (1971).

3.   See, for example, Hans A. Linde, "Who is Responsible for Republican Government?" 65 *University of Colorado Law Review* 709 (1994); Julian Eule, "Judicial Review of Direct Democracy," 99 *Yale Law Journal* 1503 (1990).

4.   See Cronin, *Direct Democracy,* p. 92.

5. Yet, contrary to the oft-expressed view that plebiscite voters will indulge their immediate gratification at the expense of the community's long-term interest, voters have often rejected proposed tax cuts. See Cronin, *Direct Democracy*, p. 206.

6. *Romer v. Evans*, 882 P.2d 1335 (Colo. 1994), affirmed, 116 S.Ct. 1620 (1996).

7. See Lynn A. Baker, "Direct Democracy and Discrimination: A Public Choice Perspective," 67 *Chicago-Kent Law Review* 707 (1991).

8. H.L. Richardson, *What Makes You Think We Read the Bills?* (Caroline House, 1978).

9. Woodrow Wilson, address in Kansas City, Missouri, May 5, 1919, reprinted in Ray Stannard Baker and William E. Dodd, eds., *The Public Papers of Woodrow Wilson* (Harper & Brothers, 1925), volume 2, pp. 287–88.

10. See Baker, "Direct Democracy and Discrimination," p. 754.

11. These statistics, initially documented in Cronin's *Direct Democracy* in 1989, appear confirmed by more recent data which the Public Affairs Research Institute of New Jersey is in the process of compiling.

12. *The Federalist* Papers No. 10, pp. 81–82 (Clinton Rossiter ed., New American Library, 1961).

13. *The Federalist* No. 21, pp. 139–40; *The Federalist* No. 43, pp. 274–78.

14. *The Federalist* No. 10, p. 80 (emphasis added).

15. *The Federalist* No. 14, p. 100.

16. *The Federalist* No. 39, pp. 240–41; *The Federalist* No. 43, p. 274.

17. *The Federalist* No. 39, pp. 240–41.

18. *The Federalist* No. 55, p. 346.

19. *The Federalist* No. 84, p. 512.

20. *The Federalist* No. 21, p. 140 (emphasis added).

21. See Deborah Jones Merritt, "The Guarantee Clause and State Autonomy: Federalism For a Third Century," 88 *Columbia Law Review* 1, 24 (1988).

22. *Chisolm v. Georgia*, 2 U.S. (2 Dall.) 419, 457 (1793).

23.   *Penhallow v. Doane's Adm'rs,* 3 U.S. (3 Dall.) 54, 93 (1795).

24.   See Richard Hofstadter, *The Idea of a Party System* (University of Chicago Press, 1969), p. 143.

25.   Jonathan Elliot, *The Debates in the Several State Conventions on the Adoption of the Federal Constitution* (J.B. Lippincott & Co., 1881), volume 4, p. 328 (emphasis added).

26.   Elliot, *Debates,* volume 2, p. 433 (emphasis added).

27.   Ibid., p. 482 (emphasis added).

28.   *The Federalist* No. 10, p. 84 (emphasis added).

29.   Max Farrand, ed., *The Records of the Federal Convention of 1787* (Yale University Press, 1937), volume 1, p. 135 (emphasis added).

30.   William M. Wiecek, *The Guarantee Clause of the U.S. Constitution* (Cornell University Press, 1972), p. 24 (emphasis added).

31.   *The Federalist* No. 71, p. 433.

32.   *The Federalist* No. 48, p. 309.

33.   Madison sought to make a virtue of necessity, extolling the notion of a large republic because the risk of majority tyranny varies inversely with the size of the polity.

34.   This much is already clear—plebiscites tend to increase voter turnout at elections. See Cronin, *Direct Democracy,* pp. 226–27.

CHAPTER 4

1.   See, for example, Douglas W. Ell, "The Right to an Incompetent Jury: Protracted Commercial Litigation and the Seventh Amendment," 10 *Connecticut Law Review* 775 (1978).

2.   For an engaging discussion of this and other criticisms of the jury system, see Steven Daniels, "The Question of Jury Competence and the Politics of Civil Justice Reform: Symbols, Rhetoric and Agenda-Building," *Law and Contemporary Problems* (Autumn 1989), pp. 269–310.

3.   See Laura Mansnerus, "Under Fire, Jury System Faces Overhaul," *New York Times,* November 4, 1995, p. A9 (noting growing discontent with the jury system "after a raft of unpopular verdicts" and quoting jury scholar Valerie Hans as saying that the discontent stems

from "the very strong belief that courts are not doing enough to punish wrongdoers").

4.   The reader is especially referred to Robert Litan, ed., *Verdict: Assessing the Civil Jury* (Brookings Institution, 1993), a collection of essays by social scientists, judges, and other observers of the jury system. The picture that emerges, especially from the social scientists who have studied the way juries actually work, is of the jury as a competent decision-making body.

5.   See, for example, William F. Woo, "Justice Was Served In The Simpson Case," *St. Louis Post Dispatch*, October 8, 1995, p. 1B (citing the axiom that "it is better that ten guilty persons escape than one innocent suffer" and arguing that "English law came to rely on the jury—even as we still do today," in service of that sentiment).

6.   See, for example, Stephen A. Saltzburg, "The Quality of Jury Decisionmaking," in Robert Litan, ed., *Verdict*, pp. 343–44 (listing advantages of juries over judges).

7.   For documentation of the Framers' views on this point, see Akhil Amar, "The Bill of Rights as a Constitution," 100 *Yale Law Journal* 1131, 1183–1185 (1991).

8.   Julian Boyd, ed., *The Papers of Thomas Jefferson, 1788–89* (1898), pp. 282–83 (letter to l'Abbé Arnoux).

9.   See Akhil Amar, "The Bill of Rights as a Constitution," 100 *Yale Law Journal* 1131, 1183–1185 (1991).

10.   Alexis de Tocqueville, *Democracy in America*, J.P. Mayer & Max Lerner, eds., (Harper & Row, 1966), p. 250. Recent cases illustrate the influence of jury verdicts on political discourse and decisionmaking. The acquittals of Jack Kevorkian have played a role in the nation's debate over assisted suicide, and the conviction of former business associates of President Clinton became an issue in the 1996 presidential campaign.

11.   Robert McCloskey, ed., The *Works of James Wilson* (Harvard University Press, 1967) volume 2, p. 537.

12.   Ibid.

13.   Tocqueville, *Democracy in America*, p. 252.

14.   Ibid., p. 253.

15. See, for example, Robert Putnam, "Bowling Alone," *Journal of Democracy* 65 (January 1995). Putnam discusses the decline of vibrant civil society, noting reduced membership in assorted civics groups and even bowling leagues.

16. In his insightful book, *Democracy's Discontent* (Harvard University Press, 1996), Michael Sandel laments the decline of public spaces where citizens engage in "self-government in small spheres" that cultivates virtue, produces loyalties to something larger than the individual, and enhances our capacity for self-government generally. Curiously, Sandel ignores the institution perhaps best suited (and constitutionally endowed) to serve this purpose—the jury.

17. Max Farrand, ed., *The Records of the Federal Convention of 1787*, (Yale University Press, 1937), volume 2, pp. 587–88.

18. Edward Dumbauld, *The Bill of Rights and What It Means Today* (University of Oklahoma Press, 1957), pp. 176, 181–84, 188, 190–91, 200, 204.

19. See, for example, *New York Times Company v. United States*, 403 U.S. 713 (1971) (per curiam).

20. Readers who doubt this assertion (and some readers will, since today's legal community looks kindly on search warrants), are referred to Akhil Amar, "Fourth Amendment First Principles," 107 *Harvard Law Review* 757 (1994).

21. Under current law, however, such civil suits are often unavailable. The courts have grossly distorted the Framers' vision in this regard. See Amar, "Fourth Amendment First Principles."

22. Edward Coke, *The Second Part of The Institutes of the Laws of England,* pp. 50–51.

23. Julian Boyd, ed., *The Papers of Thomas Jefferson, 1788–89,* (1958) pp. 676, 678 (letter to David Humphreys).

24. The Anti-Federalists were particularly keen on this point. One leading pamphlet of theirs claimed it "essential in every free country, that common people should have a part and share of influence, in the judicial as well as in the legislative department." Herbert Storing, ed., *The Complete Anti-Federalist* (University of Chicago Press, 1981), volume 2, p. 249 ("Letters from the Federal Farmer").

CHAPTER 5

1.   For a thorough exploration of the link between voting and jury service, see Vikram Amar, "Jury Service as Political Participation Akin to Voting," 80 *Cornell Law Review* 203 (1995).

2.   Alexis de Tocqueville, *Democracy in America,* J.P. Mayer & Max Lerner eds., (Harper & Row, 1966), p. 251.

3.   Ibid.

4.   Ibid., p. 702.

5.   Barbara Babcock, "Jury Service and Community Representation" in Robert Litan, ed., *Verdict: Assessing the Civil Jury* (Brookings Institute, 1993), p. 474.

6.   See, for example, *Kramer v. Union Free School District,* 395 U.S. 621 (1969) (championing a general "right to vote"); *Reynolds v. Sims,* 377 U.S. 533, 554 (1964) ("Undeniably, the Constitution of the United States protects the right of all qualified citizens to vote, in state as well as in federal elections.").

7.   See, for example, Lani Guinier, *The Tyranny of the Majority* (The Free Press, 1994), pp. 36, 124.

8.   See Joanna Grossman, "Women's Jury Service: Right of Citizenship or Privilege of Difference?" 46 *Stanford Law Review,* 1115, 1136–37 & n. 137 (1994), reviewing history and citing cases.

9.   *Carter v. Jury Commission of Greene Country,* 396 U.S. 320, 330 (1970).

10.   See *United States v. Herman,* 939 F.2d 1207, 1210 (5th Cir. 1991) ("There is no constitutionally protected right to serve on a jury."); James G. McConnell, "Blind Justice or Just Blindness?" 60 *Chicago-Kent Law Review* 209, 211 (1984) ("[T]he right to trial by jury is a right of the litigants, not a right of prospective jurors to serve. . . . [C]itizens generally have no right to insist on being included in a jury panel").

11.   *Oregon v. Mitchell,* 400 U.S. 112, 148 (1970); *United States v. Classic,* 313 U.S. 299, 314–15 (1941).

12.   *Reynolds v. Sims,* 377 U.S. 533, 554 (1964).

13.   *Batson v. Kentucky,* 476 U.S. 79 (1986); *J.E.B. v. Alabama ex rel. T. B.,* 114 S.Ct. 1419 (1994); *Taylor v. Louisiana,* 419 U.S. 522 (1975).

14.   *Powers v. Ohio,* 499 U.S. 400, 407 (1991).

CHAPTER 6

1.   The federal statute governing jury selection, discussed below in the text, was designed to "provide the best method for obtaining jury lists that represent a cross section of the relevant community." House Report No. 1076, 90th Congress, 2d Session p. 4, reprinted in 1968 *U.S. Code Congressional & Administrative News*, pp. 1792–93.

2.   28 U.S.C. 1861–74.

3.   419 U.S. 522 (1975).

4.   476 U.S. 79 (1986).

5.   George Fletcher, *With Justice For Some: Victims Rights and the Criminal Law* (Addison-Wesley, 1995), pp. 220–21.

6.   Clarence Darrow, "Attorney for the Defense," *Esquire* (May 1936).

7.   Clarence Darrow, *The Story of My Life* (Scribner's, 1932), p. 308.

8.   This history is fully recounted in Jeffrey Abramson, *We, The Jury* (Basic Books, 1994), pp. 143–76.

9.   Morton Hunt, "Putting Juries on the Couch," *New York Times*, November 28, 1992, sec. 6, p. 70.

10.   Alan Dershowitz, *The Advocate's Devil* (Time Warner, 1994), p. 190.

11.   See Alan Dershowitz, *The Best Defense* (Random House, 1982), p. xiv ("I am not unique in representing guilty clients. This is what most defense attorneys do most of the time.").

12.   St. George Tucker, ed., *Blackstone's Commentaries* (1803), volume 5, p. 353.

13.   Albert Alschuler, "The Supreme Court and the Jury: Voir Dire, Peremptory Challenges, and the Review of Jury Verdicts," 56 *University of Chicago Law Review* 153, 165–66 (1989).

14.   The Supreme Court has said that the peremptory challenge is not constitutionally required. See, for example, *Frazier v. United States*, 335 U.S. 497, 505-06, n. 11 (1948).

15.   Michael Saks, "Blaming the Jury," 75 *Georgetown Law Journal* 693, 695-96.

16.   Alschuler, "The Supreme Court and the Jury," at pp. 202-04.

CHAPTER 7

1. Jeffrey Abramson, *We, The Jury* (Basic Books, 1994), p. 168.

2. Mark Twain, *Roughing It* (Heritage Press, 1972 reprint) pp. 246–47.

CHAPTER 8

1. See, for example, *Batson v. Kentucky,* 476 U.S. 79 (1986); *Duren v. Missouri,* 439 U.S. 357 (1979).

2. 28 U.S.C. Sec. 1863(b)(4) (1968).

3. 10 U.S.C. Section 505(a). The statute also establishes the eligibility of seventeen-year-olds, provided a parent or guardian gives written consent.

4. See Vikram Amar, "Jury Service as Political Participation Akin to Voting," 80 *Cornell Law Review* 203 (1995).

5. Ibid., pp. 228–34.

6. Barbara Babcock, "Jury Service and Community Representation" in Robert Litan, ed., *Verdict: Assessing the Civil Jury* (Brookings Institute, 1993), p. 474.

7. Senate Report No. 92, 92d Congress, 1st session, p. 4 (1971, emphasis added).

8. Ibid.

9. Ibid., p. 6.

10. *Peters v. Kiff,* 407 U.S. 493, 503–04 (1972).

11. *Taylor v. Louisiana,* 419 U.S. 522, 531–32 (1975), quoting *Ballard v. United States,* 329 U.S. 187, 193–94 (1946).

12. *Hamling v. United States,* 418 U.S. 87 (1974).

13. See, for example, *Duren v. Missouri,* 439 U.S. 357, 366, 368 n. 26. (1979).

14. For a list of cases so holding, see Vikram Amar, "Jury Service," p. 214, n. 72.

15. See Donald H. Ziegler, "Young Adults as a Cognizable Group in Jury Selection," 76 *Michigan Law Review* 1045 (1978).

16. *Barber v. Ponte,* 772 F.2d 982, 999 (1st Cir. 1985) (en banc), cert. denied, 475 U.S. 1050 (1986).

17. The Court cases finding the right to jury service for blacks, women, and poor people have not relied on the voting rights amendments. Rather, the Court has relied on the Equal Protection Clause—reaching the right result for the wrong reason. See Vikram Amar, "Jury Service," at pp. 226–27, 257–58 (showing why Equal Protection Clause does not apply). Where young adults are concerned, the Court has found no equal-protection violation and has failed to consider the Twenty-Sixth Amendment, thus producing the wrong result for the wrong reason.

18. See *Reed v. Reed*, 404 U.S. 1 (1971) (administrative convenience does not justify policy resulting in gender discrimination).

CHAPTER 9

1. *Marbury v. Madison*, 5 U.S. (1 Cranch) 137, 177 (1803).

2. In his book *The Intelligible Constitution* (Oxford University Press, 1992), Yale Law School professor Joseph Goldstein argues that the constitution/statute distinction underlies Justice Marshall's famous admonition that "we must remember it is a *constitution* we are expounding." *McCulloch v. Maryland*, 17 U.S. (4 Wheat.) 316, 407 (1819) (emphasis added). According to Goldstein, Marshall meant precisely that the Constitution is a comprehensible outline of principles, not a detailed legal code inaccessible to the People.

3. Robert McCloskey, ed., *The Works of James Wilson* (Harvard University Press, 1967), volume 1, p. 186.

4. Jonathan Elliot, *The Debates in the Several State Conventions on the Adoption of the Federal Constitution* (J.B. Lippincott & Co., 1881), volume 2, p. 94.

5. See Akhil Amar, "The Bill of Rights as a Constitution," 100 *Yale Law Journal* 1131, 1193 n.76 (1991) (documenting the relevant writings of all three).

6. 25 F.Cas. 239 (C.C.D. Va. 1800) (No. 14, 709).

7. 25 F.Cas. at 253.

8. Ibid.

9. Ibid.

10. Ibid.

11.   Ring Lardner, "The Young Immigrunts," in Lardner, *Shut Up, He Explained,* Babette Rosmond and Henry Morgan, eds. (Scribners, 1962), p. 28.

12.   *Georgia v. Brailsford,* 3 U.S. (3 Dall.) 1, 4 (1794).

13.   Ibid., p. 4.

14.   Ibid.

15.   156 U.S. 51 (1895).

16.   156 U.S. at 101.

17.   156 U.S. at 77.

18.   156 U.S. at 102, 103.

19.   See, for example, Robert Bork, *The Tempting of America* (The Free Press, 1990).

20.   Herbert Storing, ed., *The Complete Anti-Federalist* (University of Chicago Press, 1981), volume 5, p. 39.

CHAPTER 10

1.   *Works of John Adams* (Charles Francis Adams, ed., Little Brown, 1850) volume 2, pp. 253–55.

2.   Peter Westen and Richard Drubel, "Towards a General Theory of Double Jeopardy," 1981 *Supreme Court Review* 81, pp. 129–31.

3.   *United States v. Dougherty,* 473 F.2d 1113, 1136 (D.C. Cir. 1972).

4.   To take just one example, the anti-abortion group Operation Rescue has taken to running newspaper advertisements advising prospective jurors of their right to acquit against the evidence anti-abortion activists charged with various crimes. See Jeffrey Abramson, *We, The Jury* (Basic Books, 1994), pp. 57–59.

5.   "Merciful Juries: The Resilience of Jury Nullification," 48 *Washington & Lee Law Review* 165, 183 (1991).

6.   Alexander Hamilton saw fit to explicate this etymological point in *The Federalist Papers* No. 81, p. 489 (Clinton Rossiter, ed., New American Library, 1961).

7.   Alan Scheflin and Jon Van Dyke "Jury Nullification: The Contours of a Controversy," 43 *Law and Contemporary Problems* 51, 87 (1990) (emphasis added).

8. Till was a black youth killed by two southern white men without justification. For an excellent account of his murder, and the acquittal of his
killers, see David Halberstam, *The Fifties* (Villard, 1993), pp. 431–41.

9. Among other things, Cochran said: "Maybe you're the right people
at the right time at the right place to say 'no more. We're not going to have
this.' . . . You're the ones who send the message. Nobody else is going to do
it in this society. They don't have the courage. Nobody has the courage. . . .
You're the ones in war. You're the ones who are on the front lines."

10. See Abramson, *We, The Jury*, pp. 49–50.

11. In the aftermath of the trial, columnist William Raspberry wrote, "It
would surprise me not at all to learn that all 12 jurors secretly believed the
mayor guilty on virtually all the counts." William Raspberry, "The Verdict for
Barry and the Verdict for the City," *Washington Post*, August 12, 1990, p. C1.

12. George Fletcher, *A Crime of Self Defense: Bernhard Goetz and the
Law on Trial* (The Free Press, 1988), p. 155.

13. Ibid.

14. See Scheflin and Van Dyke, "Jury Nullification," pp. 84–85.

CHAPTER 11

1. *Gannett Co. v. DePasquale*, 443 U.S. 368, 428–29 (1979) (Blackmun, J., concurring in part and dissenting in part).

2. 281 U.S. 276 (1930).

3. Jonathan Elliot, *The Debates in the Several State Conventions on the
Adoption of the Federal Constitution* (J.B. Lippincott & Co., 1881), volume
3, pp. 520–21 (remarks of Edmund Pendleton at the Virginia convention);
volume 4, p. 171 (remarks of James Iredell at the North Carolina convention). See also *the Federalist Papers* No. 83 at 495-95 (Clinton Rossiter,
ed., New American Library, 1961).

4. *Callan v. Wilson*, 127 U.S. 540, 549 (1888). That case involved a
slightly different issue—whether jury trials were required in the District of
Columbia. Since the Sixth Amendment speaks only of "states," the government argued that jury trials were not required. However, the Court rejected
that argument because of the mandatory language of Article III—all federal
trials must be jury trials—which the Sixth Amendment did not contradict.

5.   For a fuller review of the legislative history, see Akhil Amar, "The Bill of Rights as a Constitution," 100 *Yale Law Journal* 1131, 1197–98 (1991).

6.   *Thompson v. Utah,* 170 U.S. 343, 354–54 (1898).

7.   *Insurance Co. v. Morse,* 87 U.S. (20 Wall.) 445, 451 (1874).

8.   281 U.S. at 293.

CHAPTER 12

1.   See, for example, *Pennhurst State School & Hospital v. Halderman,* 465 U.S. 89, 100 (1984).

2.   For evidence that this was the traditional American view, see Akhil Amar, "Of Sovereignty and Federalism," 96 *Yale Law Journal* 1425 (1987).

3.   2 U.S. (4 Dall) 419 (1793).

4.   "It is a general and indisputable rule, that where there is a legal right, there is a legal remedy by suit, or action at law, where that right is invaded." *Marbury v. Madison,* 5 U.S. (1 Cranch) 137, 163 (1803).

5.   *Ex Parte Young,* 209 U.S. 123 (1908).

6.   *Edelman v. Jordan,* 415 U.S. 651 (1974).

7.   *Atascadero State Hospital v. Scanlon,* 473 U.S. 234, 239–40 n.2 (1985).

8.   *The Federalist Papers* No. 44, p. 289 (Clinton Rossiter, ed., New American Library 1961).

9.   To their credit, several Justices have protested. Most recently, Justice Souter, joined by Justices Ginsburg and Breyer, observed that "we have two Eleventh Amendments, the one ratified in 1795, the other (so-called) invented by the Court nearly a century later." *Seminole Tribe of Florida v. Florida,* 116 S.Ct 1114 (1996) (Souter, J., dissenting) (paraphrasing and endorsing views of Justice Stevens expressed in *Pennsylvania v. Union Gas,* 491 U.S. 1, 23 (1989) (Stevens, J., concurring)).

10.   For a broad critique of the Court's Eleventh Amendment doctrine, see Akhil Amar, "Of Sovereignty and Federalism."

CHAPTER 13

1.   *The Federalist Papers* No. 8, p. 70 (Clinton Rossiter, ed., New American Library, 1961).

2.   The Army Clause is Article I, Section 8, Clause 12; the Navy Clause is Article I, Section 8, Clause 13.

3.   The Framers added one additional safeguard. Article I, Section 10, Clause 3 prohibits the states themselves from maintaining troops—that is, keeping a paid standing army akin to the federal army.

4.   Jonathan Elliot, *The Debates in the Several State Conventions on the Adoption of the Federal Constitution* (J.B. Lippincott & Co., 1881), volume 3, pp. 48, 52.

5.   See, for example, *Whalen v. Roe,* 429 U.S. 589, 608 (1977) (Stewart, J., concurring) ("The Third Amendment's prohibition against the unconsented peacetime quartering of soldiers protects another aspect of privacy from governmental intrusion").

6.   David C. Williams, "Civic Republicanism and the Citizen Militia: The Terrifying Second Amendment," 101 *Yale Law Journal* 551, 562–63 (1991).

CHAPTER 14

1.   Indeed, a number of courts have explicitly asserted that there is no such right. See *Rich v. Secretary of the Army,* 735 F.2d 1220, 1226 (10 Cir. 1984); *Nieszner v. Mark,* 684 F.2d 562, 564 (8th Cir. 1982); *West v. Brown,* 558 F.2d 757, 760 (5th Cir. 1977), cert. denied, 453 U.S. 926 (1978).

2.   Ironically, one of the few Supreme Court cases to note this point—albeit in service of an improper conclusion—is the infamous *Dred Scott v. Sanford,* 60 U.S. (19 How.) 393 (1857). In holding that blacks could never be citizens, the Court drew on the fact that the first Congress excluded blacks from militia service. See ibid. at 420.

3.   David Williams, "Civic Republicanism and the Terrifying Second Amendment," 101 *Yale Law Journal* 551, 563 (1991).

4.   *Reynolds v. Sims,* 377 U.S. 533, 554 (1964).

5.   *The Federalist Papers* No. 29, pp. 184–85 (Clinton Rossiter, ed., New American Library, 1961) (envisioning the evolution of the militia into a "select corps of moderate size").

CHAPTER 15

1.   See David Burrelli, "An Overview of the Debate on Homosexuals in

the U.S. Military," in Wilbur J. Scott and Sandra Carson Stanley, eds., *Gays and Lesbians in the Military* (Gruyter, 1994), pp. 23–26.

2.   David Williams, "Civic Republicanism and the Terrifying Second Amendment," 101 *Yale Law Journal* 551, 563 (1991).

3.   Randy Shilts, *Conduct Unbecoming: Lesbians and Gays in the United States Military, Vietnam to the Persian Gulf* (St. Martin's Press, 1993), p. 111.

4.   For a full recounting of this history, see Allan Berube, *Coming Out Under Fire: The History of Gay Men and Women in World War II* (The Free Press, 1990).

5.   The policy, initially implemented by executive orders, was subsequently codified as a statute at 10 U.S.C. Sec. 654.

6.   In 1973, the American Psychiatric Association deleted homosexuality from its list of mental disorders.

7.   See, generally, Shilts, *Conduct Unbecoming;* Berube, *Coming Out Under Fire.*

8.   See Laura Miller, "Fighting for a Just Cause: Soldiers' Views on Gays in the Military," in *Gays and Lesbians in the Military,* pp. 69–85.

9.   Kenneth Karst, "The Pursuit of Manhood and the Desegregation of the Armed Forces," 38 *U.C.L.A. Law Review* 499 (1991).

10.   See Vicki Quade, "Gays in the Military: Finally Being Able To Be All That You Can Be," 18 *Human Rights* 27.

11.   *United States v. Watkins,* 847 F.2d 1329 (9th Cir. 1988), different results reached on rehearing, 875 F.2d 699 (9th Cir. 1989) (en banc), cert. denied, 111 S.Ct. 384 (1990).

12.   847 F.2d at 1350.

13.   Compare Robert Bork, *The Tempting of America,* p. 124 (The Free Press, 1990) ("Moral outrage is a sufficient ground for prohibitory legislation") with Laurence Tribe, *American Constitutional Law* (Foundation Press, 1978), pp. 981–990 (suggesting that legislation based solely on moral views is generally improper).

14.   847 F.2d at 1352.

15.   478 U.S. 186 (1986).

16.   Indeed, the dissent in the Ninth Circuit *Watkins* case discussed

above, while sympathetic with Perry Watkins' claim, found it impossible to get around *Hardwick:* "The anti-homosexual thrust of *Hardwick,* and the Court's willingness to condone anti-homosexual animus in the actions of government are clear." 847 F.d at 1355 (Reinhardt, J., dissenting).

17. See Ruth Marcus, "Powell Regrets Backing Sodomy Law," *Washington Post,* October 26, 1990, p. A3.

18. In its recent decision striking down an antigay provision in Colorado's constitution, *Romer v. Evans,* 116 S.Ct. 1620 (1996), the Court, while conspicuously avoiding mention of *Hardwick,* endorsed the notion that gays are full citizens. Justice Kennedy's opinion for the Court began as follows: "One century ago, the first Justice Harlan admonished this Court that the Constitution 'neither knows nor tolerates classes among citizens.'"

CHAPTER 16

1. *Taylor v. Louisiana,* 419 U.S. 522 (1975).

2. *Rostker v. Goldberg,* 453 U.S. 69 (1981).

3. Ibid. at 86 (Marshall, J., dissenting).

4. Less significant, but equally disturbing, statute books still limit the "unorganized militia" to able-bodied, adult *males.* 10 U.S.C. Sec. 311 (1982). This anachronistic vestige of discrimination has little practical effect but should still be declared unconstitutional.

5. Women do, of course, remain uniquely susceptible to pregnancy, a fact that has been cited as a basis for the combat exclusion. However, there is no evidence that pregnancy among soldiers has been particularly disruptive, and some evidence that men are more frequently absent from duty than women. See Martin Binkin and Shirley Bach, *Women in the Military* (The Brookings Institution, 1977), pp. 62-64.

6. Elaine Scarry, "War and the Social Contract: Nuclear Policy, Distribution, and the Right to Bear Arms," 139 *University of Pennsylvania Law Review* 1278 (1991).

7. Mary Becker, "The Politics of Women's Wrongs and the Bill of 'Rights': A Bicentennial Perspective," 59 *University of Chicago Law Review* 453, 498–99 (1992).

CHAPTER 17

1. *Selective Draft Law Cases*, 245 U.S. 366 (1918).

2. See Roger Taney, "Thoughts on the Conscription Law of the United States," in Martin Anderson. ed., *The Military Draft* (Hoover Institution Press, 1982), pp. 208–218.

3. *Kneedler v. Lane*, 45 Pa. 238 (1863).

4. Ibid. at 294–95. For an interesting discussion, see Bernstein, "The Amazing Case of *Kneedler v. Lane*," 53 *American Bar Association Journal* 708 (1967).

5. 245 U.S. at 366 (1918).

6. The issue was again raised during the Vietnam War, but the Supreme Court declined to revisit it. Thus, for example, when the Eighth Circuit declared itself troubled by conscription, but bound by Supreme Court precedent, the Court chose not to review the case. *United States v. Crocker*, 420 F.2d 307 (8th Cir. 1970), cert. denied, 397 U.S. 1011 (1970).

7. 245 U.S. at 377.

8. George Washington, "Sentiments on a Peace Establishment," in *Basic Writings of George Washington* (Saxe Cummins, ed., Random House, 1948), pp. 467–89.

9. *The Federalist Papers* No. 24, p. 161 (Clinton Rossiter, ed., New American Library, 1961).

10. See for example, *Webster's American Dictionary* (1828).

11. *Marbury v. Madison*, 5 U.S. (1 Cranch) 137, 174 (1803).

12. Taney, "Thoughts on the Conscription Law of the United States," in Anderson, ed., *The Military Draft*, p. 212.

13. Ibid.

14. See, for example, Robert Bork and Theordore Olson, "Trial Lawyers and Other Closet Federalists," *The Washington Times*, March 9, 1995, p. A21 ("Federal courts no longer defend the rights of states, so legislators must be sensitive to principles of federalism or the states will disappear").

15. It is true that the states also need their militia to deal with internal crises, but this concern pales next to national security, and it is hard to imagine the federal government not offering assistance if a state were over-

whelmed by an internal crisis and unable to respond because many of its National Guard members had been drafted by that same federal government.

16.   Max Farrand, ed., *The Records of the Federal Convention of 1787* (Yale University Press, 1937), volume 3, p. 208 (emphasis in original).

17.   For example, at Virginia's ratifying convention George Nicholas explained: "There is a great difference between having the power [to call out the militia] in three cases, and in all cases. They can not call them forth for any other purpose than to execute the laws, suppress insurrections and repel invasions." Elliot, *Debates*, volume 3, at 392.

18.   The British history and legislation is discussed in Leon Friedman, "Conscription and the Constitution," 67 *Michigan Law Review* 1493, 1499–1501 (1969).

19.   Speech on the floor of the House of Representatives, December 9, 1814, in Anderson, ed., *The Military Draft*, p. 643.

20.   Ibid., p. 644.

21.   Ibid.

22.   *The Federalist* No. 24, at 161. Hamilton was responding to concern that the militia would be sent to the Western frontier to ward off the Indians. Still more would his argument apply if the federal government wished to send the militia abroad.

23.   *The Federalist* No. 29, at 187.

24.   While many liberals use the phrase to express opposition to foreign intervention, some conservatives have used the phrase in almost the opposite vein, as a call to effective, aggressive military action. See Richard Nixon, *No More Vietnams* (Arbor House, 1985), p. 237: "'No more Vietnams' can mean that we will not *try* again. It *should* mean that we will not *fail* again" (emphasis in original).

25.   The concept of an "unorganized militia" is preserved by statute, 10 U.S.C. Sec. 311, even though Congress has ignored it by drafting citizens directly into the "army."

26.   Such a notion may have influenced the Supreme Court in the case of *Perpich v. Minnesota*, 496 U.S. 334 (1990), revolving around the rights of governors to resist the calling out of their National Guard units by the fed-

eral government. For an analysis of the case, see Alan Hirsch, "The Militia Clauses of the Constitution and the National Guard," 56 *Cincinnati Law Review* 919, 956–68 (1988).

27.　For a discussion of how such a case should arise, and how courts have (mis)handled disputes involving militiamen, see Hirsch, "The Militia Clauses," pp. 950–56.

28.　Thus, for example, the courts refused to address the claim that the Vietnam conflict was unconstitutional because Congress did not declare war. See *Massachusetts v. Laird*, 451 F.2d 26 (1st Cir. 1971); *Orlando v. Laird*, 443 F.2d 1039 (2d Cir.), cert. denied, 404 U.S. 869 (1971).

29.　Farrand, *Records of the Federal Constitutional Convention*, volume 3, p. 85.

CHAPTER 18

1.　See Elaine Scarry, "War and the Social Contract: Nuclear Policy, Distribution, and the Right to Bear Arms," 139 *University of Pennsylvania Law Review* 1257 (1991); Sanford Levinson, "The Embarrassing Second Amendment," 99 *Yale Law Journal* 637 (1989).

2.　See generally Akhil Amar, *Creation and Reconstruction* (Yale University Press, 1998).

3.　Jonathan Elliot, *The Debates in the Several State Conventions on the Adoption of the Federal Constitution* (J.B. Lippincott & Co., 1881), volume 3, p. 37.

4.　See John Locke, *The Second Treatise of Government* (T. Peardon editor, 1952).

5.　See Garry Wills, "To Keep and Bear Arms," *New York Review of Books*, September 21, 1995, p. 64. We discuss the ramifications of the arms/guns distinction below.

6.　Levinson, "The Embarrassing Second Amendment," p. 657.

7.　Dennis Henigan, "Arms, Anarchy, And The Second Amendment," 26 *Valparaiso University Law Review* 107 (1991).

8.　Ibid., p. 115 (emphasis in original).

9.　Ibid.

10. David Williams, "Civic Republicanism and the Terrifying Second Amendment," 101 *Yale Law Journal* 551, 553–54 (1991).

11. Henigan, "Arms, Anarchy, and the Second Amendment," p. 110.

12. Abraham Lincoln, First Inaugural Address, in Roy. P. Basler, ed., *The Collected Works of Abraham Lincoln* (Rutgers University Press, 1953), volume 4, p. 269.

13. See Locke, *The Second Treatise of Government,* Sections 221–43.

14. As Lincoln explained, "no government proper, ever had a provision in its organic law for its own termination." Abraham Lincoln, First Inaugural Address, in Basler, ed., volume 4, p. 264.

15. Ibid., p. 269.

16. Henigan, "Arms, Anarchy, and the Second Amendment," p. 110.

17. Ibid., p. 129.

18. See, for example, Robert Bork, *Slouching Toward Gomorrah* (HarperCollins, 1996) (arguing in favor of censorship).

19. Scarry, "War and the Social Contract." p. 1268.

20. Wendy Brown, "Guns, Cowboys, Philadelphia Mayors, and Civic Republicanism: On Sanford Levinson's Embarrassing Second Amendment," 99 *Yale Law Journal* 661 (1989).

21. Ibid. at 663.

22. Where the First Amendment is concerned, the Court may be mistaken. A persuasive case can be made that, while speech is not absolute, "freedom of speech" is. See Alexander Meiklejohn, *Political Freedom: The Constitutional Powers of the People* (Oxford University Press, 1960), pp. 26–27, 34–36.

23. See, for example, *Bolger v. Youngs Drug Products,* 463 U.S. 60, 64–65 (1983).

24. *United States v. Miller,* 307 U.S. 174 (1939).

25. 307 U.S. at 178.

CHAPTER 19

1. See, for example, Charles Reich, "The Individual Sector," 100 *Yale Law Journal* 1409, 1435–40 (1991); Peter Edelman, "The Next Century of Our Constitution: Rethinking Our Duty to the Poor," 39 *Hastings Law Jour-*

nal 1 (1987); Charles Black, "Further Reflections on the Constitutional Justice of Livelihood," 86 *Columbia Law Review* 1103 (1986); Frank Michelman, "Welfare Rights in a Constitutional Democracy," 1979 *Washington University Law Quarterly* 659.

2.   See, for example, *Pierce v. Society of Sisters*, 268 U.S. 510 (1925) on the right to attend private school.

3.   See Neal A. Lewis, "Clinton, Fearing Fight, Shuns Bid to Name Friend as Judge," *New York Times*, September 1, 1995, p. A18.

4.   Robert Bork, "The Impossibility of Finding Welfare Rights in the Constitution," 1979 *Washington University Law Quarterly* 695, 695–96.

5.   See Drew R. McCoy, *The Elusive Republic: Political Economy in Jeffersonian America* (University of North Carolina Press, 1980), p. 68: "American republicans valued property in land primarily because it provided personal independence. . . . [This] permitted a citizen to participate responsibly in the political process, for it allowed him to pursue spontaneously the common or public good."

6.   History confirms a correlation between poverty and unwillingness to participate in the political processes. See, for example, Raymond E. Wolfinger and Steven J. Rosenstone, *Who Votes?* (Yale University Press, 1980), pp. 13–36. The authors find an even stronger correlation between lack of education and nonparticipation, which dovetails with our argument later in the chapter that the uneducated are also effectively disenfranchised.

7.   See St. George Tucker, ed., *Blackstone's Commentaries* (1803), volume 1, p. 171: "The true reason of requiring a qualification, with regard to property, in voters, is to exclude such persons as are in so mean a situation that they are esteemed to have no will of their own."

8.   The most blatant examples are Article I, Section 9, preventing Congress from prohibiting the importing of slaves until 1808, and Article IV, Section 2, Clause 3, requiring free states to return escaped slaves to their masters.

9.   *The Federalist Papers* No. 43, p. 277 (Clinton Rossiter, ed., New American Library, 1961).

10.   Ibid.

11.   *The Federalist* No. 39, p. 241.

12.   See Lance Banning, *Jefferson and Madison* (Madison House, 1995), pp. 43–44.

13.   A few legal scholars have emphasized the importance of the Citizenship Clause. See, for example, Charles L. Black, Jr., *Structure and Relationship in Constitutional Law* (Louisiana State University Press, 1969); Chris Eisgruber, "The Fourteenth Amendment's Constitution," 69 *Southern California Law Review* 47 (1995).

14.   The Civil Rights Cases, 109 U.S. 3, 20 (1883).

15.   *Clyatt v. United States*, 197 U.S. 207, 216 (1905).

16.   Bork, "The Impossibility of Finding Welfare Rights," p. 1959.

17.   Lawrence Sager, "Justice in Plain Clothes: Reflections on the Thinness of Constitutional Law," 88 *Northwestern Law Review* 410 (1993).

18.   See, for example, Michael W. McConnell, "Symposium on Interpreting the Ninth Amendment: A Moral Realist Defense of Constitutional Democracy," 64 *Chicago Kent Law Review* 89, 104 (1988): the problem of finding appropriate limits to judges' authority "becomes still more acute if we recognize 'affirmative rights.'" Note, too, that the Constitution empowers Congress to compensate public officials. As Professor Charles Black has suggested, if Congress must set an amount of compensation for itself and other government officials, it hardly seems beyond the pale that it set a level of minimal entitlements for all Americans. Black, "Further Reflections," p. 1113.

19.   See *Gideon v. Wainwright*, 372 U.S. 335 (1963) (requiring appointment of counsel to indigent criminal defendants accused of a felony); *Farmer v. Brennan*, 114 S.Ct. 1970 (1994) (confirming that government must feed and shelter prisoners).

20.   See Thomas Jefferson, *Writings* (Merrill Peterson, ed., Library of America, 1984), p. 343.

21.   347 U.S. 483, 493 (1954).

22.   Chester Finn, "A Seismic Shock For Education," *New York Times*, September 3, 1989, Sec. 4, p. 13.

23.   *Wisconsin v. Yoder*, 406 U.S. 205, 221 (1972).

24.   *Plyler v. Doe*, 457 U.S. 202, 221 (1982).

25.   411 U.S. 1 (1973).

26. 411 U.S. at 36.

27. 411 U.S. at 36–37.

28. In *Rodriguez*, the plaintiff argued that the fundamental right to education required not just minimal education but greater equality among school districts. The Court may have been correct to deny the sweep of that claim, yet still incorrect in denying a fundamental right to education.

29. 411 U.S. at 35.

30. 411 U.S. at 63 (Brennan, J., dissenting).

31. Susan Ritensky, "Theoretical Foundations For a Right to Education Under the United States Constitution: A Beginning to the End of the National Education Crisis," 86 *Northwestern Law Review* 550 (1992).

32. 411 U.S. at 70. (Marshall, J., dissenting).

33. In reviving the notion of cultural literacy, E.D. Hirsch has persuasively argued that failure in education makes it difficult for Americans to talk to one another, much less govern together. See Hirsch, *Cultural Literacy* (Houghton Mifflin, 1987).

34. *Ambach v. Norwick*, 441 U.S. 68, 77 (1977).

Index

253